the **GREAT RIOTS** of NEW YORK

JOEL TYLER HEADLEY

With an Introduction by PETE HAMILL

the GREAT RIOTS of NEW YORK

1712–1873

• THUNDER'S MOUTH PRESS •
NEW YORK

THE GREAT RIOTS OF NEW YORK: 1712–1873

© 2004 by Thunder's Mouth Press
Introduction © 2004 by Pete Hamill
Afterword © 1970 by Thomas Rose and James Rodgers

Published by
Thunder's Mouth Press
An Imprint of Avalon Publishing Group Incorporated
245 West 17th Street, 11th Floor
New York, NY 10011-5300

Library of Congress Cataloging-in-Publication Data is available.

ISBN: 1-56025-552-8

9 8 7 6 5 4 3 2 1

Designed by Pauline Neuwirth, Neuwirth & Associates, Inc.

Printed in the United States of America
Distributed by Publishers Group West

• CONTENTS •

CHAPTER I.

The Great Riots of New York City.

CHARACTER OF A CITY ILLUSTRATED BY RIOTS.—NEW MATERIAL FOR HISTORY OF DRAFT RIOTS.—HISTORY OF THE REBELLION INCOMPLETE WITHOUT HISTORY OF THEM.—THE FATE OF THE NATION RESTING ON THE ISSUES OF THE STRUGGLE IN NEW YORK CITY.—THE BEST PLAN TO ADOPT FOR PROTECTION AGAINST MOBS

CHAPTER II.

The Negro Riots of 1712–1741.

ALMOST IMPOSSIBLE FOR THE PRESENT GENERATION TO COMPREHEND ITS TRUE CHARACTER AND EFFECT ON THE PEOPLE.—DESCRIPTION OF NEW YORK AT THAT TIME.—THE NEGRO SLAVES.—THE NEGRO RIOT OF 1712.—DESCRIPTION OF IT.—THE WINTER OF 1741.—GOVERNOR'S HOUSE BURNED DOWN.—OTHER FIRES.—SUSPICION OF THE PEOPLE.—ARREST AND IMPRISONMENT OF THE BLACKS.—REWARD OFFERED FOR THE SUPPOSED CONSPIRATORS.—ALARM AND FLIGHT OF THE INHABITANTS.—EXAMINATION AND CONFESSION OF MARY BURTON.—PEGGY, THE NEWFOUNDLAND BEAUTY, AND THE HUGHSON FAMILY.—THE CONSPIRACY.—EXECUTIONS.—FAST.—HUGHSON'S HEARING.—HUNG IN CHAINS.—THE BODY, AND THAT OF A NEGRO, LEFT TO SWING AND ROT IN THE

CHAPTER III.

The Stamp-Act Riot of 1765.

CHAPTER IV.

Doctors' Riot, 1788

CONTENTS

CHAPTER V.

Spring Election Riots of 1834.

CHAPTER VI.

Abolition Riots of 1834 and 1836.

CHAPTER VII.

Flour Riot of 1837.

CHAPTER VIII.

Astor-Place Riots, 1849.

CHAPTER IX.

Police Riot—Dead Rabbits' Riot—Bread Riot, 1857.

CHAPTER X.

Draft Riots of 1863.

CONTENTS

CONTENTS

CHAPTER XVIII.

Draft Riot—Fourth Day.

CHAPTER XIX.

Closing Scenes.

CHAPTER XX.

CHAPTER XXI.

Orange Riots of 1870 and 1871.

• LIST OF ILLUSTRATIONS •

· INTRODUCTION ·

by Pete Hamill

THE FEAR OF disorder was part of the fabric of Anglo-Dutch New York from its beginnings in the 17th century. After the British Crown took over for the last time, the conquered Dutch kept their own cautious, even surly distance from their conquerors. But they were not the primary cause of municipal unease among those who ruled the tiny town at the foot of Manhattan island. The population of enslaved Africans were. At one point, almost a quarter of the population was made up of human beings who were owned by others, the way horses were owned.

So it's fitting that Joel Tyler Headley opened this 1873 study of disorder with the revolt of Africans against their owners in 1712. This extraordinary event was not properly a riot. It was a rebellion, with slaves killing whites, and burning symbols of their authority, before retreating into the forests north of today's Chambers Street. At least two of the African rebels chose to kill themselves rather than return to shackles and certain doom.

That rebellion played under much of what was to come in New York history and in Headley's study. The bloodshed of 1712 was vivid proof that some human beings would not accept the authority of those who ruled them. They would not accept the power of distant kings, or any claim they might make to divine legitimacy. Nor would they accept the authority of their local agents, secular or religious. In revolt they said: we are men, not chattel. We prefer to die on our feet.

Such a declaration (its purposes must be inferred because there are no known documents of rebellious intent) certainly played under the events of 1741. Modern scholars are divided over whether this was a true revolt or an exercise in paranoia similar to the witchcraft trials in Salem. But 1712 surely offered credence to the fears of 1741, with its mysterious fires, and rumors of an alliance of Africans with underclass Irish people. Before it was over, thirteen Africans were burned at the stake and sixteen were hanged, along with four whites (two of the whites were women). More than seventy were banished from New York, the Africans sent to the West Indies for "seasoning."

Much of the fear that ruled New York in 1741 came from the grand jury testimony of a white indentured servant named Mary Burton. Headley is wrong when he describes her as a slave; she was almost certainly Irish, and wanted desperately to be free of her indenture. At the end of her many days of testimony, she was given what the grand jurors had promised in exchange for informing: her freedom, plus a considerable sum of money. She then vanished from history, presumably into a colonial form of the witness protection program.

By 1741 a primitive class structure had evolved in New York, based on the British model. The rich Anglo-Dutch, who had begun making mergers for pragmatic reasons, began assuming airs of superiority. They showed this with their grand houses, their servants, their private entertainments. This might have been unplanned, but it was certainly real, and was marked by a gradual physical separation from the lives of workmen, mechanics, and slaves. Many were enriched by the growing vitality of the port, but they maintained a physical separation from the rowdy life of the South Street wharves, with their foreign seamen, randy rented women, and hard-drinking pipe–smoking residents. They performed a kind of moral superiority by ostentatious attendance at Trinity Church on Broadway at Wall Street and assumed that their growing wealth was proof of God's blessings. In the torrid New York summers, when cholera, smallpox, or yellow fever invaded the town, they retreated to country estates.

But they were also nervous. The Sons of Liberty—many of them white or poor or both—made them very nervous when they rioted in 1765. The outbreak ten years later of the American Revolution was not a case of nerves; it was a social and cultural shock wave. The young New York aristocracy split. Some went off to join the forces of George Washington. Many maintained loyalty to the British Crown. After more than a century of British rule, freedom was finally offered to African slaves if they supported the Crown forces. All of this was too late. When the last British and Hessian troops sailed on in 1783, the exodus of Tories to Nova Scotia or the West Indies or Mother England had already begun. Some took their liberated slaves with them.

They did not take with them the notion of an American aristocracy. The returning upper class American patriots wanted a form of change that changed nothing. Slavery continued (and did not end in New York until 1827). The Electoral College was created as a form of veto against the choices of the majority. But the right to vote was the most blatant example of the aristocracy's protection of its own pre-war privileges. Voting was restricted to those who owned property. A revolutionary soldier who had fought from Valley Forge onward and did not own his house, or land, could not vote. The aristocrats, including those who served honorably in the cause of liberty, were spoken for by Gouverneur Morris, who had chosen the patriots' side. He once wrote:

"There never was, and never will be, a civilized Society without an Aristocracy."

The Federalist Party was the political arm of that American aristocracy, its leadership provided by Alexander Hamilton and John Jay. Its adherents feared what was labeled "mobocracy." At the same time, foreign events also drove fear into the New York aristocrats. The French Revolution of 1789 swiftly degenerated into bloodshed and vengeance and the endless appetite of the guillotine. The 1798 rebellion in Ireland made its own point to the Americans. The Irish rebel leaders included many Protestants, and they claimed to represent what they called The Men of No Property. That bloody class-based rebellion was brutally crushed by the British, but its ideas lived on. Some rebel leaders found their way to New York, where Catholics now had the post-revolutionary right to practice their faith openly, but not to vote unless they owned property. For some New Yorkers, notions of revolt by men without property held certain obvious attractions. Aristocratic fears were again reinforced by the rebellion in Haiti in 1804, which brought many French–speaking refugees to the port of New York, while providing a kind of inspiration to African-American slaves.

For the most part, politics warded off serious violence in post-revolutionary New York. Headley doesn't explore this in any serious way, but one key player was a brilliant scoundrel named Aaron Burr. In 1799, he and his associates managed to get $2,000,000 out of the state's rulers in Albany to provide fresh water to the parched town at the tip of Manhattan. Their agreement included a clause allowing the Manhattan Company to use any moneys left over from the water project to protect their investment. They spent $100,000 on the water pipes (which were thoroughly inadequate). They used the rest to create the Bank of Manhattan (it would evolve over the coming centuries into the Chase Manhattan Bank). Burr began arranging mortgages for the men of no property. Some of these included the first New York condominiums, with three families sharing ownership of a single house.

At the same time, Burr, whose political career ended when he killed Alexander Hamilton in a duel in 1804, began aligning himself with a group called the Society of St. Tamenend. This group had been founded in 1788, as a more fraternal version of the Order of Cincinnatti. The latter restricted its membership to those who had served as officers in the Revolution, and became an arm of the New York aristocrats and the Federalist Party. The Tamenend group was open to all former enlisted men, along with mechanics and any other men who wanted to dress up as Indians and have a good time. Burr helped politicize it (Martin van Buren would become a member), and it would soon begin demanding universal male suffrage (women would wait another century to vote), the end of debtors' prisons, and other working class protections. They began accumulating power, drawing on the successes of Andrew Jackson's imperfect populism and their own skills at organizing. For the first time, in 1834, New Yorkers would elect their own mayor, who until then had been appointed by the state's governor. Meanwhile, the Society of St. Tamenend evolved into Tammany Hall and would remain a political power in New York until the 1960s. For many years, class would be the basic armature of New York politics.

Headley himself was not immune to fears of the mob. In the 1840s, although basically a Whig, he was an active member of the Know Nothings, a semi-secret movement that evolved into the American Party whose public platform was based on fear of a new kind of mob. They were frightened of those steadily arriving immigrants (most of them Irish) who they believed were changing the character of New York. They were poorly educated (true). They were Catholic (also true, but they also contained substantial numbers of Irish Presbyterians). They were falling into the clutches of Tammany Hall (whose leaders, as they still say in New York, could count). Their growing tide would become a flood after the Irish Famine of 1847 and that immigrant flood contained possible subversive political elements among Germans (and others) who began arriving in flight from the 1848 socialist convulsions in Europe. The nativists believed they must be turned back.

Headley's account of the riot at the Astor Place Opera House in 1849 is a reasonably accurate outline of the events, but contains little social or political context. The riot, as Headley tells us, was based on the rivalry of two actors: the Englishman William Macready and the American Edwin Forrest. Their feud took place on both sides of the Atlantic. Forrest was the darling of crowds in the theaters of the Bowery, who appreciated his vigorous, muscular style of performing Shakespeare. By all accounts, Macready's style was subtler, more refined, with elocution counting more than vulgar passion. When Forrest brought his acting to London in 1846, he was heckled, and believed that Macready was one of the instigators. He went to see Macready perform and heckled back. Then Macready came to tour America in 1849, with a final stop in New York. The stage, literally, was set for confrontation.

There is an unstated suggestion in Headley's account that somehow the Irish were the principal players in what then took place at the aristocratic "uptown" Astor Place Opera House. We know that Macready's performance of Macbeth on May 7th was brought to a halt by heckling and rowdyism, and a second performance three nights later ended up in terrible bloodshed. At the time, the 36–year–old Headley lived in New York. He had worked for a year as a journalist for the *New York Tribune*, but we don't know whether he went to the Astor Place scene as a reporter or writer or even curious citizen. Reporting would have revealed that the most passionate enemies of Macready were in fact American nativists. Their intellectual leader was a slightly sinister Tammany leader named Isaiah Rynders. But the nativist commander on the spot was a man named Edward Z.C. Judson, also a writer. In the year or so before the Astor Place riots, he had been using his own publication, *Ned Buntline's Own*, to campaign against all British influence in the United States, including influence in literature and the theater. When Macready decided to risk a second performance of Macbeth on May 10 almost 10,000 people showed up on the streets. Some were drawn by a public manifesto urging protest against the "English Aristocratic Opera House". Certainly some Irishmen came up from the Five Points slum to Astor Place, and were there when the militia fired into the crowd. Twenty–two people died, including an eight–year–old boy. Seven of the dead were Irish.

Later, Judson/Buntline would serve a year in jail for his part in the riot. But Headley apparently absorbed no lessons about the potential fevers of nativism. Five years later (as Thomas Rose and James Rodgers point out in their superb introduction to the 1970 edition of this book) he was elected to the state assembly on the Know Nothing ticket. In 1971, historian Edward K. Spann would describe that movement in "The New Metropolis: New York City. 1840-1857":

"Know-Nothingism had become a popular political movement which made no secrets of its objectives: the elimination of all foreigners and Roman Catholics from public office, the establishment of a 21–year naturalization period for all aliens, the deportation of foreign paupers and criminals, Bible-reading in the public schools, and the preservation of Protestant domination in all areas of public life."

The movement swiftly faded, swamped by the arrival of more and more immigrants, and in 1858, after service as New York's

Secretary of State, Headley chose to leave the city for the comforts of upstate Newburgh, where he lived and worked for the rest of his life. But the resentments aroused by the rhetoric of the Know Nothings did not fade quickly. Inadvertently, they served as incentives to the immigrants to join the Democratic Party, thus increasing its power—the opposite of what the Know Nothings wanted. And they provided powerful and lingering emotional fuel for the Draft Riots of 1863.

These were the worst in the city's history, and they are referred to in the plural not simply because they lasted for four days and nights but because there were at least four separate riots combined in those days. One was the most obvious: a protest against Abraham Lincoln's badly–conceived draft law which allowed rich people to hire substitutes for $300. But there were at least three other riots going on at the same time: a race riot, pitting white mobs against African-Americans, with most of mob fury driven by hatred of mixed marriages with Irish women; a trade union riot, directed against the use of black strikebreakers by some city corporations; and finally a criminal riot, which included the looting of Brooks Brothers, along with many liquor and grocery stores.

Class hatred permeated most of the rioting, with attacks on the mansions of some prominent citizens. The race rioting—white against black—had a special savagery, including sexual mutilation and lacerations of the dying. One mob burned down the Colored Orphans Asylum on Fifth Avenue and 43rd Street (Irish policemen rescued all but one of these terrified children). The militia used howitzers on one mob as if their cannon were rifles. Headley, and other contemporaries, believed that a thousand people had been killed. Modern scholars have verified only one hundred twenty dead, including eighteen African–Americans. Still, the Draft Riots remain the most murderous in American history.

There were riots that Headley did not describe, most of them listed in an appendix to this book. Many were riots between Irish Catholics and Irish Protestants, re-fighting that part of the late 17th century (including the Battle of the Boyne) that continued killing human beings in Northern Ireland in the 20th century. The New York culmination of this ancient quarrel came in the two "Orange" riots of 1870 and 1871, which would leave almost seventy dead. To his credit, Headley describes them in a properly appalled way. In the aftermath, marches by the Orange Order in New York were essentially banned (through deprivation of marching permits) and most members found their way into Masonic Orders. After 1871, there were no more riots between Catholics and Protestants.

In our own time, race has often been a factor in riots, but the New York death tolls have been comparatively low. Harlem erupted in 1935, 1943 (during the Second World War), 1964, 1965, 1968, with the murder of Martin Luther King, and most recently in Crown Heights in 1991. With the exception of Crown Heights, they were not riots against people—with white corpses littering the streets—but riots against property. That is to say, they were primarily about class. Unlike the violent urban outbursts in Watts, Detroit, Miami, and other American cities during the 1960s and 1970s, the combined New York death toll was less than a dozen. That was no consolation to the dead, or their families, of course, and these deaths contributed to enduring mistrust of the police by African-Americans.

But they also showed that across the centuries New Yorkers had learned something valuable about the dangers of chaos, the techniques of containing it, and the absolute duty of intelligent people to perceive and attack its root causes. In this book, Joel Tyler Headley shows clearly that the Shining City on the Hill envisioned by so many early Americans (both aristocrats and republicans) was not a complete illusion, but needed to be seen as a whole, with the certainty that some dangers might forever lurk in the shadows. He does not suggest that violent disorder was about to vanish from human activity. Anyone today who believes that it is forever behind us is almost certain to be disappointed, and in a city like New York, prophecy is always a fool's game. Still, we have learned something, and for all of its lack of a wider context, Headley's book has been one of our instructors.

Note: The following four pages are a facsimile of material from the 1873 edition of *The Great Riots of New York: 1712–1873*.

BURNING OF THE PROVOST-MARSHAL'S OFFICE—FIRST DAY OF THE DRAFT RIOT.

THE

GREAT RIOTS

OF

NEW YORK,

1712 TO 1873.

INCLUDING A FULL AND COMPLETE ACCOUNT

OF THE

FOUR DAYS' DRAFT RIOT OF 1863.

By Hon. J. T. HEADLEY,

Author of "NAPOLEON AND HIS MARSHALS," "WASHINGTON AND HIS GEN-
ERALS," "SACRED MOUNTAINS," "SACRED HEROES AND MARTYRS," ETC.

ILLUSTRATED.

———•••———

NEW YORK:

E. B. TREAT, 805 BROADWAY,

Successor to E. B. TREAT & CO., *Formerly Subscription Department of* CHARLES SCRIBNER & CO.

1873.

Stereotyped at the
WOMEN'S PRINTING HOUSE,
56, 58 and 60 Park Street,
New York.

To

THE METROPOLITAN POLICE,

WHOSE

UNWAVERING FIDELITY AND COURAGE IN THE PAST,

ARE A

SURE GUARANTEE OF WHAT THEY WILL DO

FOR

NEW YORK CITY IN THE FUTURE,

THIS WORK IS

RESPECTFULLY INSCRIBED

BY

The Author.

· PREFACE ·

THE MATERIALS FOR the descriptions of the Negro and Doctors' Riots were gathered from the Archives of the Historical Society; those of the immediately succeeding ones, from the press of the times.

For the scenes and incidents that occurred on the stage and behind the curtain in the Astor-place Opera Riot, I am indebted to a pamphlet entitled *"Behind the Scenes."*

The materials for the history of the Draft Riots were obtained in part from the Daily Press, and in part from the City and Military Authorities, especially Commissioner Acton, Seth Hawley, General Brown, and Colonel Frothingham, who succeeded in putting them down.

Mr. David Barnes, who published, some ten years ago, a pamphlet entitled "The Metropolitan Police," kindly furnished me facts relating to the Police Department of great value, and which saved me much labor and time.

Much difficulty has been encountered in gathering together, from various quarters, the facts spread over a century and a half, but it is believed that everything necessary to a complete understanding of the subjects treated of has been given, consistent with the continuity and interest of the narrative.

Of course some minor riots—a collection of mobs that were easily dispersed by the police, and were characterized by no prolonged struggle or striking incidents—are not mentioned.

CHAPTER I

The Great Riots
of New York City.

CHARACTER OF A CITY ILLUSTRATED BY RIOTS.—NEW MATERIAL FOR
HISTORY OF DRAFT RIOTS.—HISTORY OF THE REBELLION INCOM-
PLETE WITHOUT HISTORY OF THEM.—THE FATE OF THE NATION
RESTING ON THE ISSUES OF THE STRUGGLE IN NEW YORK CITY.—THE
BEST PLAN TO ADOPT FOR PROTECTION AGAINST MOBS.

THE HISTORY OF the riots that have taken place in a great city
from its foundation, is a curious and unique one, and illustrates the peculiar changes in tone and temper that have come
over it in the course of its development and growth. They exhibit
also one phase of its moral character—furnish a sort of moral history of that vast, ignorant, turbulent class which is one of the distinguishing features of a great city, and at the same time the
chief cause of its solicitude and anxiety, and often of dread.

The immediate cause, however, of my taking up the subject, was
a request from some of the chief actors in putting down the Draft
Riots of 1863, to write a history of them. It was argued that it had
never been written, except in a detached and fragmentary way in
the daily press, which, from the hurried manner in which it was
done, was necessarily incomplete, and more or less erroneous.

It was also said, and truly, that those who, by their courage and
energy, saved the city, and who now would aid me not only officially, but by their personal recollections and private memo-
randa, would soon pass away, and thus valuable material be lost.

Besides these valid reasons, it was asserted that the history of the rebellion was not complete without it, and yet no historian of that most important event in our national life had given the riots the prominence they deserved, but simply referred to them as a side issue, instead of having a vital bearing on the fate of the war and the nation. On no single battle or campaign did the destiny of the country hinge as upon that short, sharp campaign carried on by General Brown and the Police Commissioners against the rioters in the streets of New York, in the second week of July, 1863. Losses and defeats in the field could be and were repaired, but defeat in New York would in all probability have ended the war. It is not necessary to refer to the immediate direct effects of such a disaster on the army in the field, although it is scarcely possible to over-estimate the calamitous results that would have followed the instantaneous stoppage, even for a short time, of the vast accumulations of provisions, ammunition, and supplies of all kinds, that were on their way to the army through New York. Nor is it necessary to speculate on the effect of the diversion of troops from the front that such an event would have compelled, in order to recover so vital a point. Washington had better be uncovered than New York be lost. One thing only is needed to show how complete and irreparable the disaster would have been; namely, the effect it would have had on the finances of the country. With the great banking–houses and moneyed institutions of New York sacked and destroyed, the financial credit of the country would have broken down utterly. The crash of falling houses all over the country that would have followed financial disaster here, would have been like that of falling trees in a forest swept by a hurricane. Had the rioters got complete possession of the city but for a single day, their first dash would have been for the treasures piled up in its moneyed institutions. Once in possession of these, they, like the mobs of Paris, would have fired the city before yielding them up. In the crisis that was then upon us, it would not have required a long stoppage in this financial centre of the country to have effected a second revolution. With no credit abroad and no money at home, the Government would have been completely paralyzed. Not long possession of the city was needed, but only swift destruction.

Doubtless the disastrous effects would have been increased

tenfold, if possible, by uprisings in other cities, which events showed were to follow. Even partial success developed hostile elements slumbering in various parts of the country, and running from Boston almost to the extreme West.

In this view of the case, these riots assume a magnitude and importance that one cannot contemplate without a feeling of terror, and the truth of history requires that their proper place should be assigned them, and those who put them down have an honorable position beside our successful commanders and brave soldiers. It is also important, as a lesson for the future, and naturally brings up the question, what are the best measures, and what is the best policy for the city of New York to adopt, in order to protect itself from that which to–day constitutes its greatest danger—*mob violence?* If it ever falls in ruins, the work of destruction will commence and end within its own limits. We have a police and city military which have been thought to be sufficient, but experience has shown that though this provision may be ample to restore law and order in the end, it works slowly, often unwisely, and always with an unnecessary expenditure of life. In conversing with those of largest experience and intelligence in the police department on this subject of such great and growing importance, we are convinced, from their statements and views, a vast improvement in this matter can be made, while the cost to the city, instead of being increased, will be lessened; that is, a cheaper, wiser, and more effectual plan than the present one can be adopted. Of course this does not refer to mere local disturbances, which the police force in the ordinary discharge of its duties can quell, but to those great outbreaks which make it necessary to call out the military. Not that there might not be exigencies in which it would be necessary to resort, not only to the military of the city, but to invoke the aid of neighboring States; for a riot may assume the proportions of a revolution, but for such no local permanent remedy can be furnished.

The objections to relying on the military, as we invariably do in case of a large mob, are many. In the *first* place, it takes the best part of a day to get the troops together, so that a mob, so far as they are concerned, has time not only to waste and destroy for many hours, but increase in strength and audacity. The members of the various regiments are scattered all over the city, engaged in different occupations and employments, and without previous notice being given, it is a long and tedious process to get them to their respective headquarters and in uniform. This wastes much and most valuable time. Besides, they are compelled to reach the mustering place singly or in small groups, and hence liable to be cut off or driven back by the mob, which in most cases would know the place of rendezvous.

In the second place, the members are taken out from the mass of the people, between whom there might be a strong sympathy in some particular outbreak, which would impair their efficiency, and make them hesitate to shoot down their friends and acquaintances.

In the third place, in ordinary peace times, these uniformed regiments are not the steadiest or most reliable troops, as was witnessed in the riots of 1863, as well as in those of the Astor Place in 1849.

They hesitate, or are apt to become hasty or disorganized in a close, confused fight, and driven back. In the commencement of a riot, a defeat of the military gives increased confidence, and indeed, power to a mob, and makes the sacrifice of life, in the end, far greater.

In the fourth place, clearing the streets does not always dissipate a mob. A whole block of houses may become a fortress, which it is necessary to storm before a permanent victory is gained. Half-disciplined men, unaccustomed, and unskilled to such work, make poor headway with their muskets through narrow halls, up stairways, and through scuttle-holes.

In the fifth place, the military of the city cannot be called away from their work for two or three days, to parade the city, without a heavy expense, and hence the process is a costly one.

In the last place, the firing of these troops at the best is not very judicious, and cannot be discriminating, so that those are shot down often least culpable, and of least influence in the mob— in fact, more lives usually are taken than is necessary.

The simplest, most efficient, and most economical plan would be to select five hundred or more of the most courageous, experienced, and efficient men from the police department, and form them into a separate battalion, and have them drilled in each evolutions, manoeuvres, and modes of attack or defence, as would belong to the work they were set apart to do. A battery might be given them in case of certain emergencies, and a portion carefully trained in its use. At a certain signal of the bell, they should be required to hasten, without a moment's delay, to their head-quarters. A mob could hardly be gathered and commence work before this solid body of disciplined, reliable men would be upon them. These five hundred men would scatter five thousand rioters like chaff before them. It would be more efficient than two entire regiments, even if assembled, and would be worth more than the whole military of the city for the first half day.

Besides, clubs are better than guns. They take no time to load—they are never discharged like muskets, leaving their owners for the time at the mercy of the mob. Their volleys are incessant and perpetual, given as long and fast as strong arms can strike. They are also more discriminating than bullets, hitting the guilty ones first. Moreover, they disable rather than kill—which is just as effectual, and far more desirable. In addition to all this, being trained to one purpose, instructed to one duty, a mob would be their natural enemies, and hence sympathy with them in any cause almost impossible.

• CHAPTER II •

The Negro Riots
of 1712–1741

PROBABLY NO EVENT of comparatively modern times—certainly none in our history—has occurred so extraordinary in some of its phases, as the negro riot of 1741. We cannot fully appreciate it, not merely because of the incompleteness of some of its details, nor from the lapse of time, but because of our inability to place ourselves in the position or state of mind of the inhabitants of New York City at that period. We can no more throw ourselves into the social condition, and feel the influences of that time, than we can conceive the outward physical appearance of the embryo metropolis. It is impossible to stand amid the whirl and uproar of New York to–day, and imagine men plough-ing, and sowing grain, and carting hay into barns, where the City Hall now stands. The conception of nearly all the city lying below the Park, above it farms to Canal Street, beyond that clear-ings where men are burning brush and logs to clear away the fal-low, and still farther on, towards Central Park, an unbroken wilderness, is so dim and shadowy, that we can hardly fix its out-lines. Yet it was so in 1741. Where now stands the Tombs, and clus-ter the crowded tenements of Five Points, was a pond or lakelet, nearly two miles in circumference and fifty feet deep, and encir-cled by a dense forest. Its deep, sluggish outlet into the Hudson is now Canal Street. In wet weather there was another water com-munication with the East River, near Peck Slip, cutting off the lower part of the island, leaving another island, containing some eight hundred acres. Through Broad Street, along which now rolls each day the stream of business, and swells the tumult of the Brokers' Board, then swept a deep stream, up which boatmen rowed their boats to sell oysters. The water that supplied these streams and ponds is now carried off through immense sewers, deep under ground, over which the unconscious population tread. Where Front and Water Streets on the east side, and West Greenwich and Washington on the west side, now stretch, were then the East and Hudson Rivers, laving smooth and pebbly beaches. There was not a single sidewalk in all the city, and only some half dozen paved streets. On the Battery stood the fort, in which were the Governor's and secretary's houses, and over which floated the British flag.

But all this outward appearance is no more unlike the New York of to-day than its internal condition.

The population numbered only about ten thousand, one-fifth of which was negroes, who were slaves. Their education being wholly neglected, they were ignorant and debased, and addicted to almost every vice. They were, besides, restive under their bondage and the severe punishments often inflicted on them, which caused their masters a great deal of anxiety. Not isolated as an inland plantation, but packed in a narrow space, they had easy communication with each other, and worse than all, with the reckless and depraved crews of the vessels that came into port. It is true, the most stringent measures were adopted to prevent them from assembling together; yet, in spite of every precaution, there would now and then come to light some plan or project that would fill the whites with alarm. They felt half the time as though walking on the crust of a volcano, and hence were in a state of mind to exaggerate every danger, and give credit to every sinister rumor.

The experience of the past, as well as the present state of feeling among the slaves, justified this anxiety and dread; for only thirty years before occurred just such an outbreak as they now feared. On the 7th of April, in 1712, between one and two o'clock in the morning, the house of Peter Van Tilburgh was set on fire by negroes, which was evidently meant as a signal for a general revolt.

The cry of fire roused the neighboring inhabitants, and they rushed out through the unpaved muddy streets, toward the blazing building. As they approached it, they saw, to their amazement, in the red light of the flames, a band of negroes standing in front, armed with guns and long knives. Before the whites could hardly comprehend what the strange apparition meant, the negroes fired, and then rushed on them with their knives, killing several on the spot. The rest, leaving the building to the mercy of the flames, ran to the fort on the Battery, and roused the Governor. Springing from his bed, he rushed out and ordered a cannon to be fired from the ramparts to alarm the town. As the heavy report boomed over the bay and shook the buildings of the town, the inhabitants leaped from their beds, and looking out of the windows, saw the sky lurid with flames. Their dread and uncertainty were increased, when they heard the heavy splash of soldiers through the mud, and the next moment saw their bayonets gleam out of the gloom, as they hurried forward towards the fire. In the meantime, other negroes had rushed to the spot, so that soon there were assembled, in proportion to the white population, what in the present population of the city would be fully 10,000 negroes.

The rioters stood firm till they saw the bayonets flashing in the fire-light, and then, giving one volley, fled into the darkness northward, towards what is now Wall Street. The scattered inhabitants they met, who, roused by the cannon, were hastening to the fire, they attacked with their knives, killing and wounding several. The soldiers, firing at random into the darkness, followed after them, accompanied by a crowd of people. The negroes made for the woods and swamps near where the Park now stands, and disappearing in the heavy shadows of the forest, were lost to view. Knowing it would be vain to follow them into the thickets, the soldiers and inhabitants surrounded them and kept watch till morning. Many, of course, got off and buried themselves in the deeper, more extensive woods near Canal Street, but many others were taken prisoners. Some, finding themselves closely pressed and all avenues of escape cut off, deliberately shot themselves, preferring such a death to the one they knew awaited them. How many were killed and captured during the morning, the historian does not tell us. We can only infer that the number must have been great, from the statement he incidentally makes, that "during the day *nineteen more were* taken, tried, and executed—some that turned State's evidence were transported. "Eight or ten whites had been murdered," and many more wounded.

It was a terrible event, and remembered by the present inhabitants with horror and dismay. To the little handful occupying the point of the island, it was a tragedy as great as a riot in New York to-day would be, in which was a loss of 5,000 or more on each side.

Many middle-aged men, in 1741, were young men at that time, and remembered the fearful excitement that prevailed, and it was a common topic of conversation.

The state of things, therefore, which we have described, was natural. This was rendered worse by the arrival, in the winter of 1741, of a Spanish vessel, which had been captured as a prize, the crew of which was composed in part of negroes, who were sold at auction as slaves. Those became very intractable, and in spite of the floggings they received, uttered threats that they knew would reach their masters' ears. Still, no evidence of any general plot against the inhabitants was suspected, and things were moving on in their usual way, when, on the 18th of March, a wild and blustering day, the Governor's house in the fort was discovered to be on fire. Fanned by a fierce south-east wind, the flames spread to the King's chapel, the secretary's house, barracks, and stables; and in spite of all efforts to save them, were totally consumed. The origin of the fire was supposed to be accidental, but a few days after, Captain Warren's house, near the fort, was found to be on fire. Two or three days later, the storehouse of Mr. Van Zandt was discovered on fire. Still, no general suspicions were aroused. Three more days passed, when a cow-stall was reported on fire, and a few hours later, the house of Mr. Thompson; the fire in the latter case originating in the room where a negro slave slept. The very next day, live coals were discovered under the stable of John Murray, on Broadway. This, evidently, was no accident, but the result of design, and the people began to be alarmed. The day following, the house of a sergeant near the fort was seen to be on fire, and soon after, flames arose from the roof of a dwelling near the Fly Market. The rumor now spread like wildfire through the town that it was the work of incendiaries. It seems to us a small foundation to base such a belief on, but it must be remembered that the public mind was in a state to believe almost anything.

The alarm was increased by the statement of Mrs. Earle, who said that on Sunday, as she was looking out of her window, she saw three negroes swaggering up Broadway, engaged in earnest conversation. Suddenly she heard one of them exclaim, "Fire! fire! Scorch! scorch! a little d—n by and by!" and then throwing up his hands, laughed heartily. Coupled with the numerous fires that had occurred, and the rumors afloat, it at once excited her suspicions that this conversation had something to do with a plot to burn the city. She therefore immediately reported it to an alderman, and he, next day, to the justices.

Although the number of buildings thus mysteriously set on fire was, in reality, small, yet it was as great in proportion to the town then, as three hundred would be in New York to-day. Less than that number, we imagine, would create a panic in the city, especially if the public mind was in a feverish state, as, for instance, during the recent civil war.

Some thought the Spanish negroes had set the buildings on fire from revenge, especially as those of the Government were the first to suffer. Others declared that it was a plot of the entire negro population to burn down the city. This belief was strengthened by the fact that, in one of the last fires, a slave of one of the most prominent citizens was seen to leap from the window, and make off over garden fences. A shout was immediately raised by the spectators, and a pursuit commenced. The terrified fugitive made desperate efforts to escape, but being overtaken, he was seized, and, pale as death, lifted on men's shoulders and carried to jail.

Added to all this, men now remembered it lacked but a few days of being the anniversary of the bloody riot of thirty years ago. They began to watch and question the negroes, and one of the Spanish sailors, on being interrogated, gave such unsatisfactory, suspicious answers, that the whole crew were arrested, and thrown into prison. But that same afternoon, while the magistrates, whom the alarming state of things had called together, were in consultation about it, the cry of "Fire!" again startled the entire community. The ringing of the alarm-bell had now become almost as terrifying as the sound of the last trumpet, and the panic became general. The first step was to ascertain if there were any strangers in town who might be concealed enemies, and a thorough search was made—the militia being ordered out, and sentries posted at the ends of all the streets, with orders to stop all persons carrying bags and bundles. This was done on the 13th of April. None being found, the conclusion became inevitable that some dark, mysterious plot lay at the bottom of it all, and the inhabitants thought the city was doomed, like Sodom. First, the more timorous packed up their valuable articles and fled into the country, up toward Canal Street. This increased the panic, which swelled until almost the entire population were seen hurrying through the streets, fleeing for their lives. The announcement of an approaching army would not have created a greater stampede. Every cart and vehicle that could be found was engaged at any price, into which whole families were piled, and hurried away to the farms beyond Chambers Street, in the neighborhood of Canal Street. It was a strange spectacle, and the farmers could hardly believe their senses, at this sudden inundation into their quiet houses of the people of the city. The town authorities were also swept away in the general excitement, and negroes of all ages and sexes were arrested by the wholesale, and hurried to prison. The Supreme Court was to sit in the latter part of April, and the interval of a few days was spent in efforts to get at the guilty parties. But nothing definite could be ascertained, as the conspirators, whoever they were, kept their own secret. At length, despairing of getting at the truth in any other way, the authorities offered a reward of a hundred pounds, and a full pardon to any one who would turn State's evidence, and reveal the names of the ringleaders. This was pretty sure to bring out the facts, if there were any to disclose, and almost equally sure to obtain a fabricated story, if there was nothing to tell. A poor, ignorant slave, shaking with terror in his cell, would hardly be proof against such an inducement as a free pardon, and to him or her an almost fabulous sum of money, if he had anything to reveal, while the temptation to invent a tale that would secure both liberty and money was equally strong.

On the 21st of April the court met, Judges Philips and Horsmander presiding. A jury was impanelled, but although there was no lack of prisoners, there was almost a total want of evidence sufficient to put a single man on trial. The reward offered had not borne its legitimate fruits, and no one offered to make any revelations.

Among the first brought up for examination was Mary Burton, a colored servant girl, belonging to John Hughson, the keeper of a low, dirty negro tavern over on the west side of the city, near the Hudson River. This was a place of rendezvous for the worst negroes of the town; and from some hints that Mary had dropped, it was suspected it had been the head-quarters of the conspirators. But when brought before the Grand Jury, she refused to be sworn. They entreated her to take the oath and tell the whole truth, but she only shook her head. They then threatened her, but with no better success; they promised she should be protected from danger and shielded from prosecution, but she still maintained an obstinate silence. They then showed her the reward, and attempted to bribe her with the wealth in store for her, but she almost spat on it in her scorn. This poor negro slave showed an independence and stubbornness in the presence of the jury that astonished them. Finding all their efforts vain, they ordered her to be sent to jail. This terrified her, and she consented to be sworn. But after taking the oath, she refused to say anything about the fire. A theft had been traced to Hughson, and she told all she knew about that, but about the fires would neither deny nor affirm anything. They then appealed to her conscience; painted before her the terrors of the final judgment, and the torments of hell, till at last she broke down, and proposed to make a clean breast of it. She commenced by saying that Hughson had threatened to take her life if she told, and then again hesitated. But at length, by persistent efforts, the following facts were wrenched from her by piecemeal. She said that three negroes—giving their names—had been in the habit of meeting at the tavern, and talking about burning of the fort and city and murdering the people, and that Hughson and his wife had promised to help them; after which Hughson was to be governor and Cuff Phillipse king. That the first part of the story was true, there is little doubt. How much, with the imagination and love of the marvellous peculiar to her race, she added to it, it is not easy to say. She said, moreover, that but one white person beside her master and mistress was in the conspiracy, and that was an Irish girl known as Peggy, "the Newfoundland Beauty." She had several *aliases*, and was an abandoned character, being a prostitute to the negroes, and at this time kept as a mistress by a bold, desperate negro named Cæsar. This revelation of Mary's fell on the Grand Jury like a bombshell. The long-sought secret they now felt was out. They immediately informed the magistrates. Of course the greatest excitement followed. Peggy was next examined, but she denied Mary Burton's story *in toto*—swore that she knew nothing of any conspiracy or of the burning of the stores, that if she should accuse any one it would be a lie, and blacken her own soul.

It is rather a severe reflection on the courts of justice of that period, or we might rather say, perhaps, a striking illustration of the madness that had seized on all, that although the law strictly forbade any slave to testify in a court of justice against a white person, yet this girl Mary Burton was not only allowed to appear as evidence against Peggy, but her oath was permitted to outweigh hers, and cause her to be sentenced to death. The latter, though an abandoned, desperate character, was seized with terror at the

near approach of death, and begged to be allowed another examination, which was granted, and she professed to make a full confession. It is a little singular that while she corroborated Mary
Burton's statement as to the existence of a conspiracy, she located
the seat of it not in Hughson's tavern, but in a miserable shanty
near the Battery, kept by John Romme, who, she said, had promised to carry them all to a new country, and give them their liberty, if they would murder the whites and bring him the plunder.
Like Mary Burton's confession, if truthful at all, it evidently had
a large mixture of falsehood in it.

On Saturday, May 9th, Peggy was again brought in, and under-
went a searching examination. Some of her statements seemed
improbable, and they therefore tested them in every possible way.
It lasted for several hours, and resulted in a long *detailed* confession, in which she asserted, among other things, that it was the
same plot that failed in 1712, when the negroes designed to kill
all the whites, in fact, exterminate them from the island. She
implicated a great many negroes in the conspiracy; and every one
that she accused, as they were brought before her, she identified
as being present at the meetings of the conspirators in Romme's
house. The court seemed anxious to avoid any collusion between
the prisoners, and therefore kept them apart, so that each story
should rest on its own basis. By this course they thought they
would be able to distinguish what was true and what was false.

Either from conscious guilt, or from having got some inkling
of the charge to be brought against him, Romme fled before he
could be arrested. His wife, however, and the negroes whose
names Peggy gave, were sent to jail.

On the 11th of May, or twenty days after the court convened,
the executions commenced. On this day, Cæsar and Prince, two
of the three negroes Mary Burton testified against, were hung,
though not for the conspiracy, but for theft. They were abandoned men, and died recklessly. Peggy and Hughson and his wife
were next condemned. The former, finding that her confession
did not, as had been promised, secure her pardon, retracted all
she had said, and exculpated entirely the parties whose arrest she
had caused.

An atmosphere of gloom now rested over the city; every face

showed signs of dread. In this state of feeling the Lieutenant-governor issued a proclamation, appointing a day of fasting and humiliation, not only in view of this calamity, but on account also of the want and loss caused by the past severe winter, and the declaration of war by England against Spain. When the day arrived, every shop was closed and business of all kinds suspended, and the silence and repose of the Sabbath rested on the entire community. Without regard to sect, all repaired to the places of worship, where the services were performed amid the deepest solemnity.

The day of execution appointed for Hughson, his wife, and Peggy was a solemn one, and almost the entire population turned out to witness it. The former had declared that some extraordinary appearance would take place at his execution, and every one gazed on him as he passed in a cart from the prison to the gallows. He was a tall, powerful man, being six feet high. He stood erect in the cart all the way, his piercing eye fixed steadily on the distance, and his right hand raised high as his fetters would permit, and beckoning as though he saw help coming from afar. His face was usually pale and colorless, but to-day it was noticed that two bright red spots burned on either cheek, which added to the mystery with which the superstitious spectators invested him. When the sad procession arrived at the place of execution, the prisoners were helped to the ground, and stood exposed to the gaze of the crowd. Hughson was firm and self-possessed; but Peggy, pale, and weeping, and terror-struck, begging for life; while the wife, with the rope round her neck, leaned against a tree, silent and composed, but colorless as marble. One after another they were launched into eternity, and the crowd, solemn and thoughtful, turned their steps homeward.

Hughson was hung in chains; and in a few days a negro was placed beside him, and here they swung, "blind and blackening," in the April air, in full view of the tranquil bay, a ghastly spectacle to the fishermen as they plied their vocation near by. For three weeks they dangled here in sunshine and storm, a terror to the passers–by. At length a rumor passed through the town that Hughson had turned into a negro, and the negro into a white man. This was a new mystery, and day after day crowds would come and gaze on the strange transformation, some thinking it super-natural, and others trying to give an explanation. Hughson had threatened to take poison, and it was thought by many that he had, and it was the effect of this that had wrought the change in his appearance. For ten days the Battery was thronged with spectators, gazing on these bloated, decomposing bodies, many in their superstitious fears expecting some new transformation. Under the increasing heat of the sun, they soon began to drip, till at last the body of Hughson burst asunder, filling the air with such an intolerable stench that the fishermen shunned the locality.

As simple hanging was soon thought not sufficient punishment, and they were left to swing, and slowly rot in chains, so this last was at length thought to be too lenient, and the convicts were condemned to be burned at the stake. Two negroes, named Quack and Cuffee, were the first doomed to this horrible death. The announcement of this sentence created the greatest excitement. It was a new thing to the colonists, this mode of torture being appropriated by the savages for prisoners taken in war. Curious crowds gathered to see the stake erected, or stare at the loads of wood as they passed along the street, and were unloaded at its base. It was a strange spectacle to behold—the workmen carefully piling up the fagots under the spring sun; the spectators looking on, some horrified, and others fierce as savages; and over all the blue sky bending, while the gentle wind stole up from the hay and whispered in the tree-tops overhead. On the day of execution an immense crowd assembled. The two negroes were brought forward, pale and terrified, and bound to the stake. As the men approached with the fire to kindle the pile, they shrieked out in terror, confessed the conspiracy, and promised, if released, to tell all about it. They were at once taken down. This was the signal for an outbreak, and shouts of "burn 'em, burn 'em" burst from the multitude. Mr. Moore then asked the sheriff to delay execution till he could see the Governor and get a reprieve. He hurried off, and soon returned with a conditional one. But, as he met the sheriff on the common, the latter told him that it would be impossible to take the criminals through the crowd without a strong guard, and before that could arrive, they would be murdered by the exasperated populace. They were then tied up again, and the torch applied. The flames arose around the unhappy victims. The curling smoke soon hid their dusky forms from view, while their shrieks and cries for mercy grew fainter and fainter, as the fierce fire shrivelled up their forms, till at last nothing but the crackling of the flames was heard, and the shouting, savage crowd grew still. As the fire subsided, the two wretched creatures, crisped to a cinder, remained to tell, for the hundredth time, to what barbarous deeds terror and passion may lead men.

Some of the negroes went laughing to the place of execution, indulging in all sorts of buffoonery to the last, and mocking the crowd which surrounded them.

All protested their innocence to the last, and if they had confessed previously, retracted before death their statements and accusations. But this contradiction of themselves, to–morrow denying what to–day they had solemnly sworn on the Bible to be true, instead of causing the authorities to hesitate, and consider how much terror and the hope of pardon had to do with it, convinced them still more of the strength and dangerous nature of the conspiracy, and they went to work with a determination and recklessness which made that summer the bloodiest and most terrific in the annals of New York. No lawyer was found bold enough to step forward and defend these poor wretches, but all volunteered their services to aid the Government in bringing them to punishment. The weeks now, as they rolled on, were freighted with terror and death, and stamped with scenes that made the blood run cold. This little town on the southern part of Manhattan Island was wholly given to panic, and a nameless dread of some mysterious, awful fate, extended even to the scattered farm-houses near Canal Street. Between this and the last of August, a hundred and fifty-four negroes, exclusive of whites, were thrown into prison, till every cell was crowded and packed to suffocation with them. For three months, sentence of condemnation was on an average of one a day. The last execution was that of a Catholic priest, or rather of a schoolmaster of the city, who was charged with being one. Mary Burton, after an interval of three months, pretended to remember that he was present with the other conspirators she had first named as being in Hughson's tavern.

His trial was long, and apparently without excitement. He conducted his own case with great ability, and brought many witnesses to prove his good character and orderly conduct; but he, of course, could not disprove the assertion of Mary, that she had some time or other seen him with the conspirators at Hughson's tavern—for the latter, with his wife and Peggy, and the negroes she had before named, had all been executed. Mary Burton alone was left, and her evidence being credited, no amount of testimony could avail him.

Although the proceedings were all dignified and solemn, as became an English court, yet the course the trial took showed how utterly unbalanced and one–sided it had become. To add weight to Mary's evidence, many witnesses were examined to prove that Ury, though a schoolmaster, had performed the duties of a Catholic priest, as though this were an important point to establish. The attorney–general, in opening the case, drew a horrible picture of former persecutions by the Papists, and their cruelties to the Protestants, until it was apparent that all that the jury needed to indorse a verdict of guilty was evidence that he was a Catholic priest. Still it would be unfair to attribute this feeling wholly to religious intolerance or the spirit of persecution. England was at this time at war with Spain, and a report was circulated that the Spanish priests in Florida had formed a conspiracy to murder the English colonists. A letter from Ogilthorpe, in Georgia, confirmed this. Ury, who was an educated Englishman, but had led an adventurous life in different countries, could not disprove this, and he was convicted and sentenced to be hung. He met his fate with great composure and dignity, asserting his innocence to the last. He made the eighteenth victim hung, while thirteen had been burned at the stake, and seventy-one transported to various countries.

At the average rate of two every week, one hanged and one burned alive, they were hurried into eternity amid prayers, and imprecations, and shrieks of agony. The hauling of wood to the stake, and the preparation of the gallows, kept the inhabitants in a state bordering on insanity. Business was suspended, and every face wore a terrified look. The voice of pity as well as justice was hushed, and one desire, that of swift vengeance, filled every heart. Had the press of to-day, with its system of interviewing, and minuteness of detail and description, existed then, there would have been handed down to us a chapter in human history that could be paralleled only in the dark ages.

A swift massacre, a terrible slaughter, comes and goes like an earthquake or a tornado, and stuns rather than debases; but this long, steady succession of horrible executions and frightful scenes changed the very nature of the inhabitants, and they became prey to a spirit demoniacal rather than human. The prayers and tears of those led forth to the stake, their heartrending cries as they were bound to it, and their shrieks of agony that were wafted out over the still waters of the bay, fell on hard and pitiless hearts. The ashes of the wood that consumed one victim would hardly grow cold before a new fire was kindled upon them, and the charred and blackened posts stood month after month, hideous monuments of what man may become when judgment and reason are surrendered to fear and passion. The spectacle was made still more revolting by the gallows standing near the stake, on which many were hung in chains, and their bodies left to swing, blacken, and rot in the summer air, a ghastly, horrible sight.

Where this madness, that had swept away court, bar, and people together, would have ended, it is impossible to say, had not a new terror seized the inhabitants. Mary Burton, on whose accusation the first victims had been arrested and executed, finding herself a heroine, sought new fields in which to win notoriety. She ceased to implicate the blacks, and turned her attention to the whites, and twenty-four were arrested and thrown into prison. Elated with her success, she began to ascend in the social scale, and criminated some persons of the highest social standing in the city, whose characters were above suspicion. This was turning the tables on them in a manner the upper class did not expect, and they began to reflect what the end might be. The testimony that was sufficient to condemn the slaves was equally conclusive against them. The stake and the gallows which the court had erected for the black man, it could not pull down because a white gentleman stood under their shadow.

Robespierre and his friends cut off the upper-crust of society without hesitation or remorse; but, unfortunately the crust next below this became in turn the upper-crust, which also had to be removed, until at last, they themselves were reached, when they paused. They had advanced up to their necks in the bloody tide of revolution, and finding that to proceed farther would take them overhead, they attempted to wade back to shore. So here, so long as the accusations were confined to the lowest class, it was all well enough, but when *they* were being reached, it was high time to stop. The proceedings were summarily brought to a close, further examinations were deemed unnecessary, and confessions became flat and unprofitable; and this strange episode in American history ended.

That there had been cause for alarm, there can be no doubt. That threats should be uttered by the slaves, is natural; for this would be in keeping with their whole history in this country. Nor is it at all improbable that a conspiracy was formed; for this, too, would only be in harmony with the conduct of slaves from time immemorial. The utter folly and hopelessness of such a one as the blacks testified to, has been urged against its existence altogether. If the argument is good for anything, it proves that the conspiracy thirty years before never existed, and that the Southampton massacre was a delusion, and John Brown never hatched his utterly insane conspiracy in Harper's Ferry. There have been a good many servile insurrections plotted in this country, not one of which was a whit more sensible or easier of execution than this, which was said to look to the complete overthrow of the little city. That the fires which first started the panic were the work of negro incendiaries, there is but little doubt; but how far they were a part of a wide-laid plan, it is impossible to determine.

Unquestionably, success at the outset would have made the movement general, so that nothing but military force could have arrested it.

There is one thing, however, about which there is no doubt— that a panic seized the people and the courts, and made them as unreliable as in the days of the Salem witchcraft. But these striking exhibitions of the weakness of human nature under certain circumstances have been witnessed since the world was made, and probably will continue to the end of time, or until the race enters on a new phase of existence. Panics, even among the most veteran soldiers, sometimes occur, and hence we cannot wonder they take place amid a mixed population. Popular excitements are never characterized by reason and common–sense, and never will be. In this case, there was more reason for a panic than at first sight seems to be.

In the first place, the proportion of slaves to the whites was large. In the second place, they were a turbulent set, and had shown such a dangerous spirit, that the authorities became afraid to let them assemble together in meetings. This restriction they felt sorely, and it made them more restive. All were aware of this hostile state of feeling, and were constantly anticipating some outbreak or act of violence. Besides, it was but a few years since the thing they now feared did actually take place. And then, too, the point first aimed at was significant, and showed a boldness founded on conscious strength. Right inside the fort itself, and to the Governor's house, the torch was applied. It certainly looked ominous. Besides, the very wholesale manner in which the authorities thought it best to go to work increased the panic. In a very short time over a hundred persons were thrown into prison. The same proportion to the population to–day would be over ten thousand. Such a wholesale arrest would, of itself, throw New York into the wildest excitement, and conjure up all sorts of horrible shapes. Add to this, an average of two hundred burned at the stake, and two hundred hung every week, or more than fifty a day, and nearly three times that number sentenced to transportation, and one can faintly imagine what a frightful state of things would exist in the city. The very atmosphere grew stifling from the smoke of burning men and women, while the gallows groaned under its weight of humanity. Had this been the wild work of a mob it would have been terrible enough, but when it was the result of a deliberate judicial tribunal, which was supposed to do nothing except on the most conclusive evidence, the sense of danger was increased tenfold. The conclusion was inevitable, that the conspiracy embraced every black man in the city, and was thoroughly organized. In short, the whole place was, beyond doubt, resting over a concealed volcano, and the instinct of self–preservation demanded the most summary work. Let the inhabitants of any city become thoroughly possessed of such an idea, and they will act with no more prudence or reason than the people of New York at that time did. An undoubted belief in such a state of things will confuse the perceptions and unbalance the judgment of a community anywhere and everywhere on the globe.

Still, consistent as it is with human history, one can hardly believe it possible, as he stands in New York to–day, that men have there been burned at the stake under the sanction of English law, or left to swing and rot in the winds of heaven, by order of the Supreme Court of the city.

CHAPTER III

The Stamp-Act Riot
of 1766

A T THE PRESENT day, when personal ambition takes the place of patriotism, and love of principle gives way to love of party; when the success of the latter is placed above constitutional obligations and popular rights, one seems, as he turns back to our early history, to be transported to another age of the world, and another race of beings.

Nothing shows how thoroughly understood by the common people were the principles of liberty, and with what keen penetration they saw through all shams and specious reasoning, than the decided, nay, fierce, stand they took against the stamp act. This was nothing more than our present law requiring a governmental stamp on all public and business paper to make it valid. The only difference is, the former was levying a tax without representation—in other words, without the consent of the governed. The colonies assembled in Congress condemned it; hence the open, violent opposition to it by the people rises above the level of a common riot, and partakes more of the nature of a righteous revolution. Still, it was a riot, and exhibited the lawless features of one.

The news of the determination of the English Government to pass a stamp act, raised a storm of indignation throughout the colonies, from Massachusetts to South Carolina, and it was denounced as an oppressive, unrighteous, tyrannical measure. From the wayside tavern and the pulpit alike, it was attacked with unsparing severity. The Government, however, thought it a mere ebullition of feeling, that would not dare exhibit itself in open opposition. Nor does this confidence seem strong, when we remember the weakness of the colonies on the one side, and the strength of an organized government, with the law and force both, on the other.

Cadwallader Colden, a Scotchman by birth, and a clergyman by profession, was at that time acting Governor of New York; and to guard against any resort to force on the part of the people when the stamps should arrive, had Fort George, on the Battery, reinforced by a regiment from Crown Point, its magazines replenished, the ramparts strengthened, and its guns trained on the town. The people saw all this, and understood its import; but it had the opposite effect from that which was intended, for, instead of overawing the people, it exasperated them.

At length, in October, 1765, a ship with the British colors flying came sailing tip the bay, and anchored off Fort George. In a short time the startling tidings was circulated, that she brought a quantity of stamps. It was like sounding an alarm–bell, and the streets became thronged with excited men, while all the provincial vessels in the harbor lowered their colors to half–mast, in token of mourning. In anticipation of this event, an organization of men had been formed, called "Sons of Liberty." They at once assembled, and resolved at all hazards to get hold of those stamps. They had caused the act itself to be hawked about the streets as "the folly of England and the ruin of America," and now they determined to measure their strength with the Governor of the colony. That night, when the town was wrapped in slumber, they quietly affixed on the doors of every public office and on corners of the streets, the following placard:

Pro Patria.
    The first man that either distributes or makes use of stamped paper, let him take care of his house, person, and effects.
    Vox Populi.
    "We Dare."

To the stamp distributors they said, "Assure yourselves, the spirit of Brutus and Cassius is yet alive. We will not submit to the stamp act upon any account or in any instance."

McEvers, the head stamp distributor, frightened by the bold, determined attitude of the people, refused to receive the stamps, and Colden had them sent for greater safety to Fort George. He had written to the British Secretary, *"I am resolved to have the stamps distributed."* But the people were equally resolved they should not be. Still, on the 30th day of October, he and all the royal governors took the oath to carry the stamp act into effect; but they soon discovered that they could find no one bold enough to act as distributor. All along the sea-coast, in every part of the colonies, the people were aroused, and either assembling quietly, or called together by the ringing of bells and firing of cannon, presented such a united, determined front, that not one person remained duly commissioned to distribute stamps. On the last day of October, the merchants of New York came together, and bound themselves to "send no new orders for goods or merchandise, to countermand all former orders, and not even receive goods on commission, unless the stamp act be repealed"—that is, give up commerce at once, with all its wealth and benefits, rather than submit to a tax of a few shillings on paper.

Friday, the 1st of November, was the day fixed upon for a

public demonstration of the people throughout the colonies against it, and never dawned a morning more pregnant with the fate not only of a nation, but of the world.

From New Hampshire to South Carolina it was ushered in by the tolling of muffled bells, the firing of minute–guns, and flags hung at half–mast. Eulogies were pronounced on liberty, and everywhere people left their shops and fields, and gathered in excited throngs to discuss the great question of taxation.

"Even the children at their games, though hardly able to speak, caught up the general chorus, and went along the streets, merrily carolling: 'Liberty, Property, and no Stamps.'"*

In New York the uprising was terrific, for the population rushed together as one man—as Gage, the commander of Fort George said, "by thousands."

The sailors flocked in from the vessels, the farmers from the country, and the shouts, and ringing of bells, and firing of cannon made the city fairly tremble. Colden was terrified at the storm that was raised, and took refuge in the fort. An old man, bent and bowed with the weight of eighty years, he tottered nervously to the shelter of its guns, and ordered up a detachment of marines from a ship of war in port, for his protection. In his indignation, he wanted to fire on the people, and the black muzzles of the cannon pointing on the town had an ominous look. Whether he had threatened to do so by a message, we do not know; at any rate, the people either suspected his determination or got wind of it, for during the day an unknown person handed in at the fort–gate a note, telling him if he did, the people would hang him, like Porteus of Edinburgh, on a sign–post. He wisely forebore to give the order, for if he had not, his gray hairs would have streamed from a gibbet.

At length the day of turmoil wore away, and night came on, but with it came no diminution of the excitement. Soon as it was dark, the "Sons of Liberty," numbering thousands, surged tumultuously up around the fort, and demanded that the stamps should be given up that they might be destroyed. Colden bluntly refused,

---

*Bancroft

when with loud, defiant shouts they left, and went up Broadway to "the field" (the present Park), where they erected a gibbet, and hanged on it Colden in effigy, and beside him a figure holding a boot; some said to represent the devil, others Lord Bute, of whom the *boot*, by a pun on his name, showed for whom the effigy was designed.

The demonstration had now become a riot, and the Sons of Liberty degenerated into a mob. The feeling that had been confined to words all day must now have some outlet. A torchlight procession was formed, and the scaffold and images taken down, and borne on men's shoulders along Broadway towards the Battery. The glare of flaring lights on the buildings and faces of the excited crowd, the shouts and hurrahs that made night hideous, called out the entire population, which gazed in amazement on the strange, wild spectacle.

They boldly carried the scaffold and effigies to within a few feet of the gate of the fort, and knocked audaciously for admission. Isaac Sears was the leader of these "Sons of Liberty."

Finding themselves unable to gain admittance, they went to the Governor's carriage–house, and took out his elegant coach, and placing the two effigies in it, dragged it by hand around the streets by the light of torches, amid the jeers and shouts of the multitude. Becoming at last tired of this amusement, they returned towards the fort, and erected a second gallows, on which they hung the effigies the second time.

All this time the cannon, shotted and primed, lay silent on their carriages, while the soldiers from the ramparts looked wonderingly, idly on. General Gage did not dare to fire on the people, fearing they would sweep like an inundation over the ramparts, when he knew a general massacre would follow.

The mob now tore down the wooden fence that surrounded Bowling Green, and piling pickets and boards together, set them on fire. As the flames crackled and roared in the darkness, they pitched on the Governor's coach, with the scaffold and effigies; then hastening to his carriage–house again, and dragging out a one–horse chaise, two sleighs, and other vehicles, hauled them to the fire, and threw them on, making a conflagration that illumined the waters of the bay and the ships riding at anchor. This was a galling spectacle to the old Governor and the British officers, but they dared not interfere.

What was the particular animosity against those carriages does not appear, though it was the only property of the Governor they destroyed, unless they were a sign of that aristocratic pride which sought to enslave them. There were, at this time, not a half-dozen coaches in the city, and they naturally became the symbols of bloated pride. It is said the feeling was so strong against them, that a wealthy Quaker named Murray, who lived out of town, near where the distributing reservoir now is, kept one to ride down town in, yet dared not call it a coach, but a *"leathern convenience."*

Although Sears and other leaders of the Sons of Liberty tried to restrain the mob, their blood was now up, and they were bent on destruction. Having witnessed the conflagration of the Governor's carriages, they again inarched up Broadway, and some one shouting "James' house," the crowd took up the shout, and passing out of the city streamed through the open country, to where West Broadway now is, and near the corner of Anthony Street. This James was Major in the Royal Artillery, and had made himself obnoxious to the people by taking a conspicuous part in putting the fort into a state of defence. He had a beautiful residence here, which the mob completely gutted, broke up his elegant furniture, destroyed his library and works of art, and laid waste his ornamented grounds. They then dispersed, and the city became quiet.

The excitement was, however, not quelled—the people had not yet got hold of the stamps, which they were determined to have. Colden, having seen enough of the spirit of the "Sons of Liberty," was afraid to risk another night, even in the fort, unless it was in some way appeased; and so the day after the riot, he had a large placard posted up, stating that he should have nothing more to do with the stamps, but would leave them with Sir Henry Moore, the newly appointed Governor, then on his way from England.

This, however, did not satisfy the Sons of Liberty: they wanted the stamps themselves, and through Sears, their leader, insisted on their being given up—telling him very plainly if he did not they would storm the fort, and they were determined to do it.

The Common Council of the city now became alarmed at the ungovernable, desperate spirit of the mob, which seemed bent on blood, and begged the Governor to let them be deposited in the City Hall. To this he finally though reluctantly consented, but the feeling in the city kept at fever heat, and would remain so until the act itself was repealed.

Moore, the new Governor, soon arrived, and assumed the reigns of government. The corporation offered him the freedom of the city in a gold box, but he refused to receive it, unless upon stamped paper. It was evident he was determined to enforce the stamp act. But on consulting with Colden and others, and ascertaining the true state of things, he wisely abandoned his purpose, and soon made it publicly known. To appease the people still more, he dismantled the fort, which was peculiarly obnoxious to them from the threatening attitude it had been made to assume. Still, the infamous act was unrepealed, and the people refused to buy English manufactures, and commerce languished.

At length, Parliament, finding that further insistance in carrying out the obnoxious act only worked mischief, had repealed it. When the news reached New York, the most unbounded joy was manifested. Bells were rung, cannon fired, and placards posted, calling on a meeting of the citizens the next day to take measures for celebrating properly the great event. At the appointed time, the people came together at Howard's Hotel, and forming a procession, marched gayly to "the field," and right where the City Hall now stands, then an open lot, a salute of twenty-one guns was fired. A grand dinner followed, at which the Sons of Liberty feasted and drank loyal toasts to his Majesty, and all went "merry as a marriage-bell." The city was illuminated, and bonfires turned the night into day. In a few weeks, the King's birthday was celebrated with great display. A huge pile of wood was erected in the Park, and an ox roasted whole for the people. Cart after cart dumped its load of beer on the ground, till twenty-five barrels, flanked by a huge hogshead of rum, lay in a row, presided over by men appointed to deal out the contents to the populace. A boisterous demonstration followed that almost drowned the roar of the twenty-one cannon that thundered forth a royal salute. As a fitting wind–up to the bacchanalian scene, at night twenty-five tar–barrels, fastened on poles, blazed over the "common," while brilliant fireworks were exhibited at Bowling Green. The feasting continued late in the night, and so delighted were the "Sons of Liberty," that they erected a mast, inscribed "to his most gracious Majesty, George the Third, Mr. Pitt, and Liberty." A petition was also signed to erect a statue to Pitt, and the people seemed determined by this excess of loyalty to atone for their previous rebellious spirit. The joy, however, was of short duration—the news of the riots caused Parliament to pass a "mutiny act," by which troops were to be quartered in America in sufficient numbers to put down any similar demonstration in future, a part of the expense of their support to be paid by the colonists themselves. This exasperated "the Sons of Liberty," and they met and resolved to resist this new act of oppression to the last. The troops arrived in due time, and of course collisions took place between them and the people. Matters now continued to grow worse and worse, until the "riot of the Sons of Liberty" became a revolution, which dismembered the British Empire, and established this great republic, the influence of which on the destiny of the world no one can predict.

CHAPTER IV

Doctors' Riot, 1788.

BODY-SNATCHING.—BODIES DUG UP BY MEDICAL STU-
DENTS.—EXCITEMENT OF THE PEOPLE.—EFFECT OF THE
DISCOVERY OF A HUMAN LIMB FROM THE HOSPITAL.—
MOB RANSACK THE BUILDING.—DESTRUCTION OF
ANATOMICAL SPECIMENS.—ARRIVAL OF MAYOR, AND
IMPRISONMENT OF STUDENTS.—SECOND DAY.—EXAMINA-
TION OF COLUMBIA COLLEGE AND PHYSICIANS' HOUSES.—
APPEAL OF THE MAYOR AND DISTINGUISHED CITIZENS TO
THE MOB.—MOB ATTEMPT TO BREAK INTO JAIL AND SEIZE
THE STUDENTS.—THE FIGHT.—THE MILITARY CALLED
OUT.—BEATEN BY THE MOB.—LARGER MILITARY FORCE
CALLED OUT.—ATTACKED BY THE MOB.—DEADLY FIR-
ING.—GREAT EXCITEMENT.—FLIGHT OF DOCTORS AND
STUDENTS.

IN FORMER TIMES "body-snatching," or digging up bodies for dis-
sections, was much more heard of than at present. The fear of
it was so great, that often, in the neighborhood where medical
students were pursuing their studies, persons who lost friends
would have a watch kept over their graves for several nights, to
prevent them from being dug up. Neither the high social position of parties nor sex was any barrier to this desecration of
graves, and the public mind was often shocked by accounts of the
young and beautiful being disinterred, to be cut up by medical

THE NEW YORK HOSPITAL.—Scene of the Doctors' Riot. Located formerly on Broadway at the head of Pearl Street.

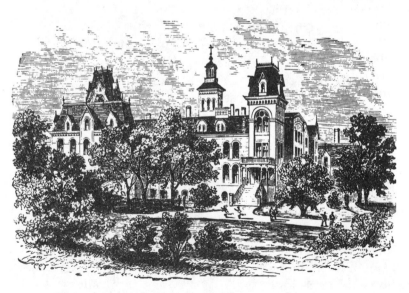

THE COLORED ORPHAN ASYLUM 143d St. The former building destroyed during the Draft Riot of 1863.

students. In the city there was, a few years ago—and perhaps there is now—a regular commercial price for bodies.

Although it was conceded that for thorough instruction in medical science, subjects for dissection were necessary, yet no one outside of the medical profession could be found to sanction "body-snatching." There is a sacredness attached to the grave that the most hardened feel. Whenever the earth is thrown over the body of a man, no matter how abject or sinful he may have been, the involuntary exclamation of every one is *"requiescat in pace."* When it comes to be one of our own personal friends, a parent, sister, or child, to this feeling of sacredness is added that of affection, and no wrong is like that of invading the tomb of those we love. Shakespeare left his curse for him who should disturb his bones; and all feel like cursing those who disturb the bones of friends who are linked to them by blood and affection.

In the winter of 1787 and 1788, medical students of New York City dug up bodies more frequently than usual, or were more reckless in their mode of action, for the inhabitants became greatly excited over the stories that were told of their conduct. Some of these, if true, revealed a brutality and indecency, shocking as it was unnecessary. Usually, the students had contented themselves with ripping open the graves of strangers and negroes, about whom there was little feeling; but this winter they dug up respectable people, even young women, of whom they made an indecent exposure.

The stories did not lose anything by repetition, and soon the conduct of physicians and medical students became a town talk. There seemed to be no remedy for this state of things; the grave-yards, which were then in the heart of the city, were easily accessible; while plenty of men could be found, who, for a small sum, would dig up any body that was desired.

A mere accident caused this state of feeling to culminate and suddenly break out into action. In the spring, some boys were playing in the rear of the hospital, when a young surgeon, from a mere whim, showed an amputated arm to them. One of them, impelled by curiosity, immediately mounted a ladder that stood against the wall, used in making some repairs, when the surgeon told him to look at his mother's arm. The little fellow's mother had recently died, and filled with terror, he immediately hastened to his father, who was a mason, and working at the time in Broadway. The father at once went to his wife's grave, and had it opened. He found the body gone, and returned to his fellow-workmen with the news. They were filled with rage, and, armed with tools, and gathering a crowd as they marched, they surged up around the hospital.

At first many seemed to be impelled only by curiosity, but as the throng increased, the masons became eager for decisive action. Threats and denunciations began to arise on every side, and then appeals for vengeance, till at length they rushed for the door, and pouring into the building, began the work of destruction. For a while there was a terrible rattling of bones, as they tore down and smashed every anatomical specimen they could lay their hands on. Valuable imported ones shared the common fate. They swarmed through the building, and finally came upon fresh subjects, apparently but just dug up. This kindled their rage tenfold, and the students, who thus far had been unmolested, were in danger of being roughly handled.

The news of the gathering of the crowd and its threatening aspect, had reached the Mayor, who immediately summoned the sheriff, and taking him with several prominent citizens, hastened to the spot. Finding the students in the hands of the infuriated mob, he released them, and to the satisfaction, apparently, of the rioters, sent them to jail for safe–keeping.

There was now nothing left for them to do, and they dispersed, and the matter was thought to be ended.

But, during the evening, knots of men were everywhere discussing the events of the day, and retailing the exciting reports that were now flying thickly around; and next morning, whether from any concert of action, or impelled by mere curiosity, is not known, crowds began to fill the street and yard in front of the city hospital. The discovery of the bodies the day before had deepened the excitement, and now a more thorough examination of the building was proposed, and also an examination of the physicians' houses. Matters were beginning to wear a serious aspect, and the Governor, Mayor, Chancellor, and some of the prominent citizens of the town, came together to consult on a course of

action. It was finally resolved to resort in a body to the spot where
the mob was assembled, and make a personal appeal to it. They
did so, and presented an imposing appearance as they advanced
up Broadway. Although representing the State and city, they did
not presume on their authority, but attempted persuasion.
Mounting the steps, they in turn addressed the throng, which now
kept momentarily increasing, and exhorted them as law–abiding
citizens to use no violence. Some made most pathetic appeals to
their feelings, their pride and self–respect; indeed, begged them,
by every consideration of home and justice, to desist, and retire
peacefully to their homes. They solemnly promised that a most
thorough investigation should be made, and they should have all
the satisfaction the laws could afford. More they ought not to ask.
These appeals and promises produced a favorable effect on many
of the mob, and they left. But the greater part refused to be paci-
fied. Their blood was up, and they insisted on making the examination themselves. They did not propose to commit any violence,
but having begun their investigations they were determined to
go through with them.

The Mayor and the Governor seemed to have an unaccountable repugnance to the use of force, and let the mob depart for
Columbia College without any resistance. The professors and students were amazed at this sudden inundation of the crowd, who
swarmed without opposition through every part of the building.
Finding nothing to confirm their suspicions, they left without
doing any material injury. Still unsatisfied, however, they repaired
to the houses of the neighboring physicians, and the leaders, act
ing as a delegation of the crowd, went through them with the
same result. It was a singularly well–behaved mob, and they
received the report of the self–constituted committees with apparently perfect satisfaction, and when they had made the round of
the houses, gradually broke up into knots and dispersed.

But the lawless spirit of a mob seldom arrests and controls
itself. Having once felt its strength and power, it is never satisfied till it measures them against those of the legal authorities,
and yields only when it must. Hence, as a rule, the quicker "it
feels the strong hand of power" the better for all parties. Promis-
ing legal satisfaction to law–breakers is a very unsatisfactory

proceeding. Obedience first and discussion afterwards is the proper order to be observed.

The Mayor had hardly time to congratulate himself on having overcome so easily a serious difficulty, before he found that he had not as yet touched it. In the afternoon, the crowd again began to assemble, and this time around the jail, with the avowed purpose of taking vengeance on the students and physicians locked up there for safe–keeping. Having asserted and exercised, against all law, the right of domiciliary visits, it was but a short and easy step to assert the right to punish also contrary to law. As they gathered in front of the jail, it was seen that a different spirit from that which they had hitherto exhibited ruled them. The tiger was unchained, and loud shouts and yells were heard. "Bring out your doctors! bring out your doctors!" arose on every side. They threatened to tear down the building unless they were given up. The inmates became thoroughly alarmed, and barricaded the doors and windows, and armed themselves the best way they could for self–defence. Attempts were made to parley with the crowd, but they would listen to nothing, and answered every appeal with loud shouts for the doctors. What they *intended* to do with them by way of punishment was not so clear, though what their fate would have been, if once at their mercy, there was little doubt. The city authorities now became alarmed, murder was imminent, and having no police force sufficient to cope with such a formidable mob, they decided that the city was in a state of insurrection, and called out the military. About three o'clock, the force marched up the street, and passed quietly through the crowd, which opened as they advanced. As they moved past, a shower of dirt and stones followed them, accompanied with taunts, and jeers, and mocking laughter. The whole military movement was evidently intended only for intimidation—to show the rioters what could be done if they resorted to violence; for the soldiers, instead of taking up their quarters, as they should have done, in the building, having exhibited themselves, marched away. But the mob, still retaining its position and threatening attitude, another force, a little later, consisting of only twelve men, was sent up. This was worse than nothing, and as the little handful marched solemnly up, the crowd broke out into derisive laughter, and all sorts of contemptuous epithets were heaped upon them. Instead of waiting for them to come near, they rushed down the street to meet them, and swarming like bees around them, snatched away their muskets, and broke them to pieces on the pavement.* The soldiers, disarmed, scattered, and hustled about, were glad to escape with whole bodies.

This first act of open resistance excited the rioters still more—they had passed the Rubicon, and were now ready for anything, and "to the jail! to the jail!" arose in wild yells, and the turbulent mass poured like a tumultuous sea around the building. They rushed against the doors, and with united shoulders and bodies endeavored to heave them from their hinges. But being secured with heavy bolts and bars, they resisted all their efforts. They then smashed in the windows with stones, and attempted to force an entrance through them; but the handful of men inside took possession of these, and, with such weapons as they could find, beat them back. Numbers were of no avail here, as only a few at a time could approach a window, while those within, being on the defensive, knocked them back as often as they attempted to climb in. The rioters, baffled in their attempts, would then fall back, and hurl paving-stones and bricks at the windows, when those who defended them would step one side. But the moment the former advanced again, the latter would crowd the windows with clubs and sticks. The enraged assailants tore off pickets, and advancing with these, made desperate efforts to clear the windows. But those within knew it was a matter of life and death with them, and stubbornly held their ground. The fight was thus kept up till dark, amid yells and shouts and a pandemonium of noises, and no efforts apparently were made to put an end to it, and release the inmates of the jail. But steps had been taken to organize and arm a large body of militia tinder an experienced officer, and now in the dim starlight their bayonets were seen gleaming, as they marched steadily forward on the dark, heaving mass that filled the street far as the eye could see. The rioters, however, instead of being intimidated at the sight, sent up a yell of defiance, and

---

*John Jay and Baron Steuben were both wounded in trying to allay the mob.

arming themselves with stones and brick–bats, hurled them in a blinding volley on the troops. So fierce was the assault, that before the latter had time to form, many were knocked down, and some badly wounded. The commanding officer, finding the fight thus forced on him, gave the order in a ringing voice, "Ready, aim, fire!" A flash broad as the street followed, lighting up the gloom, and revealing the scowling faces of the mob, the battered front of the jail, and the pale faces of those guarding the windows. They had not expected this close, point–blank volley, for the timid action of the authorities had not prepared them for it, and they stopped in amazement and hesitation. The commanding officer understood his business, and instead of waiting to see if they would disperse, poured in another volley. The rioters were con-founded as they saw their comrades fall by their side, but still stood at bay; until at last, seeing the dead and wounded on every side, they could stand it no longer, but broke and fled in every direction. In a few minutes the street was clear of all but the dead and wounded, the groans of the latter loading the night air. The poor wretches were carried away, and the troops remained on the spot all night. The next day the city was in a fever of excitement. The number of killed was greatly exaggerated, and the denun-ciations of the butchery, as it was called, were fierce and loud. On almost every corner groups of excited men were seen in angry discussion—multitudes gathered in front of the jail, and gazed with horror on the blood–stained pavement.

The soldiers who had committed the slaughter were cursed and threatened by turns, but they quietly rested on their arms, ready, it was evident, to repeat the experiment at the first open act of violence. For awhile there was danger of a general outbreak throughout the city; but the authorities had become thoroughly aroused to the danger of the situation, and seeing that the quicker they brought the conflict to a close, the better, made such a display of force, that the riotous spirit was overawed. Still, it was not entirely subdued, and it was evident that it was kept under by fear alone. The physicians of the city came in for almost as large a share of the hatred as the military. They were the origi-nal cause of the disturbance, and threats against them became so open and general, that they were in constant dread of personal violence, and many fled from the city. They scattered in every direction, and there threatened to be a general Hegira of physicians. All the medical students were secretly stowed into carriages, and hurried off into the country, where they remained till the excitement died away. It did not, however, subside readily; indeed, the danger of open revolt was so great for several days, that the military continued to keep guard at the jail.

CHAPTER V

Spring Election Riots of 1834.

FATAL ERROR IN OUR NATURALIZATION LAWS.—OUR
EXPERIMENT OF SELF GOVERNMENT NOT A FAIR ONE.—
FRUIT OF GIVING FOREIGNERS THE RIGHT TO VOTE.—BIT-
TER FEELING BETWEEN DEMOCRATS AND WHIGS.—FIRST
DAY OF ELECTION.—SHIPS "CONSTITUTION" AND
"VETO."—WHIGS DRIVEN FROM THE POLLS.—EXCITE-
MENT.—WHIGS DETERMINED TO DEFEND THEMSELVES.—
MEETING CALLED.—RESOLUTIONS.—SECOND DAY'S
ELECTION.—ATTACK ON THE FRIGATE "CONSTITUTION."—
A BLOODY FIGHT.—MAYOR AND OFFICERS WOUNDED.—
MOB TRIUMPHANT—EXCITEMENT OF THE WHIGS.—THE
STREETS BLOCKED BY FIFTEEN THOUSAND ENRAGED
WHIGS.—MILITARY CALLED OUT.—OCCUPY ARSENAL AND
CITY HALL ALL NIGHT.—RESULT OF THE ELECTION.—
EXCITEMENT OF THE WHIGS.—MASS-MEETING IN CASTLE
GARDEN.

THIS COUNTRY NEVER committed a more fatal mistake than
in making its naturalization laws so that the immense immi-
gration from foreign countries could, after a brief sojourn, exercise the right of suffrage. Our form of government was an
experiment, in the success of which not only we as a nation
were interested, but the civilized world. To have it a fair one, we
should have been allowed to build and perfect the structure with

our own material, not pile into it such ill-formed, incongruous stuff as the despotisms of Europe chose to send us. Growing up by a natural process, educating the people to the proper exercise of their high trust, correcting mistakes, and adjusting difficulties as we progressed, the noble building would have settled into greater compactness as it arose in height, and all its various proportions been in harmony. We should have built slowly but surely. But when there was thrown upon us a mass of material wholly unfit for any political structure, and we were compelled to pile it in hap–hazard, it was not long before the goodly edifice began to show ugly seams, and the despotisms of Europe pointed to them with scorn, and asked tauntingly how the doctrine of self–government worked. They emptied their prisons and poor–houses on our shores, to be rid of a dangerous element at home, and we, with a readiness that bordered on insanity, not only took them into our bosoms, but invited them to aid us in making our laws and electing our rulers. To ask men, the greater part of whom could neither read nor write, who were ignorant of the first principles of true civil liberty, who could be bought and sold like sheep in the shambles, to assist us in founding a model republic, was a folly without a parallel in the history of the world, and one of which we have not yet begun to pay the full penalty. It was a cruel wrong, not only to ourselves, but to the oppressed masses of Europe, who turned their longing eyes on us for encouragement and the moral aid which our success would give them in their struggles against despotism.

If the reason given for endowing this floating population—and dangerous element under any circumstances—with the full rights of citizens had been the true one, namely: to be just to them, and consistent with the great doctrine of equality on which our Government rested, there might be some little comfort in reflecting on the mistake we made. But this was false. The right of suffrage was given them by a party in order to secure their votes, and secure them, too, by appealing to those very passions that made them dangerous to the republic, and which the interest of all alike required should be removed instead of strengthened.

All the good the Democratic party has ever done this country will hardly compensate for the evil of this one act.

If our experiment shall finally prove a failure, we verily believe it will be owing to the extension of the political franchise to whites and blacks who were unfit to use it, and cared for it not because of its honor, or the good use to which it might be put, but as a piece of merchandise to be sold to the highest bidder or used as a weapon of assault against good order and righteous laws.

Of course, the first pernicious effect of this transfer of power to ignorant, reckless men would be felt at the polls in New York City, where this class was in the greatest number. The elections here soon became a farce, and the boasted glory of a free ballot-box a taunt and a by–word. That gross corruption and villany practised here should eventually result in the open violation of law, as it did in the charter election of 1834, was natural.

Political animosity was probably more bitter between the Democrats, under Jackson's administration, and the Whigs, than between any two political parties since the time of Federalists and Democrats, in the days of the elder Adams.

In the spring of 1834 especially, party spirit ran very high in the city. As usual, for a month or more before the election, which took place on the second Tuesday in April, all kinds of accusations and rumors were afloat. There was no registry law, and comparatively few places for the polls, so that there could be little check on voting, no end to repeating, while the gathering of an immense crowd around each place of voting became inevitable. At this election, there was a split in the Democratic party, Mr. Verplanck being the candidate of the Independent Democrats, and Mr. Lawrence of the "Tammany."

The most extensive preparations were made on both sides for the conflict, and it was generally expected there would be a personal collision in some of the wards.

Tuesday, the 8th of April, dawned dark and stormy, and the rain began to fall heavily, at times coining down in torrents. But to such a fever heat had the public feeling been carried, that no one seemed to heed the storm. The stores were closed, business of all kinds suspended; while the streets were black with men hurrying to the polls. At twelve o'clock the American flag was hoisted on the Exchange, when the building became deserted, and all gathered at the places where the voting was going on. Men stood

in long lines, extending clear out into the street, patiently enduring the pelting rain, waiting till their turn came to vote.

The famous expression of Jackson, "Perish credit, perish commerce," had been taken out of the connection in which it was
used, and paraded everywhere. The sailors had been enlisted in
the struggle, and rigged up a beautiful little frigate in complete
order, and named it the "Constitution." Mounting it on wheels,
several hundred of them paraded it through the streets and past
the polls. As they passed through Wall Street, thundering cheers
greeted them, and the excited populace, heedless of the rain, fell
into the procession, till it swelled to thousands, who, with songs
and shouts, followed after. Fearful of the effect of this demonstration on the voters, the Jackson men hastily rigged out a boat,
surmounted by a flag on which was painted in large characters,
"Veto;" and "Constitution" and "Veto" sailed after each other
through the city. This should have been prevented by the authorities, for it was impossible for these two processions to meet without a fight occurring, while it was equally certain that the Whig
one would be attacked, if it attempted to pass the polls in those
wards in which the roughs had the control. But the "Hickory
poles" had inaugurated a new mode of carrying on political campaigns. Appeals were made to the senses, and votes obtained by
outward symbols, rather than by the discussion of important
political questions. This mode of electioneering culminated with
the log–cabin excitement.

IN THE ELEVENTH Ward, the Jackson party had two private doors
through which to admit their voters to the polls, while bullies kept
back from the main entrance the Independent Republicans. In
most of the strong Jackson wards, where it was all on one side, the
voting went on peaceably enough, but in the Sixth, it was soon evident that a storm was inevitable. Oaths and threats and yells of defiance made the polls here seem more like an object on which a
mob was seeking to wreak its vengeance, than a place where
freemen were depositing their votes under sanction of law. The
babel of sound continued to grow worse in spite of the rain, and
swelled louder and louder, till at last the Jackson roughs, headed
by an ex–alderman, made a rush for the committee room where

their opponents were assembled. Some of them were armed with clubs, and others with knives, which they brandished fiercely as they burst into the room. Before the members could offer any resistance, they were assailed with such fury, that in a short time nearly twenty were stretched bleeding and maimed on the floor; one so badly wounded that he was carried out lifeless, and apparently dead. It was a savage onslaught, and those who escaped injury reached the street hatless, and with coats half–torn from their backs. The mob, now being complete masters of the room, tore down all the banners, destroyed the ballots, and made a complete wreck of everything. The Whig leaders, enraged at such dastardly, insulting treatment, despatched a messenger in all haste to the Mayor for help, but he replied that he could not furnish it, as all the available force was away in other sections of the city on duty. The excitement among the Whigs now became fearful, and they determined to take the matter in their own hands. The election was to last three days, and they concluded to let the polls, when the mob entered, take care of themselves the balance of the day, and organize a plan for self–protection on the morrow.

A call was at once issued for a meeting at Masonic Hall, and that night four thousand Whigs packed the building, from limit to limit. General Bogardus was called to the chair, who, after stating the object of the meeting, and describing the conduct of the mob in the Sixth Ward, offered the following resolutions:

"*Whereas*, The authority of the police of the city has been set at defiance by a band of *hirelings, mercenaries,* and *bullies* in the Sixth Ward, and the lives of our citizens put in jeopardy. And *whereas* it is evident that we are in a state of anarchy, which requires the prompt and efficient interposition of every friend of good order who is disposed to sustain the constitution and laws, therefore, be it

"*Resolved,* That in order to preserve the *peace* of the city, and especially of the Sixth Ward, the friends of the constitution and the liberties of the citizen will meet at this place (Masonic Hall), to–morrow (Wednesday), at half–past seven o'clock a.m., and repair to the Sixth Ward poll, for the *purpose of keeping it open to* all voters until such time as the official authorities may 'procure a sufficient number of special constables to keep the peace.'

"*Resolved,* That while at the Sixth Ward poll, those who are not residents thereof will not take part in the election, but simply act as *conservators of the peace,* until such times as the MAJESTY OF THE LAWS shall be acknowledged and respected."

These resolutions were carried with acclamations and shouts and stamping of feet.

There was no bluster in these resolutions, but their meaning was apparent enough, and the city authorities understood it. From that hall, next morning, would march at least five or six thousand determined men, and if the mob rallied in force, to repeat the action of the day before, there would be one of the bloodiest fights that ever disgraced the city. It was believed that the great mass of the rioters were Irishmen, and the thought that native–born Americans should be driven from their own ballot-box by a herd of foreigners, aroused the intensest indignation. It was an insult that could not and should not be tolerated.

The next morning, at half–past seven, Masonic Hall was filled to repletion. The excitement can be imagined, when such a crowd could be gathered at this early hour.

In the Ninth Ward a meeting was also called, and a resolution passed, tendering a committee of one hundred to the general committee; that, with a committee of the same number from each of the fourteen wards of the city, would make a battalion eighteen hundred strong, to be ready at a moment's notice, to march to any poll "to protect the sacred right of suffrage."

These measures had their desired effect. The presence of large bodies of men at the different polls, for the purpose of protecting them, overawed the unorganized mob, although in some of the wards attempts were made to get up a riot. Stones and clubs were thrown, and one man stabbed; it was thought at the time fatally. The Sixth Ward, "the Bloody Sixth," as it was called, was the point of greatest danger, and thither the Mayor repaired in person, accompanied by the sheriff and a large posse, and remained the greater part of the day. Threats and opprobrious epithets were freely used, and occasionally a paving–stone would be hurled from some one on the outskirts of the crowd; but the passage to the polls was kept open, and by one o'clock the citizens could deposit their votes without fear of personal violence.

The evil of having the election continue three days now became more apparent than ever. The disorderly class, "the roughs," by their protracted drinking, became more and more maddened, and hence riper for more desperate action. This second night was spent by them in carousing, and the next morning they turned out to the polls, not only ready, but eager for a light. Early in the forenoon, the frigate "Constitution" was again on its voyage through the streets, followed by a crowd. As it passed Masonic Hall, the head–quarters of the Whig Committee, it was saluted with cheers. This was followed by a rush upon it, on the part of the mob, who attempted to destroy it. The Whigs inside of the building, seeing the attack, poured forth with a loud cheer, and fell on the assailants with such fury, that they turned and fled. The news of what was passing, had, in the meantime, reached the Sixth Ward folks, and a shout was raised for followers. Instantly a huge crowd, composed of dirty, ragged, savage-looking men, broke away with discordant yells, and streamed up Duane Street towards the building, picking up paving–stones and brick–bats, and pulling down pickets as they ran. Coming in sight of the little frigate, they raised a shout and dashed on it. The procession had now passed the hall, but the Whigs, informed of what was going on, again sallied forth to the help of the sailors, who were fighting manfully against overwhelming odds. But they were soon overpowered, and again took refuge in the hall. This was now assailed, and stones came crashing through the windows. The Mayor was sent for, and soon appeared with the sheriff, backed by forty watchmen. Mounting the steps, he held up his staff of office, and commanded the peace. But the half–drunken mob had now got beyond the fear of the mere symbol of authority, and answered him with a shower of stones, and then charged on the force that surrounded him. A fierce and bloody fight followed. Citizens rushed out to the help of the Mayor, while the watchmen fell on the mob with their clubs. They soon stretched on the pavement more than their own number, but the odds against them was too great. The Mayor received a wound—ten or fifteen watchmen besides citizens were wounded—Captains Stewart, Munson, and Flaggs, badly injured, the latter with his skull horribly fractured, ribs broken, and face cut up. A few of the rioters were arrested, but the great mass broke through all opposition, and streaming into the hall, forced the committee to creep through back passages and windows.

The news of this high-handed outrage was carried like the wind to the lower anti–Democratic wards, and the excited Whigs came streaming up, until Duane, Elm, Pearl, Cross, Augustus, and Chatham Streets, up to Broadway, were black with determined, enraged citizens. Ten or fifteen thousand were in a short time assembled, and a fearful battle seemed inevitable. In this appalling state of things, the Mayor called a consultation, and it was decided to declare the city in a state of insurrection, and call on the military for help. A messenger was immediately despatched to the Navy Yard for a company of marines. Colonel Gamble, commanding, replied that he would be glad to comply with the request, and put himself at their head, but that he had just sent them on board the "Brandywine" and "Vincennes." Application was then made to Commodore Ridgely, commander of the station; but he refused, on the ground that he had no authority to interfere. A messenger was then hurried across to Governor's Island for help, but he met with no better success. As a last resort, General Sanford was now directed to call out the city military.

All this time the crowd kept increasing, while from out its bosom came an angry murmur like the moaning of the sea before a storm. The polls were deserted, and it seemed impossible that the opposing forces could be long kept apart. At length word passed through the Whigs that the mob were about to take possession of the arsenal. Instantly several hundred citizens made a dash for it, and occupied it. This was a brilliant piece of strategy, and no sooner did the rioters hear of it, than they swarmed around the building with yells and imprecations. The Whigs, however, held it, and some of them passed out arms to their friends.

Three terrible hours had now passed since the first outbreak, and from the Park to Duane Street, Broadway, and the cross streets on the east side of it, were packed with excited men, their shouts, calls, and curses rising over the dwellings in tones that sent terror to the heart. But for the narrow streets, in which but few

could come in contact, there would doubtless have been a collision long before.

But at this critical moment a detachment of infantry and two
squadrons of cavalry came marching down Broadway, and in
close column. The crowd divided as they advanced, and they
drew up before the arsenal. The gleaming of the bayonets and
the rattle of sabres had a quieting effect on the rioters, and they
began to disperse again to the polls, to watch the progress of the
voting. In the meantime, the infantry took up their quarters at
the arsenal, and the cavalry at the City Hall, for the night.

When the polls closed at evening, the ballot–box of the Sixth
Ward was taken under a strong guard to the City Hall, and locked
up for the night. It was followed by four or five thousand excited
men, but no violence was attempted.

The election was over. For three days the city had been heaving to the tide of human passion, and trembling on the verge of
a great disaster, and all because a few ruffians, not a fourth part
of whom could probably read or write, chose to deny the right
of suffrage to American citizens, and constitute themselves the
proper representatives of the city.

But the excitement did not end with the election. It was very
close, and as the returns came in slowly, the people assembled in
great numbers, to hear them reported. The next day, till three
o'clock at night, ten or fifteen thousand people blocked Wall
Street, refusing to disperse, till they knew the result. It was finally
announced that Mr. Lawrence, the Democratic candidate, was
elected by a small majority.

The next thing was to ascertain the character of the Common
Council. The same mighty throng assembled next day, forgetting
everything else in the intense interest they felt in the result. It
would seem impossible to get up such a state of feeling over the
election of a few local officers, but the city shook from limit to
limit as the slow returns came in. At last, it was announced that
the Whigs had carried the Common Council by a small majority.
As the news passed through the immense concourse, a shout went
up that shook Wall Street from Broadway, to the East River. It
rolled back and forth like redoubled thunder, till every throat was
hoarse.

When the crowd at last dispersed, it was only to assemble again in separate bodies in different parts of the city, and talk over the victory.

Even then the excitement was not allowed to die away. The event was too great to be permitted to pass without some especial honor, and a mass–meeting was called in Castle Garden to celebrate it. Webster was sent for to make a speech, the most distinguished speakers of New York were called upon, and a day of general rejoicing followed, great as that which succeeded Lee's surrender.

CHAPTER VI

Abolition Riots of 1834 and 1835.

MOST OF THE riots of New York have grown out of causes more or less local, and wholly transient in their nature. Hence, the object sought to be obtained was at once secured, or abandoned altogether. But those arising from the formation of Abolition societies, and the discussion of the doctrine of immediate emancipation, were of a different character, and confined to no locality or time. The spirit that produced them developed itself in every section of the country, and the question continued to assume vaster proportions, till the Union itself was involved, and what was first only a conflict between the police of the city and a few hundred or thousands of ignorant, reckless men, grew at last into the most gigantic and terrible civil war that ever cursed the earth. The Union was rent asunder, and State arrayed against State, while the world looked on aghast at the strange and bloody spectacle. The final result has been the emancipation of the slaves, and their endowment with all the rights and privileges of American citizens. But with this has come a frightful national debt, the destruction of that feeling of common interest and patriotism, which is the strongest security of a country; a contempt for the Constitution, the concentration of power in the hands of Congress, small regard for State rights, while the controlling power in the South has passed into the hands of an ignorant, incapable, irresponsible class; and, worse than all, the people have become accustomed to the strange spectacle, so fraught with danger in a republic, of seeing the legislatures and executives of sovereign States overawed and overborne by the national troops. That frightful conflict for the slave has sown dangerous seed; what the final harvest will be, the future historian alone will be able to show.

The inconsistency of having a system of slavery incorporated into a republican government was always felt by good men North and South, as well as its damaging effect on the social and political well-being of the whole community; and steps had been taken both in Virginia and Kentucky to do away with it by legislative action. Whether these incipient steps would ever have ended in relieving us of the evil, can only be conjectured. We only know that a peaceable solution of the question was rendered impossible, by the action of the Abolitionists, as they were called, who, governed by the short logic, that slavery being wrong, it could not exist a moment without sin, and therefore must be abandoned at once without regard to consequences. The system of slavery was no longer a social or political problem, calling for great wisdom, prudence, statesmanship, and patience, but a personal crime, not to be tolerated for a moment. The whole South was divided by them into two classes, the oppressor and oppressed, the kidnapper and kidnapped, the tyrant and the slave—a relationship which liberty, religion, justice, humanity, alike demanded should be severed without a moment's delay.

These views, in the judgment of the press at the time, and of sound statesmen, would eventually end in civil war, if adopted by the entire North, and hence they denounced them. The Abolitionists were considered by all as enemies to the Union, whom the lower classes felt should be put down, if necessary, by violence. This feeling was increased by the action of William Lloyd Garrison, the founder of the society, who went to England, and joined with the antislavery men there in abusing this country for its inconsistency and crime. These causes produced a state of public feeling that would be very apt to exhibit itself on the first opportunity. When, therefore, in the autumn of 1833, after Garrison's return from England, a notice appeared for an antislavery meeting in Clinton Hall, some of the most respectable men in New York determined to attend, and crush out, by the weight of their influence, the dangerous movement. Another class was resolved to effect the same project in another way, and on the 2d of October the following placard was posted in flaming letters all over the city :

NOTICE

To all persons from the South.

All persons interested in the subject of the meeting called by

J. Leavitt,   W. Goodell,

W. Green,   J. Rankin,

Lewis Tappan,

At Clinton Hall, this evening, at 7 o'clock, are requested to attend at the same hour and place.

MANY SOUTHERNERS.

New York, *October* 2d, 1833.

N. B. All citizens who may feel disposed to manifest the *true* feeling of the State on this subject, are requested to attend.

Putting the appeal in the name of the Southerners, was an artful device to call out the people.

At an early hour crowds began to assemble in front of Clinton Hall; but to their surprise they found a notice nailed on the door, that no meeting would be held. Many, seeing it, returned home; but still the crowd continued to swell to thousands, who rent the air with shouts and threats against Garrison. Determined not to be disappointed in a meeting of some kind, they forced their way upstairs, till the room in which it was to be held was crammed to suffocation. The meeting was then organized, and waited till quarter past seven, when it was moved to adjourn to Tammany Hall. There it was again organized, and a gentleman was about to address the crowd, when a man stepped forward to the president, and stated that the meeting announced to be held in Clinton Hall was at that moment under full headway in Chatham Street Chapel. Instantly several voices shouted, "Let us go there and rout them!" But the chairman said they had met to pass certain resolutions, and they should attend to this business first, and then every one could do as he liked. The resolutions were read, and after some remarks had been made upon them, adopted, and the meeting adjourned. A portion of those present, however, were not satisfied, but resolved to go to the chapel and break up the meeting there. The little handful assembled within, apprised of their approach, fled, so that when the mob arrived, the building, though the doors were open and the lights burning, was empty. It immediately took possession of the room, and giving a negro who was foremost in the sport the name of one of the Abolitionists, made him chairman. The most absurd resolutions were then offered, and carried, when the chairman returned thanks for the honor done him amid the most uproarious laughter, and what had threatened to be a serious riot ended in a wild, lawless frolic.

This was the beginning of the Abolition riots in New York City, which afterwards, to a greater or less extent, prevailed for years in different parts of the Union.

Next summer the excitement, which during the winter had nothing to call it forth, broke out afresh, ending in destruction of property and bloodshed, and the calling out of the military.

On the evening of the 7th of July, an assembly of colored persons of both sexes occupied Chatham Street Chapel, for the purpose of listening to a sermon from a negro preacher. The New York Sacred Music Society had leased the building for certain evenings in the week, of which it was asserted this was one. Justice Lowndes, of the Police Court, was president, and Dr. Rockwell vice–president of the society, and they repaired to the building during the evening, and finding it occupied, at once claimed their right to it, and demanded that the blacks should leave. But the latter, having hired and paid for it, refused to do so, when a fight ensued, in which lamps and chairs were broken, loaded canes used freely, and some persons seriously injured. The news of the fight spread rapidly, and a dense crowd gathered around the door. But the police soon arrived, and forcing their way in, drove white and black out together, and locked up the church.

The riot, however, continued for some time in the street; but the blacks, finding themselves outnumbered, fled, and peace was restored.

A portion of the crowd, having recognized Lewis Tappan, one of the leading Abolitionists, followed him home with hoots and yells, and even hurled stones at his house after he had entered it.

The next evening, at dusk, the crowd began again to assemble in front of the chapel. But the lessee of it had closed and locked the gates. The multitude determined, however, not to be disappointed of a meeting, and forcing open the gates, obtained entrance. The meeting was then organized, and Mr. William W. Wilder called to the chair. After making a speech, in which he showed the evil effects of a sudden abolition of slavery, by relating his experience in San Domingo, he moved an adjournment until the next meeting of the Antislavery Society. The motion was carried, and the assembly broke up. This was, however, altogether too quiet a termination for a part of the crowd, and a shout was made for the Bowery Theatre. The attacks on us by the English, for upholding slavery, and their sympathy and aid for Garrison, and co–operation with him in agitating the question of abolition in this country, had rekindled the old slumbering feeling of hostility to that country; and Mr. Farren, the stage manager of the Bowery, being an Englishman, it was transferred to him, especially as reports had been circulated that he had spoken disrespectfully of the Americans. This night having been selected to give him a benefit, his enemies had posted placards over the city, stating the fact of his hostility to this country—whether with the intention of causing a thin house, or breaking it up altogether, is not known. At all events, the mob resolved on the latter course, and streaming up the Bowery in one wild, excited mass, gathered with loud shouts in front of the theatre. The doors were closed in their faces, but pressing against them with their immense weight, they gave way, and like a dark, stormy wave, they surged up the aisles toward the footlights. In the garish light, faces grew pale, and turned eagerly toward the doors for a way of escape. But these were jammed with the excited, yelling mob. The play was "Metamora," and was under full headway, when this sudden inundation of the rioters took place. The actors stopped, aghast at the introduction of this new, appalling scene. Messrs. Hamlin and Forrest advanced to the front of the stage, and attempted to address them; but apologies and entreaties were alike in vain. The thundering shouts and yells that interrupted them were not those of admiration, and spectators and actors were compelled to remain silent, while this strange audience took complete possession of the house, and inaugurated a play of their own.

But the police, having received information of what was going on, now arrived, and forcing their way in, drove the rioters into the street, and restored order. But the demon of lawless violence, that was now fully raised, was not to be thus laid. Some one got hold of a bell, and began to ring it violently. This increased the excitement, and suddenly the shout arose, "to Arthur Tappan's."* The cry was at once taken up by a thousand voices, and the crowd started down the street. But instead of going to his house, they went to that of his brother, Lewis, in Rose Street, a still more obnoxious Abolitionist. Reaching it, they staved open the doors, and smashed in the windows, and began to pitch the furniture into the street. Chairs, sofas, tables, pictures, mirrors, and bedding, went out one after another. But all at once a lull

---

*A silk merchant, and one of the leading Abolitionists.

occurred in the work of destruction. In pitching the pictures out, one came across a portrait of Washington. Suddenly the cry arose, "It is Washington! For God's sake, *don't burn Washington!*" In an instant the spirit of disorder was laid, and the portrait was handed carefully from man to man, till at length the populace, bearing it aloft, carried it with shouts to a neighboring house for safety. It was one of those strange freaks or sudden changes that will sometimes come over the wildest and most brutal men, like a gleam of gentle light across a dark and stormy sea—the good in man for a moment making its voice heard above the din and strife of evil passions.

This singular episode being terminated, they returned to their work of destruction. But suddenly the cry of "Watchmen!" was heard, and the next moment the police came charging down the street. The mob recoiled before it, then broke and fled, and the former took possession of the street. But the latter, coining across some piles of brick, filled their arms and hands full, and rallying, returned. Charging the watchmen in turn with a blinding shower of these, they drove them from the ground. They then kindled a fire on the pavement, and as the flames flashed up in the darkness and gained headway, they piled on bedding and furniture, till the whole street was illuminated with the costly bonfire. This caused the fire-bells to be rung, and soon the engines came thundering down the street, before which the crowd gave way. The burning furniture was then extinguished, and the house taken possession of. It was now two o'clock in the morning, and the mob dispersed.

The next day nothing was talked about in the saloons, groggeries, and on the corners of the by-streets, but the events of the night before; and as evening came on, a crowd began to assemble in front of the battered, dilapidated house of Lewis Tappan. Another attack was imminent, when the police came up and dispersed them. They had not, however, abandoned the purpose for which they had assembled.

The little band of Abolitionists, that the year before had been composed mostly of comparatively obscure men, had now increased both in numbers and men of influence. Persecution had produced its usual effects—advanced the cause it designed to destroy. Among other well–known citizens who had joined their ranks were the two brothers, Dr. Abraham Cox, M.D., and Dr. Samuel Cox, the latter, pastor of Laight Street Church, and one of the most popular preachers of the city. Though opposed by a large majority of his congregation, he had become known as a bold, outspoken man against slavery; and now the mob, bent on mischief, streamed across the city toward his church. It was dark, and as they gathered in a black, dense mass in front of it, suddenly, as if by a common impulse, a loud yell broke forth, and the next moment a shower of stones and brick–bats fell on the windows. Babel was now let loose, and, amid the crashing of window–glass, arose every variety of sound and all kinds of calls, interspersed with oaths and curses on "Abolitionists and niggers."

Shrieks of laughter and obscene epithets helped to swell the uproar. It was evident they would not be satisfied until they left the church a ruin; but at this critical moment, the Mayor, Justice Lowndes, the District Attorney, and a posse of police officers and watchmen arrived on the ground. Expecting trouble, they had arranged to be ready at a moment's warning to hasten to any threatened point. Their unexpected presence frightened the crowd, and fearing arrest, they slunk away in squads, and the danger seemed over. But, evidently by previous arrangement, the broken fragments, arriving by different streets, came together in front of Dr. Cox's house, in Charlton Street.

The doctor, however, was not at home. He had received warnings and threats from various quarters, and knowing, from the fate of Lewis Tappan's house, what that of his own would be, he had, during the day, quietly removed his furniture, and in the afternoon put his family on board of a steamboat, and left the city.

The mob found the door barricaded, but they broke it open, and began to smash the windows and blinds of the lower story. Before, however, they had begun to sack the house, police–officers and watchmen, with two detachments of horse, arrived and dislodged them. They did not, however, disperse. A more dangerous and determined spirit was getting possession of them than they had before evinced. Crowding back on each other, they packed the street east, within four blocks of Broadway. Seizing some carts, they made a hasty barricade of them across the streets, while a neighboring fence supplied them with clubs. A large number were armed with paving–stones, which they would smite loudly together, saying in deep undertones, "*all together.*" As they thus stood savagely at bay, a collision seemed inevitable, and had they been attacked, would doubtless have made a desperate light. But being let alone they slowly dispersed. A portion, however, though it was now late at night, could not retire without venting a little more spite, and returning to the church, broke in some more windows.

Dr. Cox came back to his house next morning, to see if it was safe. As he left the mutilated building, a crowd of boys, who were looking at the ruins, immediately gave chase to him with yells and derisive laughter, and pressed him so closely, at the same time hurling dirty missiles at him, that he was compelled to take shelter in the house of a parishioner.

The crowd around the house continued to increase all the morning, but a hundred policemen arriving at one o'clock, no disturbance of the peace was attempted. In the afternoon, Mayor Lawrence issued a proclamation, denouncing the rioters, and calling on all good citizens to aid in maintaining the peace, and assuring them that he had taken ample measures to repress all attempts at violence. At the Arsenal, City Hall, and Bazaar, large bodies of troops were assembled, ready to march at a moment's notice; and it was evident that the coming night was to witness a trial of strength between the rioters and the city authorities.

As soon as it was fairly dark, large crowds gathered in front of Arthur Tappan's store, and began to stone the building. Some fifteen or twenty watchmen were stationed here, and endeavored to arrest the ringleaders, when the mob turned on them, and handled them so roughly that they were compelled to take refuge in flight. Alderman Lalagh was severely wounded; but he refused to leave, and standing fiercely at bay, denounced and threatened the maddened wretches, who in turn swore they would take his life. He told them to force open the doors if they dare; that the inside was full of armed men, who were ready to blow their brains out the moment the door gave way. This frightened them, and they had to content themselves with stoning the windows, and cursing the Abolitionist who owned the building. In the meantime, Justice Lowndes came up with a strong police force, when they fled.

While this was going on here, similar scenes were passing in other parts of the city. At dark, some three or four hundred gathered around Dr. Cox's church, in Laight Street, discussing the conduct of the Abolitionists, but making no outward demonstrations calling for the interference of the police, until nine o'clock, when a reinforcement came yelling down Varick Street, armed with stones and brick–bats. These charged, without halting, so furiously on the police–officers, and the few watchmen stationed there, that, bruised and bleeding, they were compelled to flee for their lives. The next moment stones rattled like hail against the church, and, in a few minutes, the remaining windows were smashed in. The police rallied when they reached Beach Street, and hurried off a messenger to the City Hall for the military. In the meantime, loud shouts were heard in the direction of Spring Street, and with answering shouts the mob left the church, and rushed yelling like Indians to the spot. A vast crowd was in front of a church there, under the care of Rev. Mr. Ludlow, another Abolitionist, and had already commenced the work of destruction. They had torn down the fence surrounding it, and were demolishing the windows. Through them they made an entrance, and tore down the pulpit, ripped up the seats, and made a wreck of everything destructible without the aid of fire. The session–room shared the same fate, and the splintered wreck of both was carried in their arms, and on their shoulders, out of doors, and piled into barricades in the street on both sides of the building, to stop the anticipated charge of cavalry. Carts, hauled furiously along by the mob, were drawn up behind this, and chained together, making a formidable obstruction. They then rung the bell furiously, in order to bring out the firemen. The watch–house bell in Prince Street gave a few answering strokes, but information being received of what was going on, it ceased, and the firemen did not come out. It was now near eleven o'clock, when, all at once, an unearthly yell arose from the immense throng. Word had passed through it that the military was approaching. Pandemonium seemed suddenly to have broken loose, and shouts, and yells, and oaths arose from five thousand throats, as the men sprung behind their barricades. It was a moonless night, but the stars were shining brightly, and, in their light, the sheen of nearly a thousand bayonets made the street look like a lane of steel. The Twenty-seventh Regiment of National Guards, led by Colonel Stevens, had been sent from the City Hall, and their regular heavy tramp sounded ominously, as they came steadily on. The church–bell was set ringing furiously by the mob and there was every appearance of a determined resistance. As Colonel Stevens approached the first barricade, he halted his regiment, and ordered his pioneer guard to advance. They promptly obeyed, armed with their axes. A shower of stones met them, while clubs were waved frantically in the air, accompanied with oaths and threats. They, however, moved firmly up to the barricade, and the shining steel of their axes, as they swung them in the air, was as terrific as the gleam of the bayonets, and the crowd retired precipitately behind the second barricade. The first was now speedily torn down, and the head of the column advanced. The second was a more formidable affair, in fact, a regular bastion, behind which were packed in one dense mass an immense body of desperate men, reaching down the street, till lost in the darkness. It seemed now that nothing but deadly volleys would answer. One of the city officers advised Colonel Stevens to retreat, but, instead of obeying, he ordered the pioneer guard to advance, and sustained it by a detachment of troops. Amid the raining missiles they moved forward, when the crowd fell back, some fleeing up the side streets. The guard then mounted the barricade, and in a short time it was scattered in every direction; and when the order "Forward" was given, the column marched straight on the mob. At this moment, Justice Lowndes, at the head of a band of watchmen, arrived on the ground, when the two forces moved forward together, clearing the street of the rioters. While the fight was going on, some of the gang remained inside the church, and kept the bell ringing violently, until Colonel Stevens ordered one of his officers to cut the rope.

A portion of the mob now hurried to Thompson Street, where Mr. Ludlow resided. The family had retired for the night, but their repose was suddenly broken by loud yells and the sound of stones dashing in their windows. Jumping up in wild alarm, they saw the doors broken in, through which streamed the shouting, yelling crowd.

Either from fear of the military, which they knew would soon be upon them, or some other cause, they decamped almost as suddenly as they came, and relieved the terror–stricken household of their presence.

About this time, another immense mob had collected at Five Points. The rioters here seemed to be well organized, and to act in concert. Runners were kept passing between the different bodies, keeping each informed of the actions of the other, and giving notice of the approach of the police.

The destruction at Five Points was on a more extensive scale, and the gatherings in this, then dangerous section of the city— the home of desperadoes and depraved beings of every kind— were of such a character, that for a time the city authorities seemed to be overawed. The rioters had it all their own way for several hours, and the midnight heavens became lurid with burning dwellings. It somehow got round that they had resolved to attack every house not illuminated with candles, and these dirty streets soon became brilliant with the lighted windows. Five houses of ill–fame were gutted, and almost entirely demolished. St. Philip's Church, in Centre Street, occupied by a colored congregation, was broken into, and for two hours the mob continued the work of destruction unmolested. They left it a complete ruin. A house adjoining, and three houses opposite, shared the same fate. The mob was everywhere; and although the police made some arrests and had some fights, they were too weak to effect much. About one o'clock a shout arose, "away to Anthony Street!" and thither the yelling wretches repaired.

The Mayor was at the City Hall all night, doing what he could; but the mob had arranged their plans to act in concert, appearing in separate bodies in different sections of the city at the same time, so that he hardly knew, with the force at his disposal, where to strike. The next morning he issued another proclamation, calling on the citizens to report to him and be organized into companies to aid the police. He called also on all the volunteer military companies of the city to rally to the support of the laws. They did so, and that (Saturday) night they, with most of the fire companies, who had offered their services, were stationed in strong bodies all over the city; and the rioters saw that their rule was ended. Beside, many of the most notorious ringleaders had been arrested and put in prison. A short fight occurred in Catharine Street between the police and mob, in which both had some of their men badly hurt; and an attempt was made to get up a riot in Reade Street, but it was promptly put down. The city was rife with rumors of bloody things which the mob had threatened to do; but, with the exception of the military in the streets, the city on Sunday presented its usual appearance. The lawless spirit was crushed out, and a hundred and fifty of the desperadoes who had been instrumental in rousing it were locked up to await their trial.

In June of the summer of 1835 occurred the Five Points riot, which grew out of the feeling between Americans and foreigners. It threatened for a time to be a very serious matter, but was finally quelled by the police without the aid of the military. Dr. W. M. Caffrey was accidentally killed by one of the mob, and Justice Lowndes was dangerously wounded.

In connection with the series of riots of 1834 and 1835, might be mentioned the Stonecutters' riot, though it was promptly suppressed.

STONECUTTERS' RIOT.

THE CONTRACTORS FOR the building of the New York University found that they could purchase dressed stone at Sing Sing, the work of the prisoners there, much cheaper than in New York, and so concluded to use it. This, the stonecutters of the city said, was taking the bread out of their mouths, and if allowed to go on would destroy their business. They held excited meetings on the subject, and finally got up a procession and paraded the streets with placards asserting their rights and denouncing the contractors. They even attacked the houses of some of the citizens, and assumed such a threatening attitude, that the Twenty-seventh Regiment, Colonel Stevens, was called out. Their steady, determined march on the rioters dispersed them and restored quiet.

Apprehensions were felt, however, that they would reassemble in the night and vent their rage on the University building, and so a part of the regiment encamped in Washington Square in full view of it. They remained here four days and nights, until the excitement subsided, and the work could go on unmolested.

• CHAPTER VII •

Flour Riot of 1837.

HUNGER WILL DRIVE any people mad, and once let there be real suffering for want of food among the lower classes, while grain is piled up in the storehouses of the rich, and riots will surely follow. In the French Revolution of 1789, there was a great scarcity of provisions, which caused frightful outbreaks. It will never do to treat with scorn the cry of millions for bread. When, amid the general suffering in Paris, one said to Foulon, the minister of state, the people are starving for bread, he replied, "Let them eat hay." The next day he was hung to a lamp–post. The tumultuous multitude marching on Versailles, shouting wildly for "bread," was a fearful spectacle. One can hardly blame starving men from seizing food by violence, if it can be got in no other way; and if ever a mob could be justifiable, it would be when they see their families suffering and perishing around them, in the very sight of well–stored granaries.

In the old despotisms of Europe, the poor and oppressed attribute all their want and suffering to the rich and powerful, so that they are not held back from redressing their wrongs by ignorance of their source, but fear of the strong hand of their rulers.

These men, embittered not only by their own sufferings, but by the traditions of the past, when they come to this country are easily roused to commit acts of violence by anything that reminds them of their old oppressions. They have tasted the wormwood and the gall, and refuse to have it pressed to their lips in a country where liberty is the birthright of all. This is what has made, and still makes, the foreign population among us so dangerous. The vast proportion of them are from this very class. Ignorant of everything but their wrongs, they rise in angry rebellion at any attempt, or fancied attempt, to renew them here. Unfortunately there are Americans among us, who, knowing this, work upon this sensitive, suspicious feeling, to accomplish their own ends. The politician does it to secure votes; but the worst class is composed of those who edit papers that circulate only among the scum of society, and embittered by the sight of luxuries beyond their reach, are always ready to denounce the rich and excite the lower classes against what they call the oppression of the aristocracy.

It is doubtful whether the frightful riot of 1863 would ever have taken place, but for this tone assumed by many of the city papers. So of this flour riot, it probably would never have happened, but for demagogues, who lashed the ignorant foreign population into fury against their rich oppressors. Starvation, which as we said may be a justification of violence, did not exist—it was only the high price of provisions, growing out of scarcity, that caused it, but which scarcity, they were told, was created solely by the cupidity of the rich.

The year in which the great fire occurred, was a disastrous one to the crops of the country. The mighty West, that great granary of the nation, was not then open as now, and the main supply of grain came from east of the Alleghanics. Hence the cause which would create a short crop in one section, would be apt to prevail more or less over all the grain region. We imported wheat at this time very largely; not only from England, but from the Black Sea.

In September, flour was about seven dollars a barrel, but this, as the winter came on, went up to twelve dollars—a great rise at that time.

From Virginia, a great wheat State, came disastrous tidings; not only was the crop short and the price of flour high, but it was said that the latter would probably go up to fifteen or twenty dollars a barrel. In Troy, a great depot for State flour, it was stated that there were only four thousand barrels against thirty thousand at the same time the previous year. As February came on, a report circulated in the city that there were only three or four weeks supply on hand. This was repeated in the penny papers, with the information added, that in certain stores were hoarded vast amounts of grain and flour, kept out of the market to compel a still greater advance in the price. This was very probably true, as it is a rule with merchants, when they have a large stock of anything on hand, of which there threatens to be a scarcity, to hold on in order to make the scarcity greater—thus forcing higher prices. This will always prove a dangerous experiment in this country in the article of flour. It is the prime necessary of life, and the right to make it scarce for the sake of gain, and at the expense of human suffering, will always be questioned by the poorer classes.

Although the stock of grain on hand at this time was small, there was no danger of starvation, nor was it to the instinct of self-preservation that demagogues appealed. They talked of the rich oppressing the poor by their extortions—of monopolists, caring only to increase their gains without regard to the distress they occasioned.

There was, doubtless, ranch suffering among the poorer classes, not only on account of the high price of flour, but also of all the necessary articles of living. Meat advanced materially, while from some strange fatality, coal went up to ten dollars a ton. There seemed no reason for this, as the amount sent to market was said to be largely in excess of the previous year. In Canada, coal was so scarce, that the line of steamers between Montreal and Quebec was suspended before winter set in.

This state of things excited the attention of the people generally, and in the fore–part of this month, a public meeting was called at the Tabernacle to consider what could be done. It amounted to nothing. Some speeches were made, resolutions offered, but nothing practical was proposed. The temperance people attempted to make a little capital out of it, by asserting that the high price of grain was owing to the amount used by the distilleries—rye being sold as high as one dollar and seventy cents per bushel.

But a different class of people were now discussing the subject, and in a different spirit. Their attention was directed to *men,* not *theories*—the individual oppressors, not the general causes.

Chief among those against whom the popular feeling was now directed, was Hart & Co., large commission merchants in Washington Street, between Dey and Cortlandt Streets. Their store was packed with flour and wheat, and every day men passed it with sinister looks. Sometimes a little knot of men would stop opposite it, and talk of the loads of grain stored up there, while their own families were pinched for bread. They would gaze savagely on its heavy iron doors, that seemed to defy the weak and helpless, and then walk on, muttering threats and curses. These signs of a gathering storm were, however, unheeded by the proprietors. Others, better informed, were not so tranquil; and by anonymous letters tried to arouse Mr. Hart to take precautionary measures. An anonymous letter addressed to Mr. W. Lenox was picked up in the Park, in which the writer stated that a conspiracy was formed for breaking open and plundering Mr. Hart's store, and gave the following plan of action. On some dark night, two alarms of fire were to be given, one near the Battery, and the other up town, in order to draw off the watchmen and police, when a large crowd already assembled in the neighborhood would make a sudden rush for the building, and sack it before help could arrive. This letter was handed to the High Constable Hays, who showed it to Hart & Co., but they seemed to regard it as an attempt to frighten them. This was followed by anonymous letters from other parties, that reached the Mayor, insisting on it that danger was hanging over this house. He sent them to Hart & Co., but they, thinking it was only a trick to put down the price of flour, paid no attention to them. They locked their three massive iron doors at night as usual, and went to their homes without fear, and the underground swell kept on increasing in volume.

The first plan of operation, if it ever existed, was either abandoned by the mob or deferred till after other measures were tried.

At length, on the afternoon of the 10th of Febuary, the following placard was posted up all over the city :

BREAD, MEAT, RENT, FUEL!

The voice of the people shall be heard and will prevail.

The people will meet in the park, *rain or shine,* at four o'clock on

MONDAY AFTERNOON,

to inquire into the cause of the present unexampled distress, and to devise a suitable remedy. All friends of humanity, determined to resist monopolists and extortioners, are invited to attend.

Moses Jacques.	Daniel Graham.
Paulus Hedle.	John Windt.
Daniel A. Robertson.	Alexander Ming, Jr.
Warden Hayward.	Elijah F. Crane.

NEW YORK, *Feb.* 10*th,* 1837.

The idle crowd had all day Sunday to talk over this call. Everywhere knots of men were seen gathered before these placards—some spelling out slowly, and with great difficulty, the words for themselves—others reading the call to those unable to read it. The groggeries were filled with excited men, talking over the meeting, and interspersing their oaths with copious draughts of liquor, and threatening openly to teach these rich oppressors a lesson they would not soon forget.

There was something ominous in the hour selected for the meeting; four o'clock in February meant night, before it would get under full headway. It was evident that the leaders did not mean the meeting to be one of mere speech–making. They knew that under cover of darkness, men could be incited to do what in broad daylight they would be afraid to undertake.

Before the time appointed, a crowd began to assemble, the character of which boded no good. Dirty, ragged, and rough-looking, as they flowed from different quarters together into the inclosure, those who composed it were evidently a mob already made to hand.

At length, four or five thousand shivering wretches were gathered in front of the City Hall. Moses Jacques, a man who would make a good French Communist to–day, was chosen chairman. But this motley multitude had no idea or respect for order, or regular proceedings, and they broke up into different groups, each pushing forward its favorite orator.

One of the strangest freaks of this meeting, was an address to a collection of Democrats by Alexander Ming, Jr. He forgot all about the object of the meeting, and being a strong Bentonian, launched out into the currency question, attributing all the evils of the Republic, past, present, and to come, to the issue of bank-notes; and advising his hearers to refuse to take the trash altogether, and receive nothing but specie. This was the more comical, as not one out of ten of the poor wretches he addressed had the chance to refuse either. Half starving, they would have been glad to receive anything in the shape of money that would help them through the hard winter. Yet when Mr. Ming offered a resolution, proposing a memorial to the Legislature, requiring a law to be passed, forbidding any bank to issue a note under the denomination of a hundred dollars, the deluded people, who had been listening with gaping mouths, rent the air with acclamations. It was a curious exhibition of the wisdom of the sovereign people—this verdict of a ragged mob on the currency question. They were so delighted with this lucid exposition of the cause of the scarcity of flour that they seized the orator bodily, and elevating him on their shoulders, bore him across the street to Tammany Hall, where something beside specie was received from behind the bar to reward their devotion.

There was, however, some excuse for him. He had been several times candidate for city register, and hence was more anxious to secure votes than flour—be a popular demagogue rather than a public benefactor.

But there were other speakers who kept more directly to the point. They launched at once into a bitter tirade against landlords for their high rents, and against monopolists for holding on to flour at the expense of the poor and suffering. Knowing the character of the audience before them, and their bitter hatred of the rich that had grown with their growth, and strengthened with their strength in the old country, it was not difficult to lash them into a tempest of passion. They depicted the aristocrats around them rolling in wealth, wrung from their necessities—laughing at their sufferings while rioting in luxury—nay, hoarding up the very bread without which they must starve, in order to realize a few dollars more on a barrel of flour. Loud oaths and deep muttered curses followed these appeals, and the excited multitude became agitated with passion. One of the speakers closed his bitter harangue with "Fellow-citizens, Mr. Eli Hart has now 53,000 barrels of flour in his store; let us go and offer him eight dollars a barrel for it, and if he will not take it—" It was not difficult to know how he meant to close the sentence; but just then, a friend shrewder than he, seeing the legal consequences to themselves of an open proposition to resort to violence, touched him on the shoulder, when in a lower tone of voice he concluded : "*we shall depart in peace.*" In the excitement of the moment, he had evidently forgotten the guarded language he intended to use, and was about to utter that which would have consigned him to a prisoner's cell, but checked himself in time. He was willing others should suffer the consequence of violating the law, to which his appeals urged them; but his love for the poor did not prompt him to share their fate.

It was bitterly cold, and it was a wonder that the crowd had listened patiently so long. The proposition to go to Hart's store with a demand for flour, was instantly seized, and those around the speaker started off with a shout, and streaming down Broadway, poured in one dark living stream along Cortlandt Street into Washington Street. The clerks in the store heard the turmoil, and suspecting the object of the rioters, rushed to the doors and windows, and began to close and bolt them. There were three large iron doors opening on the sidewalk, and they had succeeded in bolting and barring all but one, when the mob arrived. Forcing their way through this middle door, the latter seized the barrels, and began to roll them out into the street. Mr. Hart, who either from curiosity to hear what the meeting would propose to do, or from his suspicions being aroused from what he had previously heard, was on the spot, and as soon as he saw the crowd stream out of the Park, down Broadway, he hurried to the police, and obtaining a posse of officers, made all haste for his store. But as they were going down Dey Street, the mob, which blocked the farther end, rushed on them with such fury, that before they had time to defend themselves, their clubs, or staves as they were then called, were wrenched from their hands and broken into fragments. The crowd was not yet very great, and the disarmed officers forced their way into Washington Street and into the store. Their presence frightened the few inside, and they hastily decamped. The Mayor, who was in his room at the City Hall, had been speedily notified of the riot, and hurried to the spot. The crowd remaining in the Park had also been informed of what was going on, and dashing madly down Broadway, and through Cortlandt Street, joined with loud shouts their companions in front of the store. The Mayor mounted a flight of steps, and began to harangue the mob, urging them to desist, and warning them of the consequences of their unlawful action. He had not proceeded far, however, before brick–bats, and sticks, and pieces of ice came raining around him in such a dangerous shower, that he had to give it up, and make his way to a place of safety. The street was now black with the momentarily increasing throng, and emboldened by their numbers, they made a rush at the entrance of the store. Driving the police–officers before them, they wrenched by main force one of the heavy iron doors from its hinges. A half a score of men at once seized it, and using it as a battering–ram, hurled it with such force against the others, that after a few thundering blows, they one after another gave way, and the crowd poured in. The clerks fled, and the rioters went to work without hindrance. Mounting to the upper lofts, they first broke in all the doors and windows, and then began to roll and heave out the flour. The barrels on the ground–floor were rolled, swift as one could follow another, into the street, when they were at once seized by those waiting without, and their heads knocked in, and their contents strewn over the pavement. On the upper lofts, they were rolled to the broken windows, and lifted on to the sill, and tumbled below. Warned by their descent, the crowd backed to the farther side of the street. Part would be staved in by their fall; those that were not, were seized as they rolled off the sidewalk, and the heads knocked out. One fellow, as he stood by the window–sill and pitched the barrels below, shouted as each one went with a crash to the flagging: " *Here goes flour at eight dollars a barrel!*"

The scene which now presented itself was a most strange, extraordinary one. The night was clear and cold, and the wintry moon was sailing tranquilly through the blue and starlit heavens, flooding here and there the sea of upturned faces with its mellow light, or casting the deep shadow of intervening houses over the black mass, while the street looked as if a sudden snow–storm had carpeted it with white. The men in the windows and those below were white with flour that had sifted over their garments; while, to give a still wilder aspect to the scene, women, some bareheaded, some in rags, were roaming around like camp–followers after plunder. Here a group had seized empty boxes; there others pressed forward with baskets on their arms; and others still, empty–handed, pushed along, with their aprons gathered up like a sack. These all knelt amid the flour, and scooped it up with an eagerness that contrasted strangely with the equal eagerness of those who were scattering it like sand over the street. The heavy thud of the barrels as they struck almost momentarily on the sidewalk, could be distinctly heard above the shouts of the men. Some of the mob found their way into Mr. Hart's counting–room, and tore up his papers and scattered them over the floor. It was evident they were bent on utter destruction; but when about five hundred barrels of flour had been destroyed, together with a thousand bushels of wheat in sacks, a heavy force of police came marching along the street. These were soon after followed by detachments of the National Guards from Colonel Smith's and Hele's regiments. The flashing of the moonbeams on the burnished barrels and bayonets of their muskets, struck terror into the hearts of the rioters. The cry of "The soldiers are coming!" flew from lip to lip, causing a sudden cessation of the work of destruction, and each one thought only of self–preservation. Many, however, were arrested, and sent off to Bridewell under the charge of Officer Bowyor, with a squad of police. The latter were assailed, however, on the way, by a portion of the mob that pursued them, and a fierce fight followed. In the struggle, Bowyer and his assistants had their clothes torn from their backs, and some of the prisoners were rescued.

In the meantime, the military paraded the street, clearing it of the mob, and preventing their return. In front of the store, and far beyond it, the flour lay half–knee deep—a sad spectacle, in view of the daily increasing scarcity of grain.

Just before the military and police reached the ground, some one in the crowd shouted "Meeches'." This was another flour store at Coenties Slip, on the other side of the city, nearly opposite. A portion of the mob on the outside, that could not get to the store, and aid in the work of destruction, at once hurried away to this new field of operations. On the way over, they passed Herrick & Co.'s flour store, and stopped to demolish it. They were loaded down with brick–bats, which they hurled at the windows, smashing them in. The doors followed, and the crowd, rushing through, began to roll out the barrels of flour. But when some twenty or thirty were tumbled into the street, and about half of them staved in, they, for some cause or other, stopped. Some said that they ceased because the owner promised, if they did, he would give it all away to the poor the next day. At all events, they would soon have been compelled to abandon the work of destruction, for the police hastened to the spot, accompanied by a large body of citizens, who had volunteered their help. Some were arrested, but most of the ringleaders escaped.

How many of those who attended the meeting in the Park anticipated a mob and its action, it is impossible to say; but that a great number of them did, there can be no doubt.

By nine o'clock the riot was over, and those who had engaged in it, were either arrested or dispersed.

The next day, Mr. Hart issued a card, denying that the

exorbitant price of flour was owing to his having purchased a large quantity for the sake of monopolizing it, but to its scarcity alone.

It was certainly a very original way to bring down the price, by attempting to destroy all there was in the city. Complaining of suffering from the want of provisions, they attempted to relieve themselves by putting its possession out of their power altogether. With little to eat, they attempted to make it impossible to eat at all. A better illustration of the insensate character of a mob could not be given.

• CHAPTER VIII •

Astor Place Riots, 1849.

RIVALRY BETWEEN FORREST AND MACREADY.—MACREADY'S ARRIVAL IN THIS COUNTRY.—THE ANNOUNCEMENT OF HIS APPEARANCE AT THE ASTOR-PLACE OPERA HOUSE, AND FORREST AT THE BROADWAY THEATRE THE SAME NIGHT POSTED SIDE BY SIDE.—BOWERY BOYS CROWD THE OPERA HOUSE.—ANXIETY OF THE MANAGERS.—CONSULTATIONS AND DRAMATIC SCENES BEHIND THE CURTAIN.—STAMPING OF THE PEOPLE.—SCENE ON RAISING THE CURTAIN.— STORMY RECEPTION OF MACREADY.—HOWLED DOWN.— MRS. POPE DRIVEN FROM THE STAGE BY THE OUTRAGEOUS LANGUAGE OF THE MOB.—MACREADY NOT ALLOWED TO GO ON.—HIS FOOLISH ANGER.—FLEES FOR HIS LIFE.—HIS APPEARANCE THE SECOND NIGHT.—PREPARATIONS TO PUT DOWN THE MOB.—EXCITING SCENE IN THE THEATRE.— TERRIFIC SCENES WITHOUT.—MILITARY ARRIVE.— ATTACKED BY THE MOB.—PATIENCE OF THE TROOPS.—EFFORT TO AVOID FIRING.—THE ORDER TO FIRE.—TERRIFIC SCENE.—STRANGE CONDUCT OF FOR-REST.—UNPUBLISHED ANECDOTE OF GENERAL SCOTT.

PROBABLY THERE NEVER was a great and bloody riot, moving a mighty city to its profoundest depths, that originated in so absurd, insignificant a cause as the Astor–place riot. A personal quarrel between two men growing out of professional jealousy, neither of whom had any hold on the affections of the people, were able to create a tumult, that ended only by strewing the street with the dead and wounded.

Mr. Forrest, it is true, had a certain professional popularity, but nothing to awaken a personal enthusiasm for him. Viewing the matter in this light, some have thought there was a mysterious underground influence at work, that has never yet been discovered. But one needs not to go far to find the causes that produced it.

In the first place, ever since our revolt from England, especially since the second war with her, in which the contest for the supremacy of the seas was decided, the spirit of rivalry between the two countries has been intense and often bitter. No matter what the contest was, whether between two boats, or two bullies in the ring, it at once assumed the magnitude of a national one, and no matter how conducted, the winner was always charged with unfairness. It so happened that Forrest and Macready were the two popular tragic actors on either side of the Atlantic. If they had stayed at home, nothing would have been thought of it, but each invaded the domain of the other, and laid claim to his laurels. Of course criticism followed, national prejudices were aroused, and national peculiarities ridiculed. The press took sides, and fanned the excitement. Among other things, it was currently reported that when Forrest was in London, Macready went to see him act, and publicly hissed him. This was generally believed, and of course it alone would insure the latter an unwelcome reception from Forrest's admirers here, should he ever appear on our stage.

Apparently unconscious of this hostility toward him, Macready came over in the spring of 1840, and at once made an engagement at the Astor–place Opera House, corner of Eighth Street and Lafayette Place. He was to appear as Macbeth; and the play was announced sometime beforehand. Forrest at the same time had an engagement at the Broadway Theatre. On the 7th of May, the following two significant placards appeared side by side in all the streets.

ASTOR PLACE OPERA HOUSE.

This evening will be performed

MACBETH.

MACBETH . . . . Macready.
LADY MACBETH. . . . . Mrs. Pope.

BROADWAY THEATRE.

This evening will be performed

MACBETH.

MACBETH . . . . Mr. Forrest.
LADY MACBETH. . . . . Mrs. Wallack

This public exhibition of rivalry stimulated the hostility of those opposed to Macready, and there were borne fears of disturbance; but nothing serious was anticipated—in fact, it was rather a good advertisement, and promised full houses. Niblo, one of the managers of the Opera House, unwisely gave out tickets for more people than the building would hold, and when, before evening, he found they were taken, he was alarmed. It looked as if they had been so eagerly bought up for other purposes than merely to hear Macready. He therefore went to the Chief of Police, and requested the presence of a force in case any disturbance should be attempted. It was promised, but as it turned out, most of it came too late to be of any service.

A tremendous crowd assembled in front of the building long before dark, and the moment the doors were open, a rush was made, and the human tide poured in, and flowing swiftly over the house, soon filled every part of it, except the boxes. These filled up more slowly; but long before the curtain rose, the house was packed to repletion, while the amphitheatre and parquette were crowded with hard–looking men—a dense mass of bone and muscle. The fashionable portion of the audience in the boxes began to feel anxious, for not only were all the seats occupied, but all the aisles and every foot of standing room. Some were in their shirt–sleeves, others were ragged and dirty, while all had their hats on. Such an audience had never before been seen in the Opera House, and it boded no good. Still, this heterogeneous mass was orderly, but it was noticed that at short intervals tele-graphic signals were made by those nearest the stage to those in the wings of the amphitheatre, and answered, indicating a thor-oughly arranged plan. The time before the play was to com-mence passed slowly, but the hard–looking crowd seemed very patient. Occasionally, to vary the monotony, some joke would be passed around, and once a man who was above called out to those below, imitating the English pronunciation: "I say, Jim, come 'hup 'ere! 'ere's some of Macready's hangels—'haint they sweet 'uns?" If a lorgnette was levelled from one of the boxes, those noticing it below would put their thumbs to their noses and gyrate with their fingers in return. On the whole, however, the strange–looking crowd were orderly, although the quiet had an ominous look.

But at half–past seven, the hour for the play to commence, that regular stamping, common to most theatres, began. But in this case, it did not continue for a little while and then die away, but beginning in a low rumble, every moment gathered strength and grew louder, till it rolled like thunder through the building, shaking the very walls, and making the glasses in the great cen-tral chandelier jingle, as though, knocked together by invisible hands. As the mighty sound echoed through the recesses and dressing–room's behind the scenes, Niblo became agitated, and stepping forward on the stage, peered behind the edge of the cur-tain, and surveyed the strange scene. Turning to Mr. Bowyer, of the chief's bureau, who was by his side, he said: "This looks rather dubious, Mr. Bowyer." "Yes," he replied, "the Boys are here cer-tainly. What made you sell so many tickets? People are making a tremendous rush at the doors yet, and the house is full; over full already." Niblo then turned to his partner, and said: "What do you think, Mr. Hackett. Is there going to be a disturbance?" "I don't know," he replied; "you must ask Mr. Bowyer."

The latter, putting his eye to the crack, took a careful survey of the audience, and remarked: "There is mischief in the par-quette and amphitheatre, but probably no actual violence will be attempted; the boys will make a noise, and endeavor to prevent the play from proceeding, but possibly they will do nothing fur-ther; they seem to be patient and good–natured, but Mr. Macready may expect a rough reception."

Macready, who had been dressing, now approached and also took a peep from behind the curtain. His gaze was long and searching. The scrutiny did not satisfy him, and he turned away and began to pace backward and forward in one of the wings, moody and thoughtful. The stamping had ceased while the orchestra was playing, but it now commenced again, apparently louder than ever. Lady Macbeth in full dress now came on the stage, pale and agitated. She also took a peep from behind the curtain. The spectacle frightened her, and turning to Mr. Hack-ett, she whispered, rather than exclaimed, "My God! Mr. Hack-ett, what is the matter? Are we to be murdered tonight?" "My dear Madam," he replied, "keep calm, there is no cause for alarm; everything will go on smoothly;" but his pale face and anxious look belied his words. It seemed now as if the house would come down under the continuous, furious stamping. Hackett turned to Bowyer, and asked if the chief had come. The latter replied he did not know; and another silence followed in the group behind the curtain, while they stood and listened to the thundering tramp, tramp, that rose like muffled thunder. At length Hackett asked: "How many policemen are there in the house?" "I don't know," replied Bowyer. "But the chief should have known," retorted the former. "What do you want the police to do, Mr. Niblo?" quietly asked Bowyer. The latter hesitated a moment, when the attaches of the theatre came crowding forward in alarm, and asking by their scared looks what it all meant.

Macready and Mrs. Pope, in full costume, were at this time standing apart, talking together, evidently discussing the best course to be pursued. The uproar seemed to grow louder, and prudence dictated a suspension of the play; but Macready, after a moment's hesitation, determined to risk it, and suddenly gave the signal to raise the curtain. The bell tinkled, and the curtain slowly rose, revealing the gorgeous scene and the actors standing in a blaze of light. Instantly the tumult ceased, and a deep sudden hush succeeded. Those roughs were evidently taken aback by the dazzling splendor that burst upon them. It was a new revelation to them, and for the moment they seemed to forget the object of their coming, and to be wholly absorbed in the vision before them.

The first scene passed off quietly, and the fears of a disturbance were allayed. In the second, taking Duncan for Macbeth, the crowd began to hiss, but soon finding their mistake ceased. It was evident that some one better posted than the mass had control of this wild element, so eager to be let loose. At length Macbeth came on, and was received with deafening cheers by those in the boxes. As these died away, a hiss ran through the amphitheatre and parquette, followed by cat–calls, cock–crowing, and sounds of every imaginable description. Macready had hardly uttered a single sentence, before his voice was totally drowned in the uproar. Forced to stop he quietly folded his arms and faced the storm, expecting it would soon blow over. Finding himself mistaken—that if anything it grew louder and fiercer, his disdain turned into foolish anger, and advancing to the footlights, and throwing all the contempt and scorn into his face that he was master of, he deliberately walked the entire breadth of the stage, gazing haughtily as he did so, into the faces of the roughs nearest him, who were bawling their throats hoarse. This did not mend matters any, as he easily could have foreseen, had he known this type of American character better. He then attempted to go on and outbellow, if possible, the audience. But it was like shouting amid the roar of breakers. Nobody heard a word he said, still he stuck to it till he got through that portion of the act. It was now Lady Macbeth's turn, and the appearance of a woman, it was thought, would command that respect which in America is almost always accorded to one. But her reception was worse than that of Macready, for not content with shouts and yells they heaped disgusting epithets on her, and were so vulgar in their ribaldry that she flew in affright from the stage, "blushing," it was said, "even through the rouge on her face." Macready, however, showing, if nothing else, good English pluck, determined to go on. But he had scarcely finished the first sentence, when some potatoes struck the stage at his feet; then rotten eggs, breaking and spattering their sickening contents over his royal robes; while howls that seemed to come from the lower regions arose on every side. It was Pandemonium broke loose, and those in the boxes, thoroughly alarmed, jumped to their feet and stood as if paralyzed, gazing on the strange spectacle below. Macready's passions were now thoroughly aroused, and he stubbornly stood his ground. Suddenly a chair hurled from above, and evidently aimed at his head, struck the stage at his feet and broke into fragments, followed by the shout, "Go off the stage, you English fool! Hoo! Three cheers for Ned Forrest!" which were given with a will. Then came another chair, narrowly missing Macready's head, who, now alarmed for his personal safety, fled from the stage, and the curtain fell. But the bedlam that had been let loose did not stop. Hoots, curses, threats of vengeance, and the confused sounds of a mob given wholly over to passion, struck terror into all hearts; and Macready, fearing a rush would be made for him behind the scenes, left the theatre by a private door, and jumping into a carriage was rapidly driven to his hotel. The manager, alarmed for the safety of the building, attempted to announce his departure to the audience, but in vain. They would not listen to him, and as a last resort he chalked in large letters on a board, "*Macready has left the theatre*," and hoisted it before the footlights. This had the desired effect, and the headlong crowd, with shouts and laughter, began to tumble out. Once in the street, they sent up a loud hurrah, and dispersed in groups to their various drinking places, to talk over their victory and damn all Englishmen.

The fact that the mob refrained from damaging the theatre shows that they did not desire destruction; they had only done in their rough way what other men deemed respectable, and even legislators, have often done, and almost as boisterously, to prevent an obnoxious person from being heard. They certainly had many respectable precedents for their course, and Mr. Macready should have done what others have been compelled to do—given up the attempt and waited for a more propitious time. That a man has a right to play or speak, is true; but men of all grades have always asserted the right to show their displeasure of the acting of the one or the sentiments of the other. Not that there is any excuse for such conduct as we have described, but it can be hardly called a serious riot, although by whomsoever committed is unquestionably riotous in its character.

Of this contemptible, disgraceful interference of his friends in his quarrel, Forrest had nothing to say—he kept a studied silence. How a man with any self–respect could have refrained from denouncing it, and repudiating all sympathy and connection with it by a public card, it will be difficult for men of ordinary sensibility to imagine.

Macready now determined to throw up his engagement altogether, but after ranch consultation and deliberation changed his mind. A letter was addressed to him by many of the most wealthy and prominent citizens of the city, in which they expressed their regret at the treatment he had received, and urged him not to yield to such a lawless spirit. They promised that he should be protected in his rights, and hoped he would give the city an opportunity to wipe out the stain that had been put upon its character. This he unwisely consented to do, and the next Thursday was fixed for his appearance in the same play. When the placards announcing it were pasted up, there appeared immediately alongside of them another, announcing the appearance on the same evening of Forrest, in the Broadway Theatre, in the character of the "Gladiator." In the meantime other posters appeared, and among them the following in startling capitals :

"WORKINGMEN!

SHALL AMERICANS OR ENGLISH RULE IN THIS CITY?

The crew of the British steamer have threatened all Americans who shall dare to offer their opinions this night at the

ENGLISH ARISTOCRATIC OPERA HOUSE.

WORKINGMEN! FREEMEN! STAND UP TO YOUR LAWFUL RIGHTS."

It will be observed, that this artful appeal was like a two–edged sword, cutting both ways. It aimed at the same time to stir up the hatred of the lower classes against the upper, by the word aristocratic; and the national hatred of the English, by calling it the *English aristocratic* Opera House to be guarded by English sailors. Both parties now began active preparations for the eventful night—the rioters by increasing and organizing their forces, and setting on foot plans to get possession of the house; the friends of Macready, to prevent this from being done, and at the same time secure sufficient aid from the authorities to suppress all open violence. To keep the rowdies from occupying the house, tickets were sold or given away only to those known to be friendly to Macready; while to suppress violence, three hundred police were promised, to be supported if necessary by two regiments of soldiers, who were ordered to be under arms at their quarters, ready to march at a moment's notice.

As the day advertised for the play approached, the excitement deepened, and serious trouble seemed unavoidable. On the appointed evening, a strong body of police was quietly placed inside of the house, with definite instructions how to act. In the meantime, an immense crowd had assembled in front of the building, and, when at last the doors opened, a rush was made for them. But the police kept the crowd back, and only those who had tickets were admitted. When the house was fairly filled, the doors were closed and fastened. In the meantime the windows had been barricaded, with the exception of one, which was overlooked. This the now disappointed rabble assailed with stones, sending them through it, in among the startled audience. They tried also to break down one of the doors, but the policemen's clubs stopped them. Then commenced a series of yells and shouts, mingled with horrid oaths and threats as the baffled wretches surged around the building. Finding nothing else to vent their rage on, they attacked the lamps in the neighborhood, breaking them to pieces, and putting out the lights.

In the meantime, the play inside, with this wild accompaniment without, commenced. Notwithstanding all the care that had been taken, a large number of roughs had succeeded in procuring tickets, showing that some professedly respectable men had been in collusion with them. Although the rioters inside were in a minority, they were not daunted, and being determined that the play should not go on, commenced stamping and yelling so, that Macready's voice from the outset was completely drowned.

The police in disguise had mingled all day with the rioters, and ascertained what the mode of action inside the house was to be. At a certain point in the play, a signal was to be given, on seeing which the entire body was to make a rush for the stage and seize Macready. The Chief of Police arranged his plans accordingly, and imparted them to the force under him. He therefore made no effort to stop the noise, but waited for the expected signal. At length it was given, and the entire body of rioters rose with a yell and sprang forward. But at that moment, the chief gave *his* signal, which was lifting his hat from his head. Every eye of those determined policemen had been intently watching it, and as it now rose, they sprang with a single bound upon the astonished rowdies, and before they could recover from their surprise, most of them were outside of the building, while the ringleaders were kept back and caged inside.

The play now went on, but it was a spiritless affair. Every ear was turned to hear the muffled roar of the voices outside, which every moment increased in power as the mighty multitude kept swelling in numbers.

The afterpiece was omitted, and Macready escaping through a private door, hastened to his hotel. It seemed for a time that the building would be torn down; but at length, a regiment of the National Guard, preceded by a body of cavalry, was seen marching steadily up Broadway. The crowd parted as it advanced, and as it turned into Eighth Street, the sharp word of command, "right wheel," rang out distinct and clear over the uproar. The rioters, instead of being intimidated, rushed to a pile of paving-stones that unfortunately happened to be near, and arming themselves with these, began to pelt the horses, which soon became unmanageable, so that the cavalry force had to retire.

The infantry then advanced, but were received with such a deluge of stones that they, too, fell back to Broadway. Here they rallied, and at the order forward, moved steadily on the mob, and forced their way to the front of the Opera House. While forming line here on the sidewalk, they were assailed so fiercely with paving–stones, that the soldiers fell rapidly. The rioters were in close quarters, and the heavy stones, hurled at such a short distance, were almost as deadly as musket–balls. Captain Pond soon fell wounded, when the second in command told the sheriff that if he did not give the order to fire, the troops would be withdrawn, for they couldn't stand it. Recorder Talmadge, unwilling to resort to such a desperate measure, attempted to harangue the mob. He begged them, in God's name, to disperse and go home—if they did not, the soldiers would certainly fire on them, etc. The only reply was hoots and yells of defiance, and paving–stones. The Recorder then forced his way up to General Hall, standing at the right of the battalion, and said : "You must order your men to fire; it is a terrible alternative, but there is no other." The General asked for the Mayor, for he was doubtful of his authority to do so, without his order. "He won't be here," replied Talmadge. General Sandford then said : "Well, the National Guards will not stand and be pounded to death with stones; nearly one-third of the force is already disabled." After a little more hurried conversation, the sheriff said, "If that be so, you have permission to fire." The uproar all this time was deafening, and the order, "Ready!" of General Sandford, could hardly be heard; but the sharp, quick rattle of steel rose distinctly over the discord. Still terribly repugnant to shoot down citizens, General Hall and Colonel Duryea made another attempt to address the crowd, and begged them to cease these attacks. "Fire and be d—ned!" shouted a burly fellow. "Fire, if you dare—take the life of a free-born American for a bloody British actor! D—n it, you dassent fire!" and he boldly bared his breast to the levelled muskets. "Fire, will you?" yelled another, as he hurled a paving–stone at General Sandford, wounding his sword arm. "Hit 'em again!" shouted a third, who saw the well–directed aim. Still averse to shedding blood, General Hall told the soldiers to elevate their pieces over the heads of the people, and fire at the blank wall of Mr. Langton's house opposite, hoping thus to frighten the mob. But this only awakened derision, and the leaders shouted, "Come on, boys! they have blank cartridges and leather flints!" In the meantime, the police, who had mingled with the mob, and were making arrests, began to force their way out, in order to escape the fire that now seemed inevitable. The troops moved across the street, and faced toward the Bowery, obeying the word of command promptly, and marching with great steadiness, although the pelting they received was murderous. To retreat would be pusillanimous, to stand there and be pelted to death worse still; and General Hall finally gave tile order to fire point blank, but to aim low, so that men would be wounded, rather than killed. The command fell clear and distinct, "Fire!"

A single musket–shot on the extreme left was the only response. They were too near—their muzzles almost touching the hearts of the men, and it seemed terribly murderous to fire. "Fire!" shouted General Sandford.

Three more musket–shots, only, followed. "Fire!" Duryea then cried out, in ringing tones. A swift volley ran along the line, shedding a momentary glare on the wild faces of the mob, the streets, and adjoining houses, and then came the report. This time the dead in their midst told the rioters that it was child's play no longer, and they fell back. But getting a new supply of paving-stones, they rallied, and once more advanced on the troops. A second volley, more murderous than the first, sent them crowding back on each other in terror. The troops now wheeled, and formed line again in front of the Opera House. It had got to be eleven o'clock, and more troops were ordered up, with two cannon. The mob, though dismayed, still refused to retire, and hung sullen and threatening as a thunder–cloud on the skirts of the military, and a third volley was poured into them. The rioters now separated, and fell back into the darkness, when the troops were ordered to fire the fourth time, in different directions—one wing down Eighth Street, and the other into Lafayette Place. This last volley, judging from the testimony of reliable witnesses, was altogether needless. The conflict was over.

A lawyer of Wall Street, noted for his philanthropy and kindness, resided in Fourth Avenue, and being informed by a friend, late in the evening, that men were lying dead and wounded in Astor Place, he hastened down to see if he could be of any assistance to the poor creatures. Reaching Lafayette Place, he saw in the dim light a line of soldiers drawn up, though he saw no mob, only a fcw scattered men, who seemed to be spectators. Suddenly he heard the order to fire, and the next moment came a flash and report. He could not imagine what they were firing at; but suddenly he felt his arm numb, and the next moment he grew faint and dropped on the sidewalk, his arm broken to shivers. The brother of a well–known banker was shot in Broadway by a random bullet; and a man, while stepping out of a car in Third Avenue, was shot dead. Other innocent persons "fell victims, as they always must, if they will hang on the skirts of a mob from curiosity." Men anxious to witness a fight must take the chances of getting hurt.

Great excitement followed; an indignation meeting was called in the Park, coroners' juries stultified themselves, and a senseless outcry was made generally. Twenty-two were killed and thirty wounded. It was a terrible sacrifice to make for a paltry quarrel between two actors about whom nobody cared; and in this light alone many viewed it, forgetting that when the public peace is broken, it matters not how great or insignificant the cause, it must be preserved; and if the police or military are called out to do it, and are attacked, they must defend themselves, and uphold the laws, or be false to their trust. The authorities have to do with riots, not their causes; put them down, not deprecate their existence, or argue their justice.

If public indignation had been turned against Forrest, it would have been more sensible. He knew perfectly well that if his friends persisted in their determination to attack Macready, the second night, blood would be spilt. It was his quarrel, and yet he deliberately kept his lips closed. He neither begged them for their own sake, nor for his, or as good citizens, to forbear, and let his rival alone; nor after it was known that many had been killed, did he express a single word of regret; apparently having no feeling but gratification, that even at such a fearful sacrifice his hated rival had been driven from the field. But responsibility is not so easily shaken off, and in real life as well as in tragedy, conscience will force a man to cry:

"Out! damned blood spot! Out, I say!"

Macready left the country, and the excitement died away; but the painful memories of this absurd yet deadly riot will remain till the present generation has passed from the stage.

We cannot close this account more fitly than by relating an anecdote of General Scott connected with it, that has never been made public. He was living at the time in Second Avenue, nearly opposite Astor Place. He was occupying the upper part of the house that evening, and his wife the lower. When the first volley over the heads of the people was fired, he hastened down, and sent off a servant to ascertain what it meant. Before the latter returned, he heard a second volley. Hurrying below, he dispatched a second servant to find out what was going on, and went back to his room. A third volley smote on his ear, and deeply agitated he hurried below, and began to pace the room in an excited manner. His wife, observing how much he was moved, remarked pleasantly : "Why, General, you are frightened!" This was rather a staggerer to the old hero, and he turned and exclaimed: "Am I a man to be frightened, madam? It is *volley* firing madam—*volley* firing. They are shooting down American citizens!" The old chieftain had heard that firing too often on the field of battle, to be ignorant of its meaning. He had seen ranks of living men reel and fall before it; nay, stood amid the curling smoke when his staff was swept down by his side, calm and unmoved, but here he was unmanned. Over the ploughed and blood–stained field, he had moved with nerves as steady as steel, and pulse beating evenly; but now he paced his safe and quiet room with his strong nature painfully agitated, and all because American citizens were being shot down by American citizens. The fact speaks volumes for the nobleness of his nature, and that unsullied patriotism which sheds tenfold lustre on his well–earned laurels.

CHAPTER IX

Police Riot—Dead-Rabbits' Riot—Bread Riot, 1857.

CREATION OF THE METROPOLITAN DISTRICT.—COLLISION BETWEEN
MAYOR WOOD'S POLICE AND THE METROPOLITAN POLICE.—SEV-
ENTH REGIMENT CALLED OUT.—DEAD-RABBITS' RIOT.—SEVERE
FIGHT BETWEEN THE ROACH GUARDS AND DEAD RABBITS.—POLICE
DRIVEN BACK.—BARRICADES ERECTED.—MILITARY CALLED OUT.—
KILLED AND WOUNDED.—BREAD RIOT.—FINANCIAL DISTRESS.

THE YEAR 1857 was a remarkable one in the history of New York City, and indeed of the whole country. The year previous had been characterized by intense political excitement, for the presidential campaign had been carried on as a sectional fight or a war between the upholders and enemies of the institution of slavery as it existed in the South. Pennsylvania alone by her vote defeated the antislavery party, and the South, seeing the danger that threatened it, had already begun to prepare for that tremendous struggle, that afterwards tested to the utmost the resources and strength of the North; while a financial storm overwhelmed the entire country in disaster. To these were added local causes, which affected New York City particularly, and made it a year of uncommon disturbance.

The Republican party being largely in the ascendant in the State, determined to revolutionize the municipal government, and place the Democratic city partially under Republican rule. Many bills were passed during the session of Legislature, peculiarly obnoxious to the city authorities, but that which excited

Headquarters Metropolitan Fire Department.

Headquarters Metropolitan Police, 300 Mulberry Street.

the most bitter opposition was called the Metropolitan Police Act, by which the counties of New York, Kings, Westchester, and Richmond were made one police district, to be controlled by a board of commissioners, consisting of five members appointed by the Governor and Senate, and to hold office for five years. This board having organized, proceeded to create a police department. Mayor Wood denied the constitutionality of the act and retained the old police—so that there were two police departments existing at the same time in the city. The Mayor resorted to all kinds of legal measures to defeat the action of the board, and the question was finally referred to the Court of Appeals for decision.

In the mean time the death of a street commissioner left a vacancy to be filled. Governor King, acting under the recent law, appointed Daniel D. Conover to fill it, while the Mayor appointed Charles Devlin. A third claimant for the place appeared in the deputy, who asserted his right to act until the decision of the Court of Appeals was rendered. Conover had no idea of waiting for this, and proceeded to assume the duties of his office. The Mayor of course resisted, and so Conover got out a warrant from the Recorder to arrest the former on the charge of inciting a riot, and another on the charge of personal violence. Armed with these papers, and backed by fifty of the new policemen, he proceeded to the City Hall. The Mayor, aware of the movement, had packed the building with his own police, who refused him admittance. The new police attempted to force an entrance, when a fight followed, in which twelve policemen were severely injured. While things were in this critical condition, the Seventh Regiment passed down Broadway on its way to the boat for Boston, whither it was going to receive an ovation. A request for its interference was promptly granted, and marching into the Park they quickly quelled the riot, and the writs were served on the Mayor.

Intense excitement followed, and so great was the fear of a terrible outbreak, that nine regiments were put under arms, ready to march at a moment's notice.

But on the 1st of July the Court of Appeals decided the act to be constitutional, and the disturbance ended. But of course, while this strife was going on between the police, but little was done to arrest disorder in the city. The lawless became emboldened, and in the evening before the 4th of July a disturbance began, which for a time threatened the most serious consequences.

DEAD-RABBITS RIOT.

THE ORIGIN OF the term "Dead Rabbits," which became so well known this year from being identified with a serious riot, is not certainly known. It is said that an organization known as the "Roach Guards," called after a liquor dealer by that name, became split into two factions, and in one of their stormy meetings some one threw a dead rabbit into the room, and one party suddenly proposed to assume the name.

These two factions became bitterly hostile to each other; and on the day before the 4th of July came in collision, but finally separated without doing much damage. They were mostly young men, some of them being mere boys.

The next day, the fight was renewed at Nos. 40 and 42 Bowery Street, and clubs, stones, and even pistols were freely used. The "Dead Rabbits" were beaten and retired, yelling and firing revolvers in the air, and attacking everybody that came in their way. Their uniform was a blue stripe on their pantaloons, while that of the Roach Guards was a red stripe. People in the neighborhood were frightened, and fastened their doors and windows. No serious damage was done, however.

About ten o'clock, a policeman in Worth Street, while endeavoring to clear the sidewalk, was knocked down and severely beaten. At length, breaking away from his assailants, he hastened to the central office in White Street, and reported the state of things. A squad of police was immediately dispatched to arrest the ringleaders. On reaching Centre Street they found a desperate fight going on, and immediately rushed in, to put a stop to it. The belligerents at once made common cause against them. A bloody hand–to–hand conflict followed, but the police at length forced the mob to retreat. The latter, however, did not give up the contest, but mounting to the upper stories and roofs of the tenement-houses, rained down clubs and stones so fiercely, that the police were driven off with only two prisoners.

Comparative quiet was now restored, though the excitement spread in every direction. It lasted, however, only an hour or two, when suddenly a loud yell was heard near the Tombs, accompanied with the report of fire–arms, and crowds of people came pouring down Baxter and Leonard Streets, to get out of the way of bullets. Some wounded men were carried by, and the utmost terror and confusion prevailed. The air was tilled with flying missiles and oaths, and shouts of defiance. Now the Dead Rabbits would drive their foes before them, and again be driven back. The bloody fight thus swayed backwards and forwards through the narrow streets for a long time. At length twenty-five Metropolitan Police appeared on the scene, while fifty more were held in reserve. Though assailed at every step with clubs and stones, they marched steadily on, clearing the crowd as they advanced, and forcing the Dead Rabbits into the houses, whither they followed them, mounting even to the roof, and clubbing them at every step. After clearing the houses, they resumed their march, when they were again attacked by the increasing crowd, many of them armed with muskets and pistols. Barricades were now erected, behind which the mob rallied, and the contest assumed the aspect of a regular battle. The notorious Captain Rynders came on the ground, between six and seven o'clock, and attempted to restore quiet. Not succeeding, however, he repaired to the office of the Police Commissioners, and told Commissioner Draper, if he had not police force enough to disperse the mob, he should call out the military. The latter replied that he had made a requisition on Major–General Sandford, for three regiments, and that they would soon be on the ground. But it was nine o'clock before they made their appearance. The police then formed in two bodies of seventy-five men each, and supported, one by the Seventy-first Regiment and the other by the Eighth, marched down White and Worth Streets. This formidable display of force overawed the rioters, and they fled in every direction. This ended the riot, although the military were kept on duty during the night.

At times, the fight was close and deadly, and it was reported that eight were killed and some thirty wounded.

BREAD RIOT.

IN THE AUTUMN there came a financial crisis, that was so wide-spread and disastrous that the lower classes Buffered for want of food. Banks suspended specie payment, manufactories were forced to stop work, and paralysis fell on the whole industry of the nation. It was estimated that ten thousand persons were thrown out of employment. These soon used up their earnings, and destitution and suffering of course followed. Their condition grew worse as cold weather came on, and many actually died of starvation. At length they became goaded to desperation, and determined to help themselves to food. Gaunt men and women, clad in tatters, gathered in the Park, and that most fearful of all cries, when raised by a mob, "Bread," arose on every side. Propositions were made to break open the stores, and get what they needed. Flour was hoarded up in them because so little could be got on from the West. The granaries there were groaning with provisions; but there was no money to pay for the transportation. There was money East, but kept locked up in fear. As this became known to the mob, their exasperation increased. To know that there were both food enough and money enough, while they were starving to death, was enough to drive them mad, and there were ominous mutterings. Fortunately, the authorities saw in time the threatened danger, and warded it off. A great many were set to work on the Central Park and other public works, while soup–houses were opened throughout the city, and private associations formed to relieve the suffering; and the winter passed without any outbreak, though more than five thousand business-houses in the country failed, with liabilities reaching three hundred millions of dollars.

• CHAPTER X •

Draft Riots of 1863.

CAUSE OF THE RIOTS.—THE LONDON TIMES.—DRAFT CALLED A
DESPOTIC MEASURE.—THE DESPOTIC POWER GIVEN TO WASHINGTON
BY CONGRESS.—DESPOTIC ACTION SOMETIMES NECESSARY, IN ORDER
TO SAVE THE LIFE OF THE NATION.—THE RIGHTS OF GOVERN-
MENT.—DRAFTING THE LEGITIMATE WAY TO RAISE AN ARMY—IT IS
NOT UNEQUAL OR OPPRESSIVE.

THE OSTENSIBLE CAUSE of the riots of 1803 was hostility to the draft, because it was a tyrannical, despotic, unjust measure—an act which has distinguished tyrants the world over, and should never be tolerated by a free people. Open hostility to oppression was more than once hinted in a portion of the press—as not only a right, but a duty.

Even the London *Times* said, "It would have been strange, indeed, if the American people had submitted to a measure which is a distinctive mark of the most despotic governments of the Continent." As if the fact that a measure, because resorted to by a despotic government, was therefore necessarily wrong. It might as well be said, that because settling national difficulties by an appeal to arms has always been a distinctive feature of despotic governments, therefore the American people should refuse to sustain the government by declaring or prosecuting any war; or that because it has always been a distinctive feature of despotic governments to have naval and military–schools, to train men to the art of war, therefore the American people should not submit to

Fort Lafayette, New York Harbor.

Fort Hamilton; from whence U. S. Troops were sent to aid in suppressing the
Draft Riot of 1863

either. It is not of the slightest consequence to us what despotic governments do or not do; the simple question is, whether the measure is necessary for the protection of our own government, and the welfare of the people. To leave this untouched, and talk only about despotism, the right of the people, and all that, is mere demagogism, and shows him who utters it to be unfit to control public opinion. Besides, there is a great difference between measures that are despotic, which are put forth to save the nation's life, or honor, and those put forth to destroy freedom, and for selfish ends. Not that, intrinsically, despotic measures are always not to be deprecated and avoided, if possible; for if tolerated in one case, they may be exacted in another.

Liberty can never be guarded too carefully, or the barriers erected around the rights of every individual respected too scrupulously. But everything in this world is a choice between two evils. The greatest wisdom cannot avoid *all* evils; it can only choose the least. Sound statesmanship regards any stretch of power better than the overthrow of the nation. Probably there never was a more able and wise body of men assembled, or more jealous of any exercise of arbitrary power, than the First Congress of the United States; and yet, almost in the commencement of our struggle for independence, when events wore such a gloomy aspect that failure seemed inevitable, rising above its fears of despotic measures, in its greater fear of total defeat, it conferred on Washington powers that made him to a large extent military dictator. He was authorized to raise sixteen battalions of infantry, three thousand light-horse, three regiments of artillery, together with a corps of engineers, and *appoint the officers himself.* He had, also, full power, when he deemed it necessary, to call on the several States for the militia; to appoint throughout *the entire army all the officers under brigadiers;* fill up all vacancies; to take whatever he wanted for the use of his troops, wherever he could find it, with no other restriction than that he must pay for it, which last was nullified, because he was empowered to *seize and lock up every man who refused to receive in pay Continental money.* It would seem impossible that a body of men who were so extremely sensitive in bestowing power on a military commander, and so watchful of the rights of individuals, could have committed such an act; and yet, who does not see that, under the circumstances, it was wise. Now, granting that conscription is a despotic measure, no truthful, candid man will deny that, in case of a war, where men must be had, and can be got in no other way, that it would be the duty of government to enforce it. It is idle to reply that the supposition is absurd—that in this country such a thing can never happen; for what has been in the world can be again. Besides, this does meet the question of the *right* of the Government, that must be settled before the emergency comes. Now, we do not believe there is sounder principle, or one that every unbiased mind does not concede with the readiness that it does an axiom, that, if necessary to protect and save itself, a government may not only order a draft, but call out *every* able–bodied man in the nation. If this right does not inhere in our government, it is built on a foundation of sand, and the sooner it is abandoned the better.

But we go farther, and deny that a draft is a despotic measure at all, but is a just and equitable mode of raising an army. True, if troops enough can be raised on a reasonable bounty, it is more expedient to do so; but the moment that bounty becomes so exorbitant as to tempt the cupidity of those in whom neither patriotism nor sense of duty have any power, volunteering becomes an evil. We found it so in our recent war. The bounty was a little fortune to a certain class, the benefit of which they had no idea of losing by being shot, and hence they deserted, or shammed sickness, so that scarce half the men ever got to the front, while those who did being influenced by no motive higher than cupidity, became worthless soldiers. A draft takes in enough men of a higher stamp to leaven the mass. The first Napoleon, when asked what made his first "army of Italy" so resistless, replied that almost every man in it was intelligent enough to act as a clerk. The objection that a rich man, if drafted, can buy a substitute, while the poor man, with a large family depending upon him, must go, if of any weight at all, lies against the whole structure of society, which gives the rich man at every step immunities over the poor man. When pestilence sweeps through a city, the rich man can flee to a healthy locality, while the poor man must stay and die; and when the pestilence of war sweeps over the laud, must one attempt to reverse all this relation between wealth and poverty?

When society gets in that happy state, that the rich man has no advantages over the poor, there will be no need either of drafting or volunteering. Yet, after all, it is not so unequal as it at first sight appears. War must have money as well as men, and the former the rich have to furnish; and if they do this, it is but fair that they should be allowed to furnish with it also the men to do their fighting. Besides, there must be some rule that would exempt the men that carry on the business of the country.

We have said this much, because the riots in New York, which might have ended in national destruction, were brought about by preaching views directly the opposite of these.

The military spirit is so prevalent in the nation, that in any ordinary war the Government can get all the troops it wants by giving a moderate bounty, and wages but a little greater than can be secured at any ordinary business or occupation. Still, the right to raise them differently should never be denied it.

When the old militia system was given up in the State, and a certain number of regiments were raised and equipped and drilled for active duty, and for which the people paid taxes, it was thought they would furnish all the quota that would ever be called for from the State—and in any ordinary war will. The crisis, however, in which we found ourselves had never been anticipated, and hence not provided against, and when Congress attempted to do it in what seemed to it the best way, an outcry was raised of injustice and oppression. It was hard, doubtless, but there are a great many hard things in the world that have been and have to be borne. The feeling of hostility unquestionably would have been less intense, had not so many of those to be drafted been bitterly opposed to the war. Believing it to have been brought about by the reckless demagogism and fanaticism of their political opponents, and levied as it was against those who had been their warm political friends, indeed, chief dependence for political success, it was asking a good deal, to require them to step to the front, and fight in such a war. Whether this feeling was right or wrong, had nothing to do with the influence it actually exerted. On this feeling was based, in fact, the real hostility to the draft, in which a portion of the press shared. But, as we said before, we having nothing to do with the justice or injustice of this belief or feeling; we only state the fact, with our denial that it furnished any excuse for the denunciations uttered against the draft as a wrong use of power, or the refusal to submit to it on that account. The Government, whether wrong or right, must be supported, or abandoned and given over to revolution. In ordinary times, denunciation of its measures, and the most strenuous opposition to them, is the right and often the duty of every conscientious man. This right, exercised by the press, is one of the most effectual checks against abuses, and the most powerful lever to work reform and changes. But in a great crisis, to set one's self against a measure on which the fate of the nation hangs, is a flagrant abuse of that right; for the effort, if successful, will not work change and an improved condition of things, but immediate, irretrievable ruin, and put the nation beyond the reach of reform.

· CHAPTER XI ·

RIGHTS OF MUNICIPALITIES.—INTERFERENCE OF THE LEG-
ISLATURE WITH THE CITY GOVERNMENT.—CONFLICT
BETWEEN THE GOVERNOR AND POLICE COMMISSIONERS.—
A WRONG BECOMES A PRACTICAL BLESSING.—PROVOST
MARSHALS.—RIOT NOT ANTICIPATED.—BAD TIME TO COM-
MENCE THE DRAFT.—PREPARATIONS OF SUPERINTENDENT
KENNEDY.—THE POLICE SYSTEM.—ATTACK ON PROVOST
MARSHAL CAPTAIN ERHARDT.—TELEGRAMS OF THE
POLICE.—KENNEDY STARTS ON A TOUR OF OBSERVATION.

THE RIGHTS OF municipalities have been conceded from the first dawn of constitutional liberty—indeed municipal free- dom may be said to be the first step in the onward progress of the race toward the full recognition of its rights. To interfere with a great commercial city like New York, except by general laws, is as a rule unwise, impolitic, and, indeed, unjust. Like a separate State, it had better suffer many and great evils, than to admit the right of outward power to regulate its internal affairs. To do so, in any way, is fraught with mischief; but to do so as a political party, is infinitely more pernicious. It leaves a great metropolis, on which the welfare of the commercial business of the nation mainly depends, a foot–ball for ambitious or selfish politicians to play with. But as there are exceptions to all rules, so there may be to this—still they should always be exceptions, and not claimed as a settled policy.

We mention this, because the interference of the Legislature, or rather the dominant part of it, in the internal policy of New York, about the time the war commenced, was in itself a mischievous and tyrannical act, while, under the circumstances that soon after occurred, it proved of incalculable benefit.

With the city stripped of its military, and the forts in the harbor of their garrisons, the police, under the old regime, during the draft riots, would have been trustless and powerless, even if the city government had attempted to uphold the national authority, which is doubtful. The Republicans established a Board of Police Commissioners, the majority of which were of their own political faith, who had the entire control of the department. Under their hands, an entire different set of men from those formerly selected, composed the force, and a regular system of drills, in fact, a thorough organization, adopted.

But in 1862 the Democrats elected their governor, though they failed to secure the Legislature. Mr. Seymour, immediately on his inauguration, summoned the Commissioners to appear before him, the object of which was to change the character of the board. The latter understood it, and refused to appear. Legal proceedings were then commenced against them, but they were staved off, and in the meantime the Legislature had got to work, and took the matter in hand; and Messrs. Bowen, Acton, and Bergen, were made to constitute the board—John A. Kennedy being superintendent of police. Mr. Bowen, the president of the board, having been appointed brigadier–general, resigned, and Mr. Acton, under the law, became president. This political character of the board, so diametrically opposed to the feelings and wishes of the vast majority of the citizens, tested by the ordinary rules and principles of a Republican Government, was unjust; a palpable, deliberate encroachment on the right of self-government. But as we remarked, just now, it was fortunate for the country that such a state of things existed. In the extraordinary, not anticipated, and perilous condition in which we found ourselves, everything was changed. Neither constitutions nor laws had been framed to meet such an emergency, and both, in many cases, had to be suspended. What was right before, often became wrong now, and vice-versa. The article inserted in the Constitution of the State, that the moment a bank refused specie payment, it became bankrupt, was a wise and just provision, but to enforce it now, would be financial ruin, and it was not done.

This usurpation of the government of New York by the Republican party, which seemed so unjust, was, doubtless, under the circumstances, the salvation of the city. It was, moreover, highly important to the whole country, in the anomalous war which threatened our very existence, that the controlling power of the city should be in sympathy with the General Government, but it was especially, vitally so, when the latter put its provost marshals in it to enforce the draft. That this *mode* of enforcing the draft by provost marshals, was an encroachment on the rights and powers of the separate States, there can be no doubt. It is equally clear that the proper way was to call on the separate governors for their quota, and let *them* enforce the draft. If they refused to do it, then it was time for the General Government to take the matter in its own hand. This, however, was no encroachment on *individual* rights. The oppressive nature of the act and the result were the same to the person, whether enforced by the State or General Government. Still it was a total departure from the practice of the General Government since its first organization, and it moreover established a dangerous precedent, which the sooner it is abandoned the better. But this had nothing to do with the opposition to the draft. That was a personal objection.

With the Police Department in sympathy with the rioters, it is not difficult to see what the end would have been. We do not mean by that, that the heads of the department would not have endeavored to do their duty, but it would have been impossible to control the kind of element they would inevitably have to deal with. This even the long–tried, trusted leaders of the Democratic party acknowledged. In fact, the police force would not have been in a condition, with ever so good a will, to have acted with the skill and promptness it did.

The draft riots, as they are called, were supposed by some to be the result of a deep–laid conspiracy on the part of those opposed to the war, and that the successful issue of Lee's invasion of Pennsylvania was to be the signal for open action. Whether this be so or not, it is evident that the outbreak in New York City on the 13th of July, not only from the manner of its commencement, the absence of proper organization, and almost total absence of leadership, was not the result of a general well–understood plot. It would seem from the facts that those who started the movement had no idea at the outset of proceeding to the length they did. They simply desired to break up the draft in some of the upper districts of the city, and destroy the registers in which certain names were enrolled.

A general provost marshal had been appointed over the whole city, which was subdivided into various districts, in each of which was an assistant provost marshall. Although there had been no provision for a general assistant provost marshal or aid, yet Colonel Nugent acted in this capacity. The drafting was to take place in the separate districts, under the direction of the assistant provost marshals.

Although there had been some rumors of resistance to it, they received very little credence, and no special provision was made for such an emergency. The city was almost denuded of the military; the regiments having been called to Pennsylvania to repel Lee's invasion; yet so little fear was entertained, that even the police department was not requested to make any special preparation. The Invalid Corps, as it was called, composed of the maimed and crippled soldiers who could no longer keep the field, were thought to be quite sufficient to preserve the peace.

The draft commenced on Saturday in the Eleventh and Ninth Districts, and passed off quietly; and it was thought the same order would be maintained throughout, and if any force were necessary to repress violence, it would be when the conscripts were required to take their place in the ranks.

Still Superintendent Kennedy of the Police Department feared there might be some difficulty experienced by the officers in charge of the draft, even if no serious resistance should be offered. Some of the enrolling officers, a short time previous, while taking the names of those subject to draft, had been assailed with very abusive language, or their questions received in sullen silence or answered falsely; fictitious names often being given instead of the true ones. In the Ninth District, embracing the lower part of the city, the provost marshal, Captain Joel T. Erhardt, came near losing his life in the performance of this duty. At the corner of Liberty Street and Broadway a building was being torn down, preparatory to the erection of another, and the workmen engaged in it threatened the enrolling officer who came to take down their names, with violence, and drove him off.

Captain Erhardt, on the report being made to him, repaired to head–quarters, and requested of Colonel Nugent a force of soldiers to protect the officer in the discharge of his duty. But this the latter declined to do, fearing it would exasperate the men and bring on a collision, and requested the Captain to go himself, saying, if he did, there would be no difficulty. Captain Erhardt declined, on the ground that he was not an enrolling officer. But Colonel Nugent persisting, the Captain finally told him, if he ordered him, as his superior officer, to go, he would. Nugent replied that he might so consider it. Erhardt then said he would go, but only on one condition, that if he got in trouble and asked for help, he would send him troops. To this he agreed, and Captain Erhardt proceeded to the building on the corner of Broadway and Liberty Street, and stepping on a plank that led from the sidewalk to the floor, asked a man on a ladder for his name. The fellow refused to answer, when, an altercation ensuing, he stepped down, and seizing an iron bar advanced on the provost marshal. The latter had nothing but a light Malacca cane in his hand, but as he saw the man meant murder he drew a pistol from his pocket, and levelled it full at his breast. This brought him to a halt; and after looking at Erhardt for awhile he dropped his bar. Erhardt then put up his pistol, and went on with his enrolling. The man was dogged and angry, and watching his opportunity, suddenly made a rush at the provost marshal. The latter had only time to deal him, as he sprang forward, one heavy blow with his cane, when they closed. In a moment both reeled from the plank and fell to the cellar beneath, the provost marshal on top. Covered with dirt, he arose and drew his pistol, and mounted to the sidewalk.

The foreman sympathized with the workmen, and Erhardt could do nothing. Determined to arrest them for resisting the draft, he despatched a messenger to Colonel Nugent for the promised force. None, however, was sent. He, in the meantime, stood with drawn pistol facing the men, who dared not advance on him. Aid not arriving, he sent again, and still later a third time. He stood thus facing the workmen with his pistol for three hours, and finally had to leave without making any arrests. This failure of Colonel Nugent to fulfil his promise and perform his duty came near costing Erhardt his life, and then and there starting the riot. The next day he had the foreman arrested, and completed his work of enrolling.

The time selected for commencing the draft was unfortunate. Saturday, of all days in the week, was the worst. It was a new thing, and one under any circumstances calculated to attract universal attention among the lower classes, and provoke great and angry discussion. Hence, to have the draft commence on Saturday, and allow the names to be published in the papers on Sunday morning, so that all could read them, and spend the day in talking the matter over, and lay plans for future action, was a most unwise, thoughtless procedure. If there had been any choice as to the day, one, if possible, should have been chosen that preceded the busiest day of the week. To have the list of twelve hundred names that had been drawn read over and commented on all day by men who enlivened their discussion with copious draughts of bad whiskey, especially when most of those drawn were laboring–men or poor mechanics, who were unable to hire a substitute, was like applying fire to gunpowder. If a well–known name, that of a man of wealth, was among the number, it only increased the exasperation, for the law exempted every one drawn who would pay three hundred dollars towards a substitute. This was taking practically the whole number of soldiers called for out of the laboring classes. A great proportion of these being Irish, it naturally became an Irish question, and eventually an Irish riot. It was in their eyes the game of hated England over again—oppression of Irishmen. This state of feeling could not be wholly concealed. Kennedy, aware of it, felt it necessary, on Monday morning, to take some precautionary measures. Still, in the main, only small squads of policemen were sent to the various points where the drafting was to take place, and merely to keep back the crowd and maintain order, in case a few disorderly persons should attempt to create disturbance. It was true, a rumor had been put in circulation that a body of men had planned to seize the arsenal, and Kennedy, as a matter of precaution, sent fifty policemen to occupy it. But during the morning, word was brought him that the street–contractor's men in the Nineteenth Ward were not at work. This looked ominous, and he began to fear trouble. Thinking that Provost Marshal Maniere's office, 1190 Broadway, and that of Marshal Jenkins, corner of Forty-sixth Street and Third Avenue, would be more likely to be the points attacked, he hurried off the following telegrams :

July 13, 8.35 A.M. From Central Office to Seventeenth, Eighteenth, and Twenty-first Precincts: Send ten men and a sergeant forthwith to No 677 Third Avenue, and report to Captain Porter of Nineteenth Precinct for duty.   J. A. KENNEDY.

July 13, 8.50 A.M. To Twenty-ninth Precinct: Place a squad of ten of your men, with a competent sergeant, at No. 1190 Broadway, during the draft—if you want more, inform me.   J. A. K.

8 55 A M To Sixteenth and Twentieth Precincts: Send your reserve to Seventh Avenue Arsenal forthwith.   J. A. K.

Telegrams were now pouring in from different quarters, showing that mischief was afoot, and at nine o'clock he sent the following despatch:

"To all platoons, New York and Brooklyn: Call in your reserve platoons, and hold them at the stations subject to further orders."

It should be noted, that, ordinarily one half of the police of the Metropolitan District, which took in Brooklyn, is relieved from both patrol and reserve duty, from six o'clock in the morning till six in the evening. The other half is divided into two sections, which alternately perform patrol and reserve duty during the day. A relief from patrol duty of one of these sections takes place at eight o'clock A.M., when it goes to breakfast. Hence, the orders issued by the Superintendent to call in these could not reach them without a considerable delay.

It now being about ten o'clock, Mr. Kennedy, having despatched an additional body of men to the Twenty-ninth

Precinct, got into his light wagon, to take a drive through the districts reported to be most dangerous. He went up far as the arsenal, and giving such directions as he thought necessary, started across the town to visit Marshal Jenkins' quarters in the Twenty-ninth Precinct.

· CHAPTER XII ·

COMMENCEMENT OF THE MOB.—ITS LINE OF MARCH.—
ITS IMMENSE SIZE.—ATTACKS A PROVOST-MARSHAL'S
OFFICE, IN THIRD AVENUE.—SET ON FIRE.—TERRIBLE
STRUGGLE OF KENNEDY FOR HIS LIFE WITH THE MOB.—
CARRIED TO HEAD-QUARTERS UNCONSCIOUS.—ACTON'S
PREPARATIONS.—THE TELEGRAPH SYSTEM.—MOB CUT-
TING DOWN TELEGRAPH POLES.—NUMBER OF DESPATCHES
SENT OVER THE WIRES DURING THE RIOT.—SUPERINTEN-
DENT OF TELEGRAPH BUREAU SEIZED AND HELD PRISONER
BY THE MOB.

MEANWHILE, EVENTS WERE assuming an alarming aspect in the western part of the city. Early in the morning men began to assemble here in separate groups, as if in accordance with a previous arrangement, and at last moved quietly north along the various avenues. Women, also, like camp followers, took the same direction in crowds. They were thus divided into separate gangs, apparently to take each avenue in their progress, and make a clean sweep. The factories and workshops were visited, and the men compelled to knock off work and join them, while the proprietors were threatened with the destruction of their property, if they made any opposition. The separate crowds were thus swelled at almost every step, and armed with sticks, and clubs, and every conceivable weapon they could lay hands on, they moved north towards some point which had evidently been selected as a place of rendezvous. This proved to be a vacant lot near Central Park, and soon the living streams began to flow into it, and a more wild, savage, and heterogeneous–looking mass could not be imagined. After a short consultation they again took up the line of inarch, and in two separate bodies, moved down Fifth and Sixth Avenues, until they reached Forty-sixth and Forty-seventh Streets, when they turned directly east.

The number composing this first mob has been so differently estimated, that it would be impossible from reports merely, to approximate the truth. A pretty accurate idea, however, can be gained of its immense size, from a statement made by Mr. King, son of President King, of Columbia College. Struck by its magnitude, he had the curiosity to get some estimate of it by timing its progress, and he found that although it filled the broad street from curbstone to curbstone, and was moving rapidly, it took between twenty and twenty-five minutes for it to pass a single point.

A ragged, coatless, heterogeneously weaponed army, it heaved tumultuously along toward Third Avenue. Tearing down the telegraph poles as it crossed the Harlem & New Haven Railroad track, it surged angrily up around the building where the drafting was going on. The small squad of police stationed there to repress disorder looked on bewildered, feeling they were powerless in the presence of such a host. Soon a stone went crashing through a window, which was the signal for a general assault on the doors. These giving way before the immense pressure, the foremost rushed in, followed by shouts and yells from those behind, and began to break up the furniture. The drafting officers, in an adjoining room, alarmed, fled precipitately through the rear of the building. The mob seized the wheel in which were the names, and what books, papers, and lists were left, and tore them up, and scattered them in every direction. A safe stood on one side, which was supposed to contain important papers, and on this they fell with clubs and stones, but in vain. Enraged at being thwarted, they set fire to the building, and hurried out of it. As the smoke began to ascend, the onlooking multitude without sent up a loud cheer. Though the upper part of the building was occupied by families, the rioters, thinking that the officers were concealed there, rained stones and brick–bats against the windows, sending terror into the hearts of the inmates. Deputy Provost Marshal Vanderpoel, who had mingled in the crowd, fearing for the lives of the women and children, boldly stepped to the front, and tried to appease the mob, telling them the papers were all destroyed, and begged them to fall back, and let others help the inmates of the building, or take hold themselves. The reply was a heavy blow in the face. Vanderpoel shoved the man who gave it aside, when he was assailed with a shower of blows and curses. Fearing for his life, he broke through the crowd, and hastened to the spot where the police were standing, wholly powerless in the midst of this vast, excited throng.

In the meantime, the flames, unarrested, made rapid way, and communicating to the adjoining building, set it on fire. The volumes of smoke, rolling heavenward, and the crackling and roaring of the flames, seemed for a moment to awe the mob, and it looked silently on the ravaging of a power more terrible and destructive than its own.

At this time Superintendent Kennedy was quietly making his way across the town toward the office of the provost marshal, Jenkins. But noticing a fire as he approached, he left his wagon at the corner of Forty-sixth Street and Lexington Avenue, and walked over toward Third Avenue. The street was blocked with people, but they seemed quiet and orderly as any gathering in presence of a fire, and differed from it only in that the countenances of all seemed to wear a pleased, gratified look. As he unsuspiciously edged his way forward toward the fire, he heard some one cry out, "There's Kennedy!" "Which is him?" asked a second; and he was pointed out.

Kennedy was dressed in ordinary citizen's clothes, and carried only a slight bamboo cane. Thinking the allusion to him was prompted only by curiosity, he kept on, when suddenly he felt himself violently pushed against. Turning around, he encountered a man in a soldier's old uniform, and sternly demanded what he meant by that. The words had hardly escaped his lips, when a heavy blow was planted full in his face. Instantly the crowd closed around him, and rained blows in rapid succession on him, until he fell over and down the graded street, some six feet, into a vacant lot. The crowd, with yells, poured after him. Kennedy, springing to his feet, started on a run across the lot towards Forty-seventh Street, distancing his pursuers. But as he reached Forty-seventh Street, and attempted to ascend the embankment, another crowd, which had witnessed the pursuit, rushed upon him, and knocked him back again in front of his pursuers. He quickly sprang up, though bleeding and stunned, for he knew his only chance for life was in keeping his feet. But the crowd closing around on both sides gave him no chance to run. One huge fellow, armed with a heavy club, endeavored to break in his skull, but Kennedy dodged his blows. Careful only for his head, he let them beat his body, while he made desperate efforts to break through the mass, whose demoniacal yells and oaths showed that they intended to take his life. In the struggle the whole crowd, swaying to and fro, slowly advanced toward Lexington Avenue, coming, as they did so, upon a wide mud–hole. "Drown him! drown him!" arose at once on every side, and the next moment a heavy blow, planted under his ear, sent him head-foremost into the water.

Falling with his face amid the stones, he was kicked and trampled on, and pounded, till he was a mass of gore. Still struggling desperately for life, he managed to get to his feet again, and made a dash for the middle of the pond. The water was deep, and his murderers, disliking to get wet, did not follow him, but ran around to the other side, to meet him as he came out. But Kennedy was ahead of them, and springing up the bank into Lexington Avenue, saw a man whom he knew, and called out: "John Eagan, come here and save my life!" Mr. Eagan, who was a well-known and influential resident of that vicinity, immediately rushed forward to his assistance, and arrested his pursuers. But the Superintendent was so terribly bruised and mangled, that Eagan did not recognize him. He, however, succeeded in keeping the mob back, who, seeing the horrible condition their victim was in, doubtless thought they had finished him. Other citizens now coming forward, a passing feed wagon was secured, into which Kennedy was lifted, and driven to police head-quarters. Acton, who was in the street as the wagon approached, saw the mangled body within, but did not dream who it was. The driver inquired where he should take him. "Around to the station," carelessly replied Acton. The driver hesitated, and inquired again, "Where to?" Acton, supposing it was some drunkard, bruised in a brawl, replied rather petulantly, "Around to the station." The man then told him it was Kennedy. Acton, scanning the features more closely, saw that it indeed was the Superintendent himself in this horrible condition. As the officers gathered around the bleeding, almost unconscious form, a murmur of wrath was heard, a sure premonition what work would be done when the hour of vengeance should come.

Kennedy was carried into head–quarters, and a surgeon immediately sent for. After an examination had shown that no bones were broken, he was taken to the house of a friend, and, before the week closed, was on his feet again.

Acton, now the legal head of the police force, soon showed he was the right man in the right place. Of a nervous temperament, he was quick and prompt, yet cool and decided, and relentless as death in the discharge of his duty. Holding the views of the first Napoleon respecting mobs, he did not believe in speech–making to them. His addresses were to be locust clubs and grape–shot. Taking in at once the gravity of the situation, he, after despatching such force as was immediately available to the scene of the riot, telegraphed to the different precincts to have the entire reserve force concentrated at head–quarters, which were in Mulberry Street, near Bleecker.

He saw at once, to have his force effective it must be well in hand, so that he could send it out in any direction in sufficient strength to bear down all opposition. Subsequent events proved the wisdom of his policy, for we shall see, after it had been accomplished, the police never lost a battle.

There being thirty-two precincts in the limits of the Metropolitan Police, a vast territory was covered. These were reached by a system of telegraph wires, called the Telegraph Bureau, of which James Crowley was superintendent and Eldred Polhamus deputy. There were three operators—Chapin, Duvall, and Lucas. A telegraph station was in each precinct—thus making thirty-two, all coming to a focus at head–quarters. These are also divided into five sections—north, south, east, west, and central. The Commissioners, therefore, sitting in the central office, can send messages almost instantaneously to every precinct of the city, and receive immediate answers. Hence, Mr. Acton was a huge Briareus, reaching out his arms to Fort Washington in the north, and Brooklyn in the south, and at the same time touching the banks of both rivers. No other system could be devised giving such tremendous power to the police—the power of instant information and rapid concentration at any desired point. That it proved itself the strong right arm of the Commissioners, it needs only to state, that during the four days of the riot, between five and six thousand messages passed over the wires, showing that they were worked to their utmost capacity, day and night. The more intelligent of the mob understood this, and hence at the outset attempted to break up this communication, by cutting down the poles on Third Avenue. This stopped all messages to and from the precincts at Fort Washington, Manhattanville, Harlem, Yorkville, and Bloomingdale, as well as with the Nineteenth Precinct.

But fortunately, the orders to these had passed over the wires before the work was completed. Subsequently, the rioters cut down the poles in First Avenue, in Twenty-second Street, and Ninth Avenue, destroying communication between several other precincts.

Mr. Crowley, the Superintendent of the Telegraph Bureau, was made acquainted early, Monday, by mere accident with this plan of the rioters. Coming to town in the Third Avenue cars from Yorkville, where he resided, he suddenly found the car arrested by a mob, and getting out with the other passengers, discovered men chopping furiously away at the telegraph poles; and without stopping to think, rushed up to them and ordered them to desist. One of the ruffians, looking up, cried out, "he is one of the d—d operators." Instantly yells arose, "Smash him," "Kill him," when those nearest seized him. By great adroitness he disarmed their suspicions sufficiently to prevent further violence, though they held him prisoner for an hour. At last, seeing an opportunity when more important objects attracted their attention, he quietly worked his way out and escaped.

• CHAPTER XIII •

SOLDIERS BEATEN BY THE MOB.—GALLANT FIGHT OF SERGEANT McCREDIE.—MOB TRIUMPHANT.—BEAT POLICE OFFICERS UNMERCIFULLY.—FEARFUL SCENES.— FIFTY THOUSAND PEOPLE BLOCK THIRD AVENUE.—A WHOLE BLOCK OF HOUSES BURNING.—ATTACK ON A GUN FACTORY.—DEFEAT OF THE BROADWAY SQUAD.—HOUSES SACKED IN LEXINGTON AVENUE.—TELEGRAPH DISPATCHES.—BULL'S HEAD TAVERN BURNED.—BLOCK ON BROADWAY BURNED.—BURNING OF THE NEGROES' ORPHAN ASYLUM.—ATTACK ON MAYOR OPDYKE'S HOUSE.—A CRISIS NOBLY MET.—GALLANT FIGHT AND VICTORY OF SERGEANT CARPENTER.—A THRILLING SPECTACLE.

IN THE MEANTIME, the mob that stood watching the spreading conflagration in Third Avenue increased rapidly, fed by tributaries from the tenement–houses, slums, and workshops in that vicinity. But they were soon startled from their state of comparative quietness, by the cry of "the soldiers are coming." The Invalid Corps, a small body sent from the Park, was approaching. As it came up, the soldiers fired, either blank cartridges, or over the heads of the crowd, doubtless thinking a single discharge would disperse it. The folly of such a course was instantly shown, for the mob, roused into sudden fury, dashed on the small body of soldiers before they could reload, and snatching away their muskets, pounded them over the head, and chased them like sheep for ten blocks. One soldier was left for dead on the pavement, beaten to a jelly. Another, breaking from the crowd, attempted to climb some rocks near Forty-second Street, when his pursuers grabbed him and dragged him to the top, where they tore off his uniform, and beat him till he was senseless, and then threw him down to the bottom and left him.

In the meantime, Sergeant McCredie, "fighting Mac," as he was called, from the Fifteenth Precinct, Captain C. W. Caffrey, arrived on the scene with a few men. Marching down Forty-third street to Third Avenue, they looked up two blocks, and to their amazement beheld the broad avenue, as far as they could see, blocked with the mob, while before it, bearing swiftly down on them, and running for life, came the terror–stricken Invalid Corps. At this juncture, other squads sent from various precincts arrived, swelling this force to forty-four. It was a mere handful among these enraged thousands; but McCredie, who at once took command, determined to stand his ground, and meet as best he could the overwhelming numbers that came driving down like a storm, filling the air with yells and oaths, and brandishing their clubs over their heads. He thought that another police force was beyond the mob, on the north, and if he could press through and form a junction with it, the two combined would be strong enough to hold their own. He therefore quickly formed his men in line across the street, and awaited the shock. As the disorderly mass following up the fugitives drew near, McCredie ordered a charge, and this mere handful of men moved swiftly and steadily upon it. The rioters, stunned by the suddenness and strength of the blow, recoiled, and the police, following up their advantage, drove them back, step by step, as far as Forty-sixth street. Here the sergeant, instead of meeting another body of police, as he expected, met a heavier body of rioters that were blocking up Forty-sixth Street on both sides of the avenue. Backed by these, the main body rallied and charged on the exhausted police force in turn, and almost surrounded them. To render their already desperate situation hopeless, another mob suddenly closed in behind them from Forty-fifth street.

Thus attacked in front and rear with clubs, iron bars, guns and pistols, and rained upon with stones and brick–bats from the roofs of the houses, they were unable longer to keep together, and broke and fled—part up the side streets, and some down the avenue—bruised, torn, and bleeding.

The desperate nature of this first conflict can be imagined, when, out of the fourteen men composing Sergeant McCredie's original force, only five were left unwounded. At the very outset of the charge, the sergeant himself was struck with an iron bar on the wrist, which rendered the arm almost useless. In the retreat, four men assailed him at once. Knocking down two, he took refuge in the house of a German, when a young woman told him to jump between two mattresses. He did so, and she covered him up just as his pursuers forced their way in. Streaming through the house from cellar to garret, they came back, and demanded of the young woman where the man was hid. She quietly said he had escaped by the rear of the house. Believing she told the truth, they took their departure. Officer Bennett was knocked down three times before he ceased fighting. The last time he was supposed to be dead, when the wretches began to rob him even of his clothing, stripping him of every article except his drawers. He was soon after taken up and carried to St. Luke's Hospital, and placed in the dead–house, where he lay for several hours. When the sad news was brought to his wife, she hastened to the hospital, and fell weeping on the lifeless form of her husband. She could not believe he was dead, and laying her hand on his heart, found to her joy that it pulsated. She immediately flew to the officials of the hospital, and had him brought in, and restoratives applied. He revived, but remained unconscious for three days, while the riot raged around him. Officer Travis, in the flight down the avenue, saw, as he looked back, that his foremost pursuer had a pistol. Wheeling, he knocked him down, and seized the pistol, but before he could use it, a dozen clubs were raining blows upon him, which brought him to the ground. The infuriated men then jumped upon him, knocking out his teeth, breaking his jaw–bone and right hand, and terribly mutilating his whole body. Supposing him to be dead, they then stripped him stark naked and left him on the pavement, a ghastly spectacle to the passers–by. Officer Phillips ran the gauntlet almost unharmed, but was pursued block after block by a portion of the mob, till he reached Thirty-ninth street. Here he attempted to enter a house, but it was closed against him. As he turned down the steps, one of the pursuers, in soldier's clothes, levelled his musket at him and fired. Missing his aim, he clubbed his weapon, and dealt him a deadly blow. Phillips caught the musket as it descended, and wrenching it from his grasp, knocked the fellow down with it, and started and ran across some vacant lots to Fortieth Street. But here he was headed off by another portion of the mob, in which was a woman, who made a lunge at him with a shoemaker's knife. The knife missed his throat, but passed through his ear. Drawing it back, she made another stab, piercing his arm. He was now bleeding profusely, and his death seemed inevitable, when a stranger, seeing his condition, sprang forward, and covering his body, declared he would kill the first man that advanced. Awed by his determined manner, the fiends sullenly withdrew. Officers Sutherland and Mingay were also badly beaten. Officer Kiernan, receiving a blow on his head with a stone, another on the back of his neck with a hay–bale rung, and two more on the knees, fell insensible, and would doubtless have been killed outright, but for the wife of Eagan, who saved Kennedy. Throwing herself over his body, she exclaimed, "for God's sake do not kill him." Seeing that they had got to attack this lady to get at Kiernan, they passed on.

The scene in Third Avenue at this time was fearful and appalling. It was now noon, but the hot July sun was obscured by heavy clouds, that hung in ominous shadows over the city, while from near Cooper Institute to Forty-sixth Street, or about thirty blocks, the avenue was black with human beings,—sidewalks, house–tops, windows, and stoops all filled with rioters or spectators. Dividing it like a stream, horse–cars arrested in their course lay strung along as far as the eye could reach. As the glance ran along this mighty mass of men and women north, it rested at length on huge columns of smoke rolling heavenward from burning buildings, giving a still more fearful aspect to the scene. Many estimated the number at this time in the street at fifty thousand.

In the meantime the fire–bell had brought the firemen on the ground, but the mob would not let them approach the burning houses. The flames had communicated with the adjoining block

and were now making fearful headway. At length Engineer
Decker addressed the mob, which by this time had grown thin-
ner by the main mass moving farther down town, who told them
that everything relating to the provost marshal's office was
destroyed, and now the fire was destroying private property, some
of which doubtless belonged to persons friendly to them, and
finally persuaded them to let the engines work. Water was soon
deluging the buildings, and the fire at length arrested, but not
until four were consumed with all their contents.

The drawing commenced in the Eighth District, 1190 Broadway, Captain Maniere provost marshal, on the same morning, and
continued quietly until about 12 o'clock, when it was adjourned,
and policemen who had been stationed there to guard it were
sent over to the Ninth District, where the mob was carrying everything before it. But coming in small bodies, they were easily overcome and scattered. Sergeant Ellison, especially, got badly beaten;
and Sergeant Wade, who came up soon after, and charged gallantly on the mob, shared the same fate, and had to be taken to
St. Luke's Hospital. The work of destruction having commenced,
it went on after this with the wild irregularity characteristic of
mobs. The news of the uprising and destruction of property, as
it spread through those portions of the city where the low Irish
dwelt, stirred up all the inmates, and they came thronging forth,
till there were incipient mobs on almost every corner. From this
time no consecutive narrative can be given of the after doings. This
immense mass seemed to split up into three or four sections, as
different objects attracted their attention; and they came together
and separated apparently without any concert of action. A shout
and a cry in one direction would call off a throng, while a similar
shout in another would attract a portion thither. Some feeling the
need of arms, and remembering that a gun factory was at the corner of Second Avenue and Twentieth Street, called out to the
crowd, and soon a large body was rushing in that direction. The
Police Commissioners had also thought of this, and hastily sent
off the Broadway squad to occupy it, and they succeeded, by
going singly and in pairs, in reaching it—thirty-five all told. These
men, selected for their size, being all six feet or upward, were
ordered to hold the place at all hazards.

In the meantime the mob endeavored to gain admittance, but warned off by Sergeant Burdick, left. But scarcely a quarter of an hour had elapsed, when they returned heavily reinforced, armed with all kinds of weapons, and yelling and hooting like fiends. Stones and bricks came crashing through the windows, but still the squad, though every man was armed with a carbine, did not fire.

The mob then tried to set the factory on fire, but failed. Enraged at being baffled, a powerful man advanced on the door with a sledge–hammer, and began to pound against it. At length one of the panels gave way, and as a shout arose from those looking on, he boldly attempted to crawl through. The report of a solitary carbine was heard, and the brains of the man lay scattered on the floor. This staggered the mob for a moment, but soon fear gave way to rage, and shots and stones were rained against the building, smashing in the windows, and rapidly making a clean breach through the door. Burdick sent to Captain Cameron for aid, but he replied that he could not reach him.

At 3.45 the following telegram was sent from the Eighteenth Precinct:

"The mob have attacked the armory, Second Avenue and Twenty-first Street. There is danger of firing the building."

Fifteen minutes later came: "It is impossible for us to protect the armory at Second Avenue and Twenty-first Street."

Answer—"Draw your men off. D. C."

The squad, in evacuating the building, found themselves cut off both in front and at the sides.

The only mode of escape was through a hole in the rear wall, some eighteen feet from the ground, and scarcely a foot and a half in diameter. Piling up boxes to reach this aperture, these large men squeezed themselves through one by one, feet foremost, and swinging to a gutter–trough, dropped into the yard below. Climbing from thence over a wall into a stone–yard, they sped across it to the Eighteenth Precinct Station in Twenty-second Street. Here taking off their uniforms, they made their way singly, or in groups of two or three, back to the central office.

No sooner did they leave the building than the mob entered it, and the work of pillage commenced. Every man armed himself with a musket. The stacks of weapons left, after they had taken all they wanted, were broken up or rendered useless. One thrown out of the window fell on a man's head in the street and killed him.

While the armory was being attacked, another mob was sacking and burning houses on Lexington Avenue, near Forty-seventh Street. Within five minutes from the announcement of this fact, came from the Sixth Precinct the following dispatch: "A mob of about seven hundred attacked some colored people in Baxter Street, and then went to the saloon of Samuel Crook, in Chatham Street, and beat some colored waiters there."

A few minutes later from Sixteenth came: "A crowd of about three hundred men have gone to the foot of Twenty-fourth Street, to stop men in the foundry from working."

At the same time the following was received from the Twenty-first Precinct: "The mob avow their determination of burning this station. Our connection by telegram may be interrupted at any moment."

Another from the Twentieth said : "A very large crowd is now going down Fifth Avenue, to attack the Tribune building."

As fast as the wires could work, followed from the Twenty-fourth Precinct:

"The mob have fired the buildings corner of Broadway and Twenty-fourth Street."

All this time, while new notes of alarm were sounded, and the police department was struggling to get its force in band, the work of destruction was going on in the upper part of the city. Bull's Head Tavern, in Forty-sixth Street, attracted the attention of the mob. The sales of the immense herds of cattle in the adjoining yard had been suspended, and the hotel closed. The crowd, however, forgetting the draft, and intent only on pillage, streamed up around it, and shouted, " Fire it! fire it!" While some were calling for axes and crowbars, ten powerful men jumped on the stoop, and with a few heavy blows sent the hall door flying from its hinges. The yelling crowd then rushed in, and after helping themselves to what they wanted, applied the torch, and soon the entire building was a mass of flame.

At this time another mob was sacking houses in Lexington Avenue. Elegant furniture and silver plate were borne away by the

The riot in Lexington Avenue.

crowd, while the ladies, with their children and servants, fled in terror from the scene. The provost marshal's head–quarters were also set on fire, and the whole block on Broadway, between Twenty-eighth and Twenty-ninth Streets, was burned down, while jewelry stores and shops of all kinds were plundered and their contents carried off. A vast horde followed the rioters for the sole purpose of plunder, and loaded down with their spoils, could be seen hastening home in every direction.

While these fires were under full headway, a new idea seemed to strike the mob, or at least a portion of it. Having stopped the draft in two districts, sacked and set on fire nearly a score of houses, and half killed as many men, it now, impelled by a strange logic, sought to destroy the Colored Orphan Asylum on Fifth Avenue, extending from Forty-third to Forty-fourth Street. There would have been no draft but for the war—there would have been no war but for slavery. But the slaves were black, ergo, all blacks are responsible for the war. This seemed to be the logic of the mob, and having reached the sage conclusion to which it conducted, they did not stop to consider how poor helpless orphans could be held responsible, but proceeded at once to wreak their vengeance on them. The building was four stories high, and besides the matrons and officers, contained over two hundred children, from mere infants up to twelve years of age. Around this building the rioters gathered with loud cries and oaths, sending terror into the hearts of the inmates. Superintendent William E. Davis hurriedly fastened the doors; but knowing they would furnish but a momentary resistance to the armed multitude, he, with others, collected hastily the terrified children, and carrying some in their arms, and leading others, hurried them in a confused crowd out at the rear of the building, just as the ruffians effected an entrance in front. Then the work of pillage commenced, and everything carried off that could be, even to the dresses and trinkets of the children, while heavy furniture was smashed and chopped up in the blind desire of destruction. Not satisfied with this, they piled the fragments in the different rooms, and set fire to them. At this juncture Chief Engineer Decker arrived, and determined, if possible, to save the building, addressed the crowd, as he had in the morning, hoping to induce them to forbear further violence, and let him extinguish the flames. But they had now got beyond argument of any kind, and knocking him down twice, pitched him into the street. But ten brave firemen at this juncture rushed to his side, and together fought their way through the crowd into the building, where they were joined by two assistant engineers, Lamb and Lewis. They at once began to scatter and extinguish the burning fragments, keeping back for a while, by their bold bearing, the rioters. The latter, however, soon rallied in force, and some mounting to the loft, set it on fire in every part. Decker and his few gallant allies, finding it impossible to save the building, retreated into the street, and soon the massive structure was a sheet of flame.

The crowd now proceeded to Mayor Opdyke's house, and gathering in front of it, sent up shouts and calls for the Mayor. They were, however, deterred at that time from accomplishing their purpose by an appeal from Judge Barnard, who addressed them from the steps of an adjoining house.

Soon after, an immense mob was reported coming down Broadway, for the purpose, some thought, of attacking the negro waiters in the Lafarge House, between Amity and Bleecker Streets, but in fact to attack police head–quarters in Mulberry Street, and break up the very centre of operations. It was a bold stroke, but the ringleaders had been drinking all day, and now, maddened by liquor, were ready for the most desperate attempts. When the news of this movement reached head–quarters, the commissioners saw that a crisis had come. The mob numbered at least five thousand, while they could not muster at that moment two hundred men. The clerk, Mr. Hawley, went to the commissioners' room, and said : "Gentlemen, the crisis has come. A battle has got to be *fought now, and won too,* or all is lost." They agreed with him. "But who," they asked, "will lead the comparatively small force in this fight?" He replied that he thought that Sergeant Carpenter should be selected, as one of the oldest and most experienced officers on the force. "Well," they said, "will you go down to his room and see what he says about it?" He went, and laid before him the perilous condition of things, and that an immediate and successful battle *must* be fought.

Carpenter heard him through, and taking in fully the perilous condition of things, paused a moment, and then rising to his full height and lifting his hand, said, with a terrible oath, "I'll go, and I'll win that fight, or *Daniel Carpenter will never come back a live man.*" He walked out and summoned the little force, and as "Fall in, men; fall in," was repeated, they fell into line along the street. When all was ready, Acton turned to Carpenter, every lineament of whose face showed the stern purpose that mastered him, and quietly said, "*Sergeant, make no arrests.*"

It was to be a battle in which no prisoners were to be taken. "All *right*," replied Carpenter, as he buttoned up his coat and shouted "Forward." Solid, and silent save their heavy, measured tread on the pavement, they moved down Bleecker Street towards Broadway. As they turned into the latter street, only a block and a half away, they saw the mob, which filled the entire street far as the eye could reach, moving tumultuously forward. Armed with clubs, pitchforks, iron bars, and some with guns and pistols, and most of them in their shirt–sleeves and shouting as they came, they presented a wild and savage appearance. Pedestrians fled down the side streets, stores were hastily closed, stages vanished, and they had the street to themselves. A huge hoard, on which was inscribed "No Draft," was borne aloft as a banner, and beside it waved the Stars and Stripes.

The less than two hundred policemen, compact and firm, now halted, while Carpenter detached two companies of fifty each up the parallel streets to the right and left, as far as Fourth Street. Coming down this street from both directions, they were to strike the mob on both flanks at the same time he charged them in front. He waited till they had reached their positions, and then shouted, "*By the right flank Company front, double-quick,* charge." Instantaneously every club was swung in air, and solid as a wall and swift as a wave they swept full on the astonished multitude; while at the same time, to cut the monster in two, the two companies charged in flank. Carpenter, striding several steps in advance, his face fairly blazing with excitement, dealt the first blow, stretching on the pavement a powerful ruffian, who was rushing on him with a huge club. For a few minutes nothing was heard but the heavy thud of clubs falling on human skulls, thick and fast as hailstones on windows. The mob, just before so confident and bold, quailed in terror and would have broke and fled at once, but for the mass behind which kept bearing down on them. This, however, soon gave way before the side attacks and the panic that followed. Then the confusion and uproar became terrible, and the mass surged hither and thither, now rolling up Broadway, and again borne back or shoved up against the stores, seeking madly for a way of escape. At length, breaking into fragments, they rushed down the side streets, hotly pursued by the police, whose remorseless clubs never ceased to fall as long as a fugitive was within reach. Broadway looked like a field of battle, for the pavement was strewn thick with bleeding, prostrate forms. It was a great victory and decisive of all future contests.

Having effectually dispersed them, Carpenter, with the captured flag, marched up to Mayor Opdyke's house, when, finding everything quiet, he returned to head–quarters. This successful attack of the police was received with cheers by those spectators who had witnessed it.

CHAPTER XIV

No Military in the City.—The Mayor calls on General Wool, commanding Eastern Department, for Help.—Also on General Sandford.—General Wool sends to General Brown, commanding Garrison in the Harbor, for U. S. Troops.—Marines of the Navy Yard ordered up.—Eventually, West Point and several States appealed to for Troops.—General Brown assumes Command.—Attack of Mob on the *Tribune* Building.—Its severe Punishment.—Government Buildings Garrisoned.—Difficulty between Generals Brown and Wool.—Head-Quarters.—Police Commissioners' Office Military Head-Quarters.

THE TERRIBLE PUNISHMENT the rioters received at the hands of Carpenter had, however, only checked their movements for a time; and, as the sun began to hang low in the summer heavens, men looked forward to the coming night with apprehension.

In the meantime, however, the authorities, conscious of the perilous condition of the city, had resorted to every means of defence in their power. Unfortunately, as mentioned before, nearly the whole of its military force, on which it depended in any great emergency, was absent. Lee's brilliant Hank movement around Hooker and Washington, terminating in the invasion of Pennsylvania, had filled the country with consternation. His mighty columns were moving straight on Philadelphia, and the Government at Washington, roused to the imminent danger, had called for all the troops within reach, and New York had sent forward nearly every one of her regiments. Ordinary prudence would have dictated that the draft should be postponed for a few days, till these regiments, now on their way hack, or preparing to return, should arrive. It was running a needless risk to urge it in such a crisis—indeed, one of the follies of which the Administration at this time was so needlessly guilty.

General Wool, at this juncture, commanded the Eastern Department, with his head–quarters at the corner of Bleeeker and Greene Streets. Mayor Opdyke immediately called on him for help, and also on Major–general Sandford, commanding the few troops that were left in the city. The latter immediately issued an order requesting the Seventh Regiment to meet that evening, at their drill–rooms, at eight o'clock, to consult on the measures necessary to be taken in the present unexpected crisis, and another to the late two–years' volunteers then in the city, to report at the same hour in Grand Street, to Colonel William H. Allen, for temporary duty.

General Wool, also, during the afternoon, while the rioters were having it all their own way, sent an officer to the adjutant-general of General Brown, commanding the troops in garrison in New York harbor, ordering up a force of about eighty men immediately.

General Brown, on his way from his office to Fort Hamilton, was informed by Colonel Stinson, chief clerk, that a serious riot was raging in the city, and that General Wool had sent to Fort Hamilton for a detachment of some eighty men, and that a tug had gone for them. Surprised at the smallness of the number sent (he was, by special orders of the War Department, commandant of the city, and commander of all the forts and troops in the harbor except Fort Columbus), he immediately ordered the company at Fort Wood to the city, and sent a tug for it. He then made a requisition on the quartermaster for transportation of all the other companies, and proceeded without delay to Fort Hamilton. General Brown's office was close to General Wool's; but he did not think proper to consult him on the movement.

General Brown, immediately on his arrival at Fort Hamilton, directed that all the troops there, as well as at Forts Lafayette and Richmond, be got in readiness to move at a moment's notice, and also that a section of artillery be organized, in case it should be wanted. Having taken these wise precautions he hastened up to the city, and reported to General Wool. The result proved the wisdom of his forecast. A new order was at once dispatched for the remaining troops, and just at twilight, Lieutenant McElrath saw two steamers making directly for the fort. They were hardly fastened to the dock, when an officer stepped ashore and handed him an order from General Brown to send up at once all the efficient troops in the forts, and have their places supplied as best he could with some volunteer artillery companies.

The reports coming in to police head–quarters had shown that it was no common uprising of a few disaffected men to be put down by a few squads of police or a handful of soldiers. The Mayor, after consulting with the Police Commissioners, felt that it was the beginning of a general outbreak in every part of the city, and by his representations persuaded General Wool to apply to Rear–admiral Paulding, commanding the Navy Yard, for a force of marines, and eventually to Colonel Bowman, Superintendent of West Point, and also to the authorities of Newark, and Governors of New York, New Jersey, Massachusetts, Connecticut, and Rhode Island for troops.

General Brown, after reporting to General Wool, repaired to police head–quarters, which he adopted as his own, and issued the following order:

"HEAD–QUARTERS, New York, July 13, 1863.

"In obedience to the orders of the Major–general commanding the Eastern Department, the undersigned assumes command of the United States troops in this city.

"Lieutenant–colonel Frothingham and Captain Revolle are of the staff of the undersigned, and will be obeyed accordingly.

"HARVEY BROWN,

"*Brevet Brigadier-general.*"

He also sent a dispatch to General Sandford, at the arsenal, notifying him of his action, and requesting him to come down and consult with him on the course to be pursued. General Sandford, after awhile, did come down, and, to General Brown's amazement, insisted that all the troops should be sent up to the arsenal. General Brown, seeing the utter madness of such a disposition of his force, refused decidedly to permit it to be done. This was of course denying Sandford's claim to be his superior officer. It was well for the city that he took this ground.

Mayor Opdyke also issued a proclamation, calling on the rioters to disperse.

But while these measures were being set on foot, the rioters were not idle.

All day long a crowd had been gathering in the Park around the City Hall, growing more restless as night came on. The railroad-cars passing it were searched, to see if any negroes were on board, while eyes glowered savagely on the *Tribune* building. They had sought in an eating-house for the editor, to wreak their vengeance on him. Not finding him, they determined that the building, from which was issued the nefarious paper, should come down, but were evidently waiting for help to arrive before commencing the work of destruction. The mob, which Carpenter had so terribly punished in Broadway, were marching for it, designing to burn it after they had demolished police head-quarters. Their dispersion delayed the attack, and doubtless broke its force, by the reduction of numbers it caused. There seemed enough, however, if properly led, to effect their purpose, for the Park and Printing-house Square were black with men, who, as the darkness increased, grew more restless; and "Down with it! burn it!" mingled with oaths and curses, were heard on every side.

At last came the crash of a window, as a stone went through it. Another and another followed, when suddenly a reinforcing crowd came rushing down Chatham Street. This was the signal for a general assault, and, with shouts, the rabble poured into the lower part of the building, and began to destroy everything within reach. Captain Warlow, of the First Precinct, No. 29 Broad Street, who, with his command, was in the gallant fight in Broadway, after some subsequent fighting and marching, had at length reached

The Attack On the Tribune Building.

his headquarters in Broad Street, where a dispatch met him, to proceed at once to the *Tribune* building, he immediately started off on the double-quick. On reaching the upper end of Nassau Street, he came to a halt, and gave the club signal on the pavement, to form column. Captain Thorne, of the City Hall, in the meantime, had joined his force to him, with the gallant Sergeant Devoursney. Everything being ready, the order to "Charge" was given, and the entire force, perhaps a hundred and fifty strong, fell in one solid mass on the mob, knocking men over right and left, and laying heads open at every blow. The panic-stricken crowd fled up Chatham Street, across the Park, and down Spruce and Frankfort Streets, punished terribly at every step. The space around the building being cleared, a portion of the police rushed inside, where the work of destruction was going on. The sight of the blue-coats in their midst, with their uplifted clubs, took the rioters by surprise, and they rushed frantically for the doors and windows, and escaped the best way they could. In the meantime, those who had taken refuge in the Park found themselves in the lion's jaws. Carpenter had hardly rested from his march up Fifth Avenue to Mayor Opdyke's house, when he, too, received orders to hasten to the protection of the *Tribune* building. Taking one hundred of his own men, and one hundred under Inspector Folk of Brooklyn, who had been early ordered over, and been doing good service in the city, he marched down Broadway, and was just entering the Park, when the frightened crowd came rushing pell-mell across it. Immediately forming "company front," he swept the Park like a storm, clearing everything before him. Order being restored, Folk returned with his force to Brooklyn, where things began to wear a threatening aspect, and Carpenter took up his station at City Hall for the night.

This ended the heavy fighting of the day, though minor disturbances occurred at various points during the evening. Negroes had been hunted down all day, as though they were so many wild beasts, and one, after dark, was caught, and after being severely beaten and hanged to a tree, left suspended there till Acton sent a force to take the body down. Many had sought refuge in police-stations and elsewhere, and all were filled with terror.

The demonstrations in the lower part of the city excited the greatest anxiety about the Government buildings in that section—the Custom House and Sub–treasury were tempting prizes to the rioters. General Sandford, commanding the city military, had sent such force as he could collect early in the day to the arsenal, to defend it; for, should the mob once get possession of the arms and ammunition stored there, no one could tell what the end would be. United States troops also were placed in Government buildings to protect them. Almost the last act of the mob this evening was the burning of Postmaster Wakeman's house, in Eighty-sixth Street. Mrs. Wakeman was noted for her kindness to the poor and wretched, who now repaid her by sacking and burning her house. The precinct station near by was also destroyed.

In the meanwhile, an event happened which threatened to disarrange all the plans that had been laid. Military etiquette often overrides the public good, and here, at this critical moment, General Wool chose to consider that, as General Sandford was Major–general, though not in the United States service, he, therefore, ranked Brigadier–general Brown of the regular army, and required him to act under the other's orders. This, Brown promptly refused to do, and asked to be relieved, telling General Wool that such a proceeding was an unheard of thing. That he was right the order below will show* that his troops must be under his own command, as he was responsible for their action to the Government, and Sandford was not. Wool, however, continued obstinate, and a total disruption seemed inevitable. Mayor Opdyke, President Acton, Governor Seymour, with several prominent American citizens, were present, and witnessed this

---

*[General Order No. 36.]   War Department, *Adjutant–general's Office, Washington,* April 7th, 1863.

6. The military commander's duties in reference to all troops and enlisted men who happen to serve within the limits of his command will be *precisely those of a commanding officer of a military post.*

The duties of military commanders above defined, will devolve in the *City of New York, and the military posts in that vicinity,* on Brevet Brigadier-general H. Brown, Colonel Fifth U. S. Artillery.

By order of the Secretary of War,

(Signed)   L. Thomas, *Adjutant–general.*

disagreement with painful feelings. They knew that it would work mischief, if not paralyze the combined action they hoped to put forth in the morning. General Brown, finding Wool inflexible, turned away, determined to retire altogether. The Mayor and others followed him, and begged him not to abandon them in the desperate strait they were in—to think of nothing but saving the city. General Brown had been too hasty, sticking on a point of mere etiquette, with, perhaps, too much tenacity. True, an officer must insist on his rank as a rule, but there are emergencies when everything of a personal nature must be forgotten—crises where it may be an officer's duty to serve in any capacity, however subordinate, and trust to being righted afterwards. Luckily, General Brown, on a sober second thought, took the proper view, and returned to General Wool, and asked to be reinstated in his command, but giving him to understand that, though he would cooperate in every possible way with General Sandford, he still must retain distinct and separate command of his own troops. This was right, and whether General Wool perfectly understood the arrangement, or seeing how deeply the gentlemen present felt on the subject, chose not to press a mere point of etiquette, does not appear. We only know that if General Brown had given up the command of his troops, the results to the city would have been disastrous.

While these events were passing in the St. Nicholas Hotel, the streets were comparatively quiet. It had been a hard day for the rioters, as well as for the police, and they were glad of a little rest. Besides, they had become more or less scattered by a terrific thunderstorm that broke over the city, deluging the streets with water. In the midst of it, there came a telegraphic dispatch to the commissioners, calling for assistance. The tired police were stretched around on the floor on boxes, seeking a little rest, when they were aroused, and summoned to fall in; and the next moment they plunged into the darkness and rain. They were drenched to the skin before they had gone a block, but they did not heed it—and then, as to the end, and under all circumstances, answered promptly and nobly to every call.

Acton had now gathered a large force at head–quarters, and felt ready to strike at any moment.

While the men flung themselves on the hard floor, like soldiers on the field of battle, ready to start on duty at the first call, Acting Superintendent Acton and his assistants never closed their eyes, but spent the night in telegraphing, organizing, and preparing for the fiercer fights of next day. Much was to be done to cover and protect a district that reached from Brooklyn to Westchester, and it was an anxious night. They had one consolation, however: though taken unawares, they had at the close of the day come out victors, which gave them confidence in the future, especially as now Brown and his trained soldiers were with them.

Some fifteen or twenty policemen had been more or less severely injured, while the number of the killed and wounded of the mob was wholly unknown. Both the dead and maimed were left by the police where they fell, and were almost immediately hurried away by their friends.

The destruction of property on this first day consisted of four buildings on Third Avenue burned, also a block on Broadway between Twenty-eighth and Twenty-ninth Streets; two brownstone dwellings in Lexington Avenue; Allerton's Hotel near Bull's Head; a cottage, corner of Forty-fifth Street and Fifth Avenue; the Colored Orphan Asylum, and the armory corner of Twenty-first Street and Second Avenue.

· CHAPTER XV ·

TELEGRAPH BUREAU.—ITS WORK.—SKILL AND DARING
AND SUCCESS OF ITS FORCE.—INTERESTING INCIDENTS.—
HAIRBREADTH ESCAPES.—DETECTIVE FORCE.—ITS ARDU-
OUS LABORS.—ITS DISGUISES.—SHREWDNESS, TACT, AND
COURAGE.—NARROW ESCAPES.—HAWLEY, THE CHIEF
CLERK.—HIS EXHAUSTING LABORS.

ONE THING COMMISSIONERS Acton and Bergen in their consultation settled must be done at all hazards—telegraphic
communication must be kept open with the different precincts.
Otherwise it would be impossible to concentrate men at any given
point, quick enough to arrest the mob before they spread devastation and conflagration far and wide. Every hour gained by a mob
in accumulating or organizing its forces, increases the difficulty
of dispersing it. The rioters understood this partially, and had
acted accordingly; but the rich spoils they had come across during the day, had driven, for the time being, all other thoughts but
plunder out of their heads. Some communications had already
been destroyed, and the rioters would evidently by morning have
their eyes open to the importance of doing this everywhere, and
their efforts must be foiled, no matter what the risk or sacrifice
might be. They had already cut down over sixty poles, and rendered upwards of twelve miles of wire useless; and how much more
would share the same fate the next day, no one could tell.

The superintendent and deputy of the Telegraph Bureau, Messrs. Crowley and Polhamus, with the operators mentioned before, were, therefore, set at work this very evening in the storm to restore the broken lines.

This was a perilous undertaking, for if once discovered, their lives would be instantly sacrificed.

The details of their operations, their disguises, ingenious contrivances, deceptions, and boldness in carrying out their object, would make an attractive chapter in itself. Often compelled to mingle with the mob, always obliged to conceal what they were about, not daring to raise a polo or handle a wire unless cautiously or secretly, they yet restored the lines in the north section by morning, and those in the south by Wednesday evening. Sometimes they were compelled to carry a wire over the top of a house, sometimes round it, through a back–yard; in short, every device and expedient was resorted to by these daring, sharp–witted men. Once Polhamus had his boots burned off in tramping through the burning ruins of a building after the wires. Once he and Mr. Crowley came near being clubbed to death by the police, who mistook them for rioters, so ingeniously and like them were they at work among the ruins. Captain Brower rescued them, or their services might have ended on the spot.

This work was kept steadily up during the continuation of the riots. On one occasion, Mr. Crowley, hearing that the wires were down in the Ninth and Tenth Avenues, hastened thither alone, when he encountered a large mob. Fearing to pass through it he hesitated a moment, when he noticed a carriage driving in the direction he wished to go, in which was a Catholic priest, he immediately hailed it and was taken in. As the carriage entered the mob, the latter surrounded it, and supposing the inmates were reporters, began to yell "Down with the d— d reporters;" but the moment they recognised the priest, they allowed it to pass. Often the two would take a hack; and passing themselves off as drivers, go through infected districts, and search points to which they otherwise could not have gone. One time they were returning from an expedition through Third Avenue, and had reached Houston Street, when they were hailed by a gang of rioters, who demanded to be taken downtown. They had to comply, for the men were armed with pistols, and so took them in and kept along Houston Street, under the pretence of going down through Broadway, knowing that when they reached Mulberry Street they would be in hailing distance of the head–quarters of the police. It was just after daybreak, and Crowley and Polhamus urged on the horses, expecting in a few minutes to have their load safely locked up. The fellows evidently not liking the vicinity to which the drivers were taking them, ordered them to wheel about, which they were compelled to do, and drive under their direction to an old house in the Tenth Ward. There they got out, and offering the drivers a drink and fifty cents, let them go. On one occasion, Crowley, while examining the wires in Second Avenue, was suspected by the mob, who fell upon him, and it was only by the greatest coolness and adroitness he convinced them he was a rioter himself, and so escaped. At another time they were going along in a common wagon, when they were hemmed in by a crowd, and escaped by passing themselves off as farmers from Westchester. Had they been discovered, they would have been killed on the spot.

DETECTIVE FORCE.

THE DUTIES OF this force are well known, but during the riots they had something more important to do than to work up individual cases. The force, with John Young as chief, and M.B. Morse as clerk, consisted in all of seventeen persons. These men are selected for their superior intelligence, shrewdness, sagacity, and undoubted courage. Full of resources, they must also be cool, collected, and fearless. During the riots they were kept at work day and night, obtaining knowledge of facts that no others could get, and thus supplying the different precincts and head-quarters with invaluable information. Their duty was a most perilous one, for it called them to go into the very heart of the turbulent districts; nay, into the very midst of the mob, where detection would have been followed by death, and that of the most horrible kind. Chief Young, with his clerk, was engaged at head–quarters, so that fifteen men had to perform the required work for the whole city. Sometimes alone, sometimes two or three together, they seemed omnipresent. In all sorts of disguises, feigning all sorts of employments and characters, sometimes on horseback and again driving an old cart or a hack, they pressed with the most imperturbable effrontery into the very vortex of danger. Ever on the watch, and accustomed to notice every expression of the countenance, they would discover at a single glance when they were suspected, and remove the suspicion at once by some clever device. Sometimes one of them, seeing himself watched, would quietly ascend the stops of a residence, and ringing the bell, make some inquiry as though he were on business, and then deliberately walk off; or if he thought it would not do to have his face too closely scanned, he would step inside and wait till the crowd moved on. Sometimes, with a stone or club in their hands, they would shout with the loudest, and engaging in conversation with the ringleaders themselves, ascertain their next move; then quietly slip away to the nearest station, and telegraph to head-quarters the information. When the telegraph had been cut off, they had to take the place of the wires, and carry through the very heart of the crowd their news to the department.

On their ears again and again would ring the fearful cry, "There goes Kennedy's spies;" and it required the most consummate acting and self-possession to allay the suspicion. Often on a single word or act hinged their very lives. Some of these men were in the mob that made the first attack on Mayor Opdyke's house, and while apparently acting with it, learned of the intended movement down to police head-quarters, and at once telegraphed the fact, which enabled Carpenter to prepare for them, and give them the terrible beating we have described. At the burning and sacking of different buildings they were present, and often would follow unnoticed the ringleaders for hours, tracking them with the tireless tenacity of a sleuth hound, until they got them separate from the crowd, and then pounce suddenly upon them, and run them into the nearest station. The lawlessness that prevailed not only let loose all the thieves and burglars of the city, but attracted those from other places, who practiced their vocation with impunity. To lessen this evil, the detectives one night quietly made visits to some half a dozen "lushing cribs," as they are called, in Eighth and Fourteenth Streets, and seized about thirty noted thieves, burglars, and garroters, and locked them up for safe-keeping. They also warned the negroes of threatened danger, and directed them to places of safety; and in case of emergency acted as guides to the military in their operations. In short, they were ubiquitous, indefatigable, and of immense service. They played the part of unerring pointers to the commissioners, telling them when and where to strike; yet strange to say, such was their skill, their ingenuity, and exhaustless resources, that they all escaped being assaulted, save one named Slowly. He was passing through the very heart of the riotous district, in Second Avenue, when some one who had evidently been once in his clutches, recognized him, and pointing him out, shouted "Detective!" Instantly a rush was made for him, and he was knocked down, and kicked and stamped upon. Regaining, with a desperate effort, his feet, he sprang up the steps of a house, and fought his assailants fiercely, till the lady of the house, seeing his perilous situation, courageously opened the door and let him in, and then bolted and barred it in the face of the mob. Through some strange apprehension, the baffled wretches, though they howled, and swore, and threatened, did not force an entrance, and he escaped.

In this connection, while speaking of those whose duties were uniform and running through the whole period of the riots, might be mentioned Seth C. Hawley, the chief clerk. Like Acton, he has a nervous, wiry temperament. This often makes a man rash and headlong, and hence not reliable; but when combined, as in him, with perfect self–possession and self–control, imparts enormous power. It matters not how nervous and excitable a man is, if danger and responsibility instead of confusing and unsettling him, only winds him up to a higher tension, till he becomes like a tightly–drawn steel spring. Excitement then not only steadies him, but it quickens his perceptions, clears his judgment, gives rapidity to his decisions, and terrible force to his blow. Mr. Hawley's duties were of a various and exhausting kind, so that during all the riots, he allowed himself only one hours' rest out of every twenty-four. Besides his ordinary supervisory duties over the clerks, etc., he had to see to the execution of the almost incessant orders of the commissioners, provide and issue arms, see to the refugees and prisoners, and act as commissary to over four thousand men on duty in and around head–quarters. Two men more perfectly fitted to work together in such a crisis as this, than he and Acton, could not well be found.

CHAPTER XVI

Draft Riot—Second Day.

THE EARLY JULY morning broke tranquilly over the great city,
and the rattling of vehicles was heard in some of the streets,
where men were going to their places of business. In a large

portion of it everything wore its usual air of tranquillity, yet a close observer would notice an uneasiness resting on the countenances of men. Furtive glances were cast down side streets, and people seemed on the watch, as though in expectation of something to come, and the very atmosphere appeared laden with evil omens. Around police head–quarters, and inside the building, were large bodies of policemen and the U. S. troops under General Brown. But uptown, in the vicinity of Thirteenth Street and Second and Third Avenues, crowds of men begun early to assemble, though perfectly quiet in their demeanor, while smaller knots in the adjoining wards could be seen discussing the events of the day before. In the meantime, exciting reports came from Harlem and Yorkville—as early as five o'clock, the following telegram was sent to the Twentieth Precinct: "Notify General Sandford to go immediately to Eighty-sixth Street and Harlem—mob burning." Indeed the air was charged with electricity, but the commissioners now felt ready to meet the storm whenever and wherever it should burst. A large force of special policemen had been sworn in, while General Brown had over seven hundred troops, ready to co–operate with the police. The public buildings were all well guarded—Sandford had a strong force in the arsenal, and the military and civil authorities stood waiting the next movement of the mob. Telegrams arriving, showed that the northern part of the city was alive with gathering crowds, while from Sixth Avenue on the west nearly to Second Avenue in the east, and down almost to Broome Street, the streets were black with excited men. Stores were closed, factories emptied of their hands, who voluntarily joined the rioters, or were forced into their ranks, and there was evidently a gathering of the elements in those directions for a fearful storm. Soon immense crowds began to patrol the streets in different wards, showing that simultaneous action would be required at various points. The troops were called out and marshalled in Mulberry Street, and those companies selected for immediate action drawn up in line. Colonel Frothingham, after an earnest conversation with the officers, addressed the soldiers. He told them that the fate of the city was in their hands, and everything depended on their good conduct. Knowing the temptations to disorderly conduct in the midst of the great city, he

The Fight Between Rioters and Militia.

urged on them especially to obey implicitly their officers under all circumstances. His manner and words were earnest, and listened to with profound attention. Soon a company headed by Sergeant Carpenter, with a police force two hundred and fifty strong, started for Second and Third Avenues, where the greatest gatherings were reported to be.

At this time the rioters seemed hesitating about their course of action. There was apparently no recognized leader, no common understanding and purpose, though all were engaged in animated discussions of some topic. Dirty, ferocious–looking women were scattered through the crowd; some of the men were armed, while all looked defiant and determined.

There were doubtless many who had come from mere curiosity, and a few attempted to allay the excitement, among them a Catholic priest, who harangued them, urging them to maintain peace. His address seemed to have considerable influence on those immediately around him; but as soon as he left, his words were forgotten, and the mighty throng, estimated by some at ten thousand, began to be agitated by passion. What would have been the first act of violence, it is impossible to say, had they been left undisturbed. But at the cry of "the police and soldiers are coming," everything else was forgotten.

Inspector Carpenter, coming down Twenty-first Street, struck Second Avenue, and wheeling, moved in solid column through the crowd up to Thirty-second Street. The force was assailed with hoots and yells, and all kinds of opprobrious epithets, but no violence was shown, until it had crossed Thirty-second Street. The mob not only filled the street, but numbers, with piles of stones and brick–bats, had climbed to the roofs of the houses. These deeming themselves secure, suddenly, with one accord, rained their missiles on the rear of the column.

The men fell rapidly, and two were dangerously hurt. Carpenter immediately hailed his command, and ordered fifty men to enter the houses, and mounting to the roof, clear them of the assailants. Barricaded doors were at once broken in, and every one that opposed their progress clubbed without mercy, as they made their way to the upper floors. Captain Mount of the Eleventh Precinct, led this storming party. Officers Watson and

Cole distinguished themselves by being the first on the roof, fighting their way through a narrow scuttle. As the police, one by one, stepped on to the roof, they rushed on the desperadoes with their clubs, and felled them rapidly. Those who attempted to escape through the scuttles were met by the police in the rooms below; or if one chanced to reach the street, he was knocked down by those keeping guard there. Some dropped from second and third story windows, and met with a worse fate than those who stayed behind. One huge fellow received such a tremendous blow, that he was knocked off his feet and over the edge of the roof, and fell headlong down a height of four stories to the pavement beneath. Crushed to death by the force of the fall, he lay a mangled heap at the feet of his companions.

The fight was sharp and fierce, and kept up for nearly an hour, and bodies scattered around showed with what deadly force the club had been wielded. But with the clearing of the houses there came a lull in the conflict, and the immense crowd looked on in sullen silence as the police reformed in the street, and recommenced their march. The military force that had accompanied the police had formed on the avenue, about a block and a half above where the latter were stationed, while the detachment was clearing the houses. Two howitzers were placed in position commanding the avenue. Colonel O'Brien, of the Eleventh New York Volunteers, who was raising a regiment for the war, had gathered together, apparently on his own responsibility, about fifty men, and appearing on the field, from his superior rank, assumed command. For a short time the rioters remained quiet, but as the police marched away, they suddenly awoke out of their apparent indifference. Maddened at the sight of the mangled bodies of their friends stretched on the pavement, and enraged at their defeat by the police, they now turned on the soldiers, and began to pelt them with stones and brick–bats. O'Brien rode up and down the centre of the street a few times, evidently thinking his fearless bearing would awe the mob. But they only jeered him, and finding the attack growing hotter and more determined, he finally gave the order to fire. The howitzers belched forth on the crowd, the soldiers levelled their pieces, and the whistling of minic–balls was heard on every side. Men and women reeled and fell on the sidewalk and in the street. One woman, with her child in her arms, fell, pierced with a bullet. The utmost consternation followed. The crowd knew from sad experience that the police would use their clubs, but they seemed to think it hardly possible that the troops would fire point–blank into their midst. But the deadly effect of the fire convinced them of their error, and they began to jostle and crowd each other in the effort to get out of its range. In a few minutes the avenue was cleared of the living, when the wounded and dead were cared for by their friends. Order had been restored, and O'Brien, with some twenty or thirty men, marched down to police head–quarters, and offered his services to General Brown. Colonel Frothingham thanked him, but soon saw that the Colonel was not in a fit state to have command of troops, and so reported to General Brown. O'Brien appeared to comprehend the state of things, and asked to be excused on the plea of sickness. He was excused, and rode away. Whether he disbanded his handful of men, or they disbanded themselves, was not stated, but *he* was soon back again at the scene of the riot. His residence was close by, but had been deserted that morning by the family, which had fled in alarm to Brooklyn. Scowling visages lowered on the colonel, as he rode slowly back among the crowd, and low muttered threats were heard. Although an Irishman, and well–known in that neighborhood, his sympathy with the Government had awakened more or less hostile feeling against him, which his conduct to–day kindled into deadly hate. Apparently unconscious or reckless of this, he dismounted, and entered a neighboring drug–store or saloon. After remaining a few moments, he came out, and paused as he beheld the crowd that had assembled around the door. There was little said, but dark and angry countenances were bent on him from every side, and he saw that mischief was intended. Drawing his sword, and taking a revolver in the other hand, he deliberately walked out into the street. He had taken but a few steps, when a powerful blow on the back of his head made him stagger forward. In an instant a rush was made for him, and blows were rained so fast and fierce upon him, that he was unable to defend himself. Knocked down and terribly mangled, he was dragged with savage brutality over the rough pavement, and swung from side to side like a billet of wood, till the large, powerful body was a mass of gore, and the face beaten to a pumice. The helpless but still animate form would then be left awhile in the street, while the crowd, as it swayed to and fro, gazed on it with cool indifference or curses. At length a Catholic priest, who had either been sent for, or came along to offer his services wherever they might be needed, approached the dying man and read the service of the Catholic Church over him, the crowd in the meantime remaining silent. After he had finished, he told them to leave the poor man alone, as he was fast sinking. But as soon as he had disappeared, determined to make sure work with their victim, they again began to pound and trample on the body. In the intervals of the attack, the still living man would feebly lift his head, or roll it from side to side on the stones, or heave a faint groan.

The whole afternoon was spent in this fiendish work, and no attempt was made to rescue him. Towards sundown the body was dragged into his own back–yard, his regimentals all torn from him, except his pantaloons, leaving the naked body, from the waist up, a mass of mangled flesh clotted with blood.

But the dying man could not be left alone in his own yard. A crowd followed him thither, among which were women, who committed the most atrocious violence on the body, until at last, with one convulsive movement of the head, and a deep groan, the strong man yielded up his life.

While this tragedy was being enacted here, similar scenes were occurring all over the city. Mobs were everywhere, the spirit of pandemonium was abroad, and havoc and revenge let loose.

Lieutenant Wood, whom General Brown had sent off with a company of regulars, came in conflict with a mob, two thousand strong, in Pitt and Delancey Streets. Marching along Houston to the Bowery, he turned down the latter, and kept on to Grand. On reaching Pitt Street, he beheld the hooting, yelling crowd coming straight towards him. He immediately formed his little force of one hundred and fifty men in line across the street, and brought them to "shoulder arms." One of the ringleaders stepped forward to speak to him, when Lieutenant Wood waved him off. This was the signal for the attack, and immediately a shower of stones fell among the soldiers. The officer ordered the men to fire—it was said over the heads of the rioters—in order to disperse them. The result was scattering shots in return from the latter. Wood then ordered a point–blank volley, when men tumbled over right and left. The crowd did not wait for a second, but fled in every direction. Wood then marched back to headquarters, but on the way slipped and sprained his ankle, which caused a report that he had been wounded.

A bloody conflict also took place between the police and mob in the same avenue where Colonel O'Brien fell, below Thirtieth Street. There was a wire factory here, in which several thousand carbines were stored. Of this, some of the rioters were aware, and communicated the fact to others, and a plan was formed to capture them. Having discovered from the morning's experience that the military had been called in to aid the police, arms became imperatively necessary, if they hoped to make a successful resistance. All public depositories of arms they knew were guarded, but this factory was not, and hence they resolved to capture it without delay. Swarming around it, they forced the entrance, and began to throw out the carbines to their friends. The attack, however, had been telegraphed to head–quarters, and Inspector Dilks was despatched with two hundred men to save the building, and recover any arms that might be captured. He marched rapidly up to Twenty-first Street, and down it to the avenue. Here he came suddenly upon the mob, that blocked the entire street. As the head of the force appeared, the rioters, instead of being frightened, greeted it with jeers and curses. It was two hundred against a thousand; but the inspector did not hesitate a moment on account of the inequality of numbers, but instantly formed his men and ordered a charge. The mob, instead of recoiling, closed desperately on the police, and a fierce hand–to–hand encounter took place. The clubs, however, mowed a clean swath along the street, and the compact little force pushed like a wedge into the throng, and cleared a bloody space for itself. The orders were to recapture all the arms; for this was of more vital importance than the capture of men. Wherever, therefore, a musket was seen, a man would dash for it, and, seizing it, fight his way back into line. On the pavement, the sidewalk, and in the

gutters, men lay bleeding and dying, until at last, the more res-
olute having been knocked on the head, the vast crowd, like a
herd of buffalo, broke and tore madly down the street. One of
the leaders was a man of desperate courage, and led on the mob
with reckless fury, though bleeding freely from the terrible punishment he received. As his comrades turned to flee, leaving
him alone, a fearful blow sent him reeling and staggering towards
the sidewalk. As he reached it, he fell heavily over against the iron
railing, and his chin striking one of the iron pickets, the sharp
point entered it and penetrated through to the roof of his mouth.
No one noticed him, or if they did, paid no attention to him in
the headlong flight on the one hand, and swift pursuit on the
other. Thus horridly impaled, his body hanging down along the
sidewalk, the wretched man was left to die. At length Captain
Hedden noticed him, and lifting up the corpse, laid it down on
the sidewalk. It was found, to the surprise of all, to be that of a
young man of delicate features and white, fair skin. "Although
dressed as a laborer, in dirty overalls and filthy shirt, underneath
these were fine cassimere pants, handsome, rich vest, and fine
linen shirt."* He was evidently a man in position far above the
rough villains he led on, but had disguised himself so as not to
be known. He never was known. The corpse, during the fight that
followed, disappeared with the bodies of many others. The street
being cleared, Dilks turned his attention to the factory, which was
filled with armed rioters, who were determined to defend it to
the last. Detaching a portion of his force, he ordered it to take the
building by storm. Dashing over all obstacles, the men won the
stairway step by step, and entering the main room on the second
story, felled a man at almost every blow. Those who succeeded in
escaping down–stairs were knocked on the head by the force in
the street, and soon no rioters were left but the dead and dying.
How many fell in this fight it is impossible to tell; but one physician

---

*D. M. Barnes.
　　[Note: This refers to David M. Barnes, The Draft Riots in New York, July 1863,
based on his articles in the *New York Times* (New York: Baker and Godwin,
1863)—Editor.]

alone dressed the wounds of twenty-one desperately wounded men. Taking what guns they could find and had captured in the street, the force marched triumphantly back, cheered on their way by the spectators.

In the meantime, Mayor Opdyke's house in Fifth Avenue had again been attacked and partially sacked. Captain Maniere, one of the provost marshals, however, assembled a small force, and drove out the rioters, who were mostly young men and boys, before the work of destruction was complete. The news of this attack had been telegraphed to head–quarters of the police, and Captain Helme, of the Twenty seventh Precinct, dispatched to its defence. At his approach the rioters dispersed. Soon after, he was ordered with his command over to the Second Avenue, accompanied by a detachment of troops under Captain Franklin. This was in the afternoon—the mob had reassembled, and rein-forced by those who had been dispersed at Thirty-fourth Street, where Colonel O'Brien fell, had overcome the small body of police at the wire factory, and again taken possession of it. They had found some boxes of guns that had been overlooked by Dilks, and having armed themselves, determined to hold it. Even women joined in the defence. As the force approached, it was greeted with shouts of defiance and missiles of every kind. An immense crowd was gathered outside, while the windows of the five–story building were filled with angry, excited faces, and arms wildly gesticulating. Charging on this dense mass, and clubbing their way to the building, the police entered it, and streaming up the stairways, cleared it floor by floor, some being knocked sense-less, others leaping from windows, to be killed by the fall, and oth-ers escaping down–stairs, to be met by the force in the street. A thorough search was now made for arms, and the building emptied of them. Taking possession of these, the police and military took up their line of march for head–quarters. They had not pro-ceeded far, however, before the mob that had scattered in every direction began to pour back again into the avenue, and close on the military that were bringing up the rear. Following them with hoots and yells that were unheeded, they became embold-ened, and pressing nearer, began to hurl stones and bricks, and everything they could lay their hands on, against the soldiers. The latter bore it for awhile patiently; but this only made the wretches more fierce and daring. Seeing there was but one way to end this, Captain Franklin ordered his men to "About face;" and "ready, aim, fire," fell in quick succession. The yelling, shouting crowd were in point–blank range, and the volley told with deadly effect. The street was strewed with dead and dying, while the living fled down the avenue.

In the meantime, mobs had sprung up in every part of the city; some larger and some smaller; some after negroes, others tiring buildings or sacking them.

Some idea of the pressure on the Police Commissioners during this forenoon, and the condition the city was in, may be gathered from the following despatches, which are only a small portion of those received and answered in two hours:

10.20. From Thirteenth. Send military here immediately.

10.22. To Seventh. Find military and send them to Thirteenth Street forthwith.

10.45. From Sixteenth. A mob has just attacked Jones' soap factory; stores all closed.

10.50. To Twenty-sixth. Tell Inspector Leonard to send one hundred men here forthwith.

10.55. To Twentieth. From General Brown. Send to arsenal and say a heavy battle is going on. Captain Wilkins and company of regulars will report to me here at once.

11.18. From Sixteenth. Mob is coming down to Station-house; we have no men.

11.20. From Eighteenth. The mob is very wild, corner Twenty-second Street and Second Avenue. They have attacked the Union steam factory.

11.35. To Twenty-sixth. Send another one hundred men here forthwith.

11.35. From Twentieth. Send one hundred men to disperse mob assailing Mayor Opdyke's house.

11.38. To Twenty-first. Can you send a few men here?

11.40. From Twenty-second. The mob has gone to Mr. Higgins' factory, foot of Forty-third Street, to burn it.

11.45. From Eighteenth. What shall we do? The mob is about 4,500 strong.

Answer. Clear them down, if you can.

11.50. From Eighteenth. We must leave; the mob is here with guns.

11.50. From Twentieth. Mob tearing up track on Eleventh Avenue.

11.58. The mob have just sacked a large gun–store in Grand Street, and are armed, and are on the way to attack us.

12.10. To Fifteenth. Send your men here forthwith.

12.35. From Twentieth. Send two hundred men forthwith to Thirty-fifth Street arsenal.

12.36. From Twenty-first. The mob have just broken open a gun–store on Third Avenue, between Thirty-sixth and Thirty-seventh Streets, and are arming.

12.40. From Twenty-first. Send help—the crowd is desperate.

And so on.

Between these rapid telegrams asking for help, were others making and answering inquiries. And so it was kept up from daylight till midnight for three days in succession. These urgent calls for help coming from every quarter at the same time, would have thrown into inextricable confusion a less clear head than Acton's. It was a terrible strain on him, and had it continued a little longer, would have cost him his life. In the midst of it all he received anonymous letters, telling him he had but one more day to live.

But while the police head–quarters were thus crowded with business, and the commissioners were straining every nerve to meet the frightful state of things in the city, other means were being taken to add to their efficiency.

Governor Seymour had reached the city, and after being closeted with Mayor Opdyke, had issued a proclamation, calling on the rioters to disperse, and saying that they would be put down at all hazards.

At a meeting of the merchants and bankers in Wall Street, it was resolved to close up business, and form volunteer companies of a hundred men each, to serve under the military. General Wetmore was one of the first to offer his services. The high–spirited citizen, William E. Dodge, was among the most prominent advocates of the measure, and soon found himself a captain under orders. The steamboat of the harbor police was busy in bringing troops and cannon from Hiker's and Governor's Island, and rapidly steaming from point to point on the river, to prevent destruction around the docks. Around the arsenal cannon were placed. At the city armory, corner of White and Elm Streets, were a company of the Eighty-fourth New York Militia, and some of the Zouaves and other troops. The Sub–treasury and Custom House were defended by the Tenth National Zouaves and a hundred and fifty armed citizens. In front of the Government stores in Worth and White streets, the Invalid Corps and a company of marines patrolled, while howitzers loaded with grape and canister stood on the corner of the street. Nearly four hundred citizens had been sworn in at police head–quarters as special policemen, and had been furnished with clubs and badges. All this time the fight was going on in every direction, while the fire–bells continually ringing increased the terror that every hour became more widespread. Especially was this true of the negro population. From the outset, they had felt they were to be objects of vengeance, and all day Monday and today those who could leave, fled into the country. They crowded the ferryboats in every direction, fleeing for life. But old men and women, and poor families, were compelled to stay behind, and meet the fury of the mob, and today it became a regular hunt for them. A sight of one in the streets would call forth a halloo, as when a fox breaks cover, and away would dash a half a dozen men in pursuit. Sometimes a whole crowd streamed after with shouts and curses, that struck deadly terror to the heart of the fugitive. If overtaken, he was pounded to death at once; if he escaped into a negro house for safety, it was set on fire, and the inmates made to share a common fate. Deeds were done and sights witnessed that one would not have dreamed of, except among savage tribes.

At one time there lay at the corner of Twenty-seventh Street and Seventh Avenue the dead body of a negro, stripped nearly naked, and around it a collection of Irishmen, absolutely dancing or shouting like wild Indians. Sullivan and Roosevelt Streets are great negro quarters, and here a negro was afraid to be seen in the street. If in want of something from a grocery, he would carefully open the door, and look up and down to see if any one was watching, and then steal cautiously forth, and hurry home on his errand. Two boarding–houses here were surrounded by a mob, but the lodgers, seeing the coming storm, fled. The desperadoes, finding only the owner left behind, wreaked their vengeance on him, and after beating him unmercifully, broke up the furniture, and then fired the buildings. A German store near by, because it was patronized extensively by negroes, shared the same fate, after its contents had been distributed among themselves. A negro barber's shop was next attacked, and the torch applied to it. A negro lodging–house in the same street next received the visit of these furies, and was soon a mass of ruins. Old men, seventy years of age, and young children, too young to comprehend what it all meant, were cruelly beaten and killed. The spirit of hell seemed to have entered the hearts of these men, and helpless womanhood was no protection against their rage. Sometimes a stalwart negro would break away from his murderers, and run for his life. With no place of safety to which he could flee, he would be headed off in every direction, and forced towards the river. Driven at last to the end of a pier, he would leap off, preferring to take his chances in the water rather than among these bloody men. If bruised and beaten in his desperate struggle for life, he would soon sink exhausted with his efforts. Sometimes he would strike out for a ship, but more often dive under the piers, and hold on to a timber for safety, until his yelling pursuers had disappeared, when he would crawl stealthily out, and with terrified face peer in every direction to see if they had gone.

Hanging and Burning a Negro in Clarkson Street.

Two were thus run off together into the East River. It was a strange spectacle to see a hundred Irishmen pour along the streets after a poor negro. If he could reach a police station he felt safe; but, alas! if the force happened to be away on duty, he could not stay even there. Whenever the police could strike the track of the mad hunt, they stopped it summarily, and the pursuers became the pursued, and received the punishment they had designed for the negro. All this was in the nineteenth century, and in the metropolis of the freest and most enlightened nation on earth.

The hunt for these poor creatures became so fearful, and the utter impossibility to protect them in their scattered localities so apparent, that they were received into the police stations. But these soon proved inadequate, and they were taken to headquarters and the arsenal, where they could be protected against the mob. Here the poor creatures were gathered by hundreds, and slept on the floor, and were regularly fed by the authorities.

It is impossible to give a detailed account of what transpired in every part of the city. If there had been a single band of rioters, no matter how large, a force of military and police, properly armed, could have been concentrated to have dispersed it. But bodies of men, larger or smaller, bent on violence and devastation, were everywhere; even out at Harlem eight buildings were burned, and the lower end of Westchester was in a state of agitation and alarm. A mob of thousands would be scattered, only to come together at other points. A body of police and military plunging through the heaving multitude, acted often only as a stone flung into the water, making but a momentary vacuum. Or, if they did not come together again, they swung off only to fall in, and be absorbed by a crowd collected in another part of the city. The alarm of Monday had only been partial, but today it culminated. Families, husbands, and sons left their business, and with arms patrolled the streets. Stores were shut up, stages and cars stopped running, and all business was suspended.

The blood flowing through the thousand arteries of this great mart seemed suddenly frozen in its channels, and its mighty pulsations to stop at the mandate of lawless men. The city held its breath in dread, but there were firm hearts at police head-quarters.

Acton never flinched, and in General Brown he found a soldier that knew his duty, and would do it at all hazards. Still, the uprising kept swelling into vaster proportions, embracing a still larger territory.

Broadway was deserted. A few hacks could be seen, but with very different occupants than those which they ordinarily contained. The iron shatters were closed, on the Fifth Avenue Hotel, and a stack of arms stood in the hallway. Crowds of respectable citizens, not on duty, were making all haste toward railroad depots and steamboat landings. Every boat, as it swung from the dock, was loaded to its utmost capacity with people leaving a city that seemed doomed to destruction; going, many knew not where, only out of New York. Cars were packed, and long trains were made up to carry the crowds in haste to get away. But travel on the Hudson River Road was soon stopped by the mob, that tore up the track to prevent communication with other parts of the State, and the arrival of troops.

The Harlem and Third Avenue tracks were also torn up, as the rioters were determined to isolate the great city, which they had doomed to destruction. Passing from one object to another, now acting as if from plan, and now intent only on destruction and plunder, the crowd streamed from point to point with shouts and yells, that sent terror through the adjoining streets. Suddenly, some one remembered that they were in the vicinity of Colonel Nugent's house, in Yorkville, the assistant provost marshal general, and shouting out the news, a rush was made for it, and it was sacked from top to bottom.

As the police were gathered together either at the precinct stations or head–quarters, ordinary patrol duty was out of the question; hence, many isolated acts of violence could be committed with impunity. This freedom from close surveillance, coupled with the contagion of the lawless spirit which was abroad, made every section of the city where the lower classes lived more or less restless. It was impossible for the police to divide itself up so to furnish protection in individual cases, and yet be in sufficient force to cope with the mobs, that numbered by thousands. Although the whole city was heaving like a troubled sea, yet the main gathering this day had been in the upper part and on both sides of it. The terrific contests we described farther back were in the Second Avenue, on the east side, but, nearly opposite, in the Sixth Avenue, crowds had been gathering since early in the forenoon.

For a long time they swayed backward and forward, apparently without any definite purpose, and moved only by the spirit of disorder that had taken possession of the city. But about two o'clock, these various bodies began by mutual attraction to flow together, and soon became one immense mass, and impelled by some information or other, gathered threateningly around a large mansion on the corner of Forty-sixth Street and Fifth Avenue. They had supplied themselves with all sorts of weapons, revolvers, old muskets, stones, clubs, barrel–staves—in short, everything that could be found, that might be of service in a fight—and soon commenced plundering the residence. But their movements had been telegraphed to head–quarters, and Captain Walling, of the Twentieth Precinct, was dispatched thither, with a company of regulars under Captain Putnam, a descendant of "Old Put." The report soon spread through the crowd, that bayonets could be seen coming up the avenue. Marching up to Forty-sixth Street, the force turned into it, towards the Fifth Avenue, and breaking into the charge step, with the order "no prisoners" ringing in their ears, struck the mob almost in the centre, cutting it in two, like a mighty cleaver. There was no need of bayonets—the police, at the head of the military, went right through it, and scattered the men in every direction. The force then divided into squads, and each one taking a section of the mob, followed it upon a swift run, and smote them right and left for several blocks. The larger portion went down Sixth Avenue, and seeing only a portion of the police pursuing, turned and showed fight, when the leader received a bullet in the head and fell. Seeing their leader fall, the mob wheeled and took to their heels.

Captain Walling in one instance saw a crowd with fire–arms standing in an alley–way. Just then a fire–engine and company came down the street, and he with his small force got behind it, and kept concealed until opposite the unsuspecting crowd, when, with a shout, they dashed on it. A volley received them—with answering volley, the police charged into the narrow opening.

The rioters fled into a tenement–house, from which came yells and screams of terrified women and children. Walling had some sharpshooters with him, to pick off those beyond the reach of the clubs. One fellow, armed, was seen astraddle of the ridge pole of a house. The next moment a sharpshooter covered him, and he tumbled headlong to the ground. The same afternoon he saw some twenty or thirty men attempting to stave in a hardware store, evidently after pistols. Walling charged on them alone, and with one terrible blow, his club sent the leader to the pavement with his brains oozing out.

Although the draft was almost forgotten by the rioters, in the thirst for plunder and blood, still men in the streets and some of the papers talked of its being unconstitutional, and to be contested in the courts—others that it had been and would be suspended, as though any disposal of it now could affect the conduct of the rioters. Force was the only argument they would listen to. The riot had almost ceased to wear any political aspect since the attack on the *Tribune* office, the day before, had been defeated. An occasional shout or the sight of a negro might now and then remind one of its origin, but devastation and plunder were the great objects that urged on the excited masses. The sacking of Opdyke's house was done chiefly by a few youngsters, who were simply following the example set them the day before; while the burning of negro buildings, the chasing and killing of negroes, seemed to have only a remote connection with the draft, and was simply the indulgence of a hatred they were hitherto afraid to gratify. So the setting fire to the Weehawken ferry afterwards, could be made to grow out of politics only so far as a man who kept a liquor saloon there was a known Republican. This seemed a weak inducement to draw a crowd so far, when more distinguished victims were all around them. It is more probable that some personal enemy of parties in the vicinity, finding the mob ready to follow any cry, led them thither; for one man seemed to be the leader, who, mounted on a fine cavalry horse, and brandishing a sword, galloped backwards and forwards through the crowd, giving his orders like a field officer. Mobs springing up everywhere, and flowing together often apparently by accident, each pursuing a different object : one chasing negroes and firing their dwellings; others only sacking a house, and others still, wreaking their vengeance on sta-tion-houses, while scores, the moment they got loaded down with plunder, hastened away to conceal it—all showed that the origi-nal cause of the uprising had been forgotten. A strong uncertainty seemed at times to keep them swaying backwards and forwards, as though seeking a definite object, or waiting for an appointed signal to move, and then at some shout would rush for a build-ing, a negro, or station–house.

The mob was a huge monster—frightful both in proportions and appearance, yet not knowing where or how to use its strength. The attack on Mr. Gibbon's house at Twenty-ninth Street and Eighth Avenue, during this afternoon, was attributed to the fact that he was Mr. Greeley's cousin, and that the former sometimes slept there—rather a far–fetched inference, as though a mob would be aware of a fact that probably not a dozen imme-diate neighbors knew.

Some one person might have raised a cry of "Greeley's house," which would have been sufficient to insure its destruction. The police being notified of this attack, sent a squad of men with a military force to disperse the mob. Captain Ryer formed his troops in front of the house, and Sergeant Devoursney did the same with a part of his men, while the other portion was sent into the building, that was filled with men, women, and children, loading themselves down with the spoils. The appearance of the caps and clubs in the rooms created a consternation that would have been ludicrous, but for the serious work that followed. No defence was made, except by a few persons singly. One fellow advanced to the door with a pistol in his hand, and fired, send-ing a ball through Officer Hill's thigh. The next instant the lat-ter felled him to the floor with his club, and before he could even attempt to rise he was riddled with balls. Some of the women fell on their knees, and shrieked for mercy; while one strong Irish woman refused to yield her plunder, and fought like a tigress. She seized an officer by the throat, and trying to strangle and bite him, would not let go till a blow sobered her into submission.

Some were loaded with shawls and dresses, and one burly, ferocious–looking Irishman carried under his arm a huge bun-dle of select music. As the police chased the plunderers down–stairs, and out into the street, in some unaccountable way the troops got so confused that they fired a volley that swept the police as well as the rioters. Officer Dipple was so severely wounded that he died the following Sunday, while Officers Hodson and Robinson both received flesh wounds.

In the upper part of the city, few buildings, except those too near police and army head–quarters, or too well defended, offered much spoil except private houses, and these had been the chief objects of attack. But Brooks and Brothers' clothing store in Catharine Street, situated in a part of the city thickly populated with the very class mobs are made of, became toward evening an object of great attraction to groups of hard–looking men and women. As night settled down, the heavens being overcast, it became very dark; for in all the neighboring houses the lights were extinguished by the inmates, who were terribly alarmed at the rapidly increasing crowd in the street. To deepen and complete the gloom the rioters turned off the gas. Officer Bryan, of the Fourth Ward, telegraphed to head–quarters the threatening appearance of things, and a force of fifty or sixty men were at once despatched to the spot. In the mean time Sergeant Finney, with Platt and Kennedy, stood at the entrance to defend the building till the police could arrive.

For awhile the three determined police officers, standing silent in the darkness, overawed the leaders. But soon from the crowd arose shouts, amid which were heard the shrill voices of women, crying, "Break open the store." This was full of choice goods, and contained clothing enough to keep the mob supplied for years. As the shouts increased, those behind began to push forward those in front, till the vast multitude swung heavily towards the three police officers. Seeing this movement, the latter advanced with their clubs to keep them back. At this, the shouts and yells redoubled, and the crowd rushed forward, crushing down the officers by mere weight. They fought gallantly for a few minutes; but, overborne by numbers, they soon became nearly helpless, and were terribly beaten and wounded, and with the utmost exertions were barely able to escape, and make their way back to the station. The mob now had it all its own way, and rushing against the doors, burst bolts and bars asunder, and streamed in. But it was dark as midnight inside, and they could not distinguish one thing from another; not even the passageways to the upper rooms of the building, which was five stories high. They therefore lighted the gas, and broke out the windows. In a few minutes the vast edifice was a blaze of light, looking more brilliant from the midnight blackness that surrounded it. The upturned faces of the excited, squalid throng below presented a wild and savage spectacle in the flickering light. Men and women kept pouring in and out, the latter loaded with booty, making their way home into the adjacent streets, and the former rushing after their portion of the spoils. Coats and pantaloons, and clothing of every description, were rapidly borne away; and it was evident, give them time enough, the crowd would all disappear, and there would be scarcely enough left to finish the work of destruction. Thinking only of the rich prize they had gained, they seemed to forget that retribution was possible, when suddenly the cry of "Police! police!" sent a thrill of terror through them. Sergeant Delaney, at the head of his command, marched swiftly down the street, until close upon the mob, when the order, "Double-quick," was given, and they burst with a run upon them. For a moment, the solid mass, by mere weight, bore up against the shock; but the clubs soon made a lane through it broad as the street. Just then a pistol–shot rung from a house, almost over their heads. Many of the rioters were armed with muskets, and the comparatively small police force, seeing that firearms were to be used, now drew their revolvers, and poured a deadly volley right into their midst. Several fell at the first discharge; and immediately terror seized that portion of the multitude nearest the police, especially the women, and many fell on their knees, crying for mercy. Others forced their way recklessly over their companions, to get out of reach. As the police made their way to the front of the store, they formed line, while Sergeant Matthew, of the First Precinct, with his men, entered the building. The scene here became more frightful than the one without. The rioters on the first floor made but little resistance, and, thinking only of escape, leaped from the windows, and rushed out of doors like mad creatures. But as they attempted to flee, those without knocked them over with their clubs. Having cleared this story, the police mounted to the second, where the rioters, being more closely penned, showed fight. Pistol–shots rang out, and some of the police officers had narrow escapes. One powerful bully fought like a tiger, till two policemen fell upon him with their clubs, and soon left him stark and stiff. At last they drove the whole crowd into a rear building, and kept them there till they had time to secure them.

Just as the store was cleared, Sergeant Carpenter, who had been sent as a reinforcement in case of need, came up with a hundred and fifty men, and charging on the crowd, sent them flying down the narrow streets. After quiet had been restored, a military force arrived and took possession of the building.

Just previous to this, another attempt was made to burn the *Tribune* building, but was easily repelled. The *Times* office, nearby, warned by the fate of its neighbor the night before, had established a regular garrison inside, while it brilliantly illuminated the open space all around it, in the circle of which the rioters did not care to come.

The invaluable service of the telegraph was tested today, not merely in enabling General Brown and the commissioners to despatch men quickly to a threatened point, but to keep a force moving from one ward to another, as messages came in, announcing the incipient gathering in different districts. Word sent to the station in the neighborhood where they were acting, would instantly change their route; and knots of men, which if left alone would soon have swelled into formidable mobs, were broken up, for they found military and police force marching down on them before they could form a plan of action. Nor was this all. A force sent to a certain point, after dispersing the mob, would be directed to make a tour through the disaffected districts—all the time keeping up its communication with head–quarters, so that if any serious demonstration was made in that section of the city, it could be ordered there at once, thus saving half the time it would take to march from head–quarters. Thus, for instance, Captain Petty was ordered this morning to head–quarters from the City Hall, where he had passed the night, and directed to take two hundred men (including his own precinct force), and go to the protection of a soap factory in

Sixteenth Street, Eighth and Ninth Avenues. He moved off his command, marching rapidly up Broadway and down Sixteenth Street. The mob saw it coming two blocks off, and immediately scattered in every direction, which awakened the supreme contempt of the captain. He now marched backward and forward, and through the cross streets, up as far as Nineteenth Street, scattering every fragment of the mob that attempted to hold together, and finally returned to head–quarters. This was a long march, but the men had scarcely rested, when the captain was hurried off to aid in the protection at the wire factory in Second Avenue. In the fierce fight that, followed, he, with ten men at his back, charged up the broad stairway, lighting his way step by step to the fifth story. Caught up here at the top of the building, the rioters were clubbed without mercy. Some, to escape the ter rible punishment, plunged down the hatchway; others attempted to dash past the men, and escape down the stairs. At one time eight bodies lay in the doorway, blocking it up. He then marched back to head–quarters. He had been marching and fighting all day. Similar exhausting duties were performed by other commands, both police and military. Inspector Bilks, with his force gathered from various precincts, passed the entire day in marching and fighting. The men, weary and hungry, would reach head–quarters or certain points, hoping to get a little rest and refreshment, when the hurried order would come to repair to a point a mile off, where the mob was firing and sacking houses, and off they would start on the double–quick. Uncomplaining and fearless of danger, and never counting numbers, both police and soldiers were everywhere all this day, and proved themselves as reliable, gallant, and noble a set of men as ever formed or acted as the police force of any city in the world.

In the meantime, Governor Seymour and the Mayor of the city were not idle. The latter at the City Hall, fearing an attack, asked Acton for a guard of protection, and fifty men were sent him. Report of the mob assembled there reached Governor Seymour, at the St. Nicholas, and he immediately hastened thither, and addressed the crowd from the steps, which allayed excitement for the time. This speech was variously commented upon. Some of the criticisms were frivolous, and revealed the partisan, rather than the honest man. If the Governor had not previously issued a proclamation to the whole city, in which he declared without reservation that the mobs should be put down at all hazards — if this speech had been his only utterance, then the bitter denunciations against him would have been deserved. It would have been pusillanimous, cowardly, and unworthy the Governor of the State. But he spoke in his official capacity, not only firmly, emphatically, and in no ambiguous terms, but he had hurried up the military, and used every means in his power to accumulate and concentrate the forces under his control to put down the riot. No faint–heartedness or sentimental qualmishness marked any of his official acts. Prompt, energetic, and determined, he placed no conditions on his subordinates in the manner of putting down the mob, and restoring the supremacy of the law. But here in this address he was speaking to men who, as a body at least, had as yet committed no overt act; and many doubtless were assembled expecting some public declaration from the City Hall. He was not addressing the plunderers and rioters that were firing houses and killing negroes, but a mixed assembly, the excitement of which he thought best to allay, if possible. Some said he began his address with "My friends;" others, "Fellow-citizens." Whether he did one, or the other, or neither, is of no consequence and meant nothing. To have commenced, "Ye villains and cut-throats, disperse at once, or I'll mow you down with grape-shot!" might have sounded very brave, but if that was all he was going to say, he had better kept his room.

A *proclamation* like this address would have been infamous. Hero is where the mistake was made in the criticisms heaped upon it. His official acts were all such as became the Chief Magistrate of New York. The speech, therefore, must be judged rather by the rules of taste and propriety, than by those which apply to him officially. If a man's official acts are all right, it is unjust to let them go for nothing, and bring into prominence a short address made without premeditation in the front of an excited, promiscuous assembly, moved by different motives. That it was open to criticism in some respects, is true. It should have been imbued more with the spirit of determination to maintain order and suppress violence, and less been said of the measures that had or would be taken to test the constitutionality of the draft, and of his purpose, if it were decided in the courts to be wrong, to oppose it. Such talk had better be deferred till after order is restored. When men begin to burn and plunder dwellings, attack station–houses, hang negroes, and shoot down policemen, it is too late to attempt to restore peace by talking about the constitutionality of laws. The upholding of laws about the constitutionality of which there is no doubt, is the only thing deserving of consideration. The Common Council of the city exhibited in this respect a most pusillanimous spirit, by offering resolutions to have the constitutionality of the law tested, when the entire constitution and laws of the State were being subverted! Unquestionably, some charity should be extended to men who are pleading for those whose votes elevated them to office. Brutuses are rare nowadays; and politicians do not like to shoot down their own voters—they would much rather make more voters out of men no more fit to exercise the right of suffrage than horses and mules.

Governed by a similar spirit, Archbishop Hughes, although he had yielded to the pressure made on him and issued an address to the Irish, calling on them to abstain from violence, yet accompanied it with a letter to Horace Greeley, directly calculated to awaken or intensify, rather than allay their passions, he more than intimated that they had been abused and oppressed, and thought it high time the war was ended. The proclamation was short, but the letter was a long one, full of a vindictive spirit, and showing unmistakably with whom his sympathies were.

Towards evening a mob assembled over in Ninth Avenue, and went to work with some system and forethought. Instead of wandering round, firing and plundering as the whim seized them, they began to throw up barricades, behind which they could rally when the military and police came to attack them. Indeed, the same thing had been done on the east side of the city; while railroads had been torn up, and stages stopped, to keep them from carrying policemen rapidly from one quarter to another. During the day, Colonel Frothingham had stood in Third Avenue, and stopped and emptied every car as it approached, and filled it with soldiers, to be carried to the upper part of the city. Acton, too, had sent round to collect all the stages still running in Broadway and the Bowery, and in a short time they came rumbling into Mulberry Street, forming a long line in front of head–quarters. A telegram from Second Avenue demanded immediate help, and the police were bundled into them and hurried off. One driver refused to stir, saying, roughly, he was not hired to carry policemen. Acton had no time to argue the case, and quickly turning to a policeman, he said: "Put that man in cell Number 92." In a twinkling he was jerked from his seat and hurried away. Turning to another policeman, he said: "Mount that box and drive." The next moment the stage, with a long string of others, loaded inside and out with the blue-coats, was whirling through the streets. He had done the same with the Sixth Avenue care. The son–in–law of George Law remonstrated, saying that it would provoke the mob to tear down the railroad buildings. There was no time to stand on ceremony; the cars were seized, and the company, to save their property, paid a large sum to the ringleaders of the rioters. In fact, a great many factories and buildings were bought off in the same way; so that the leaders drove quite a thriving business.

But, as before remarked, the commencement of barricades to obstruct the movements of the police and military, after the Parisian fashion, was a serious thing, and must be nipped in the bud; and Captain Walling, of the Twentieth Precinct, who had been busy in this part of the city all the afternoon in dispersing the mob, sent to head–quarters for a military force to help remove them. He also sent to General Sandford, at the arsenal, for a company of soldiers, which was promised, but never sent. At six o'clock a force of regulars arrived from General Brown, and repaired to the Precinct station–house. Captain Slott, of the Twentieth Precinct, took command of the police force detailed to cooperate with the troops, but delayed action till the arrival of the company promised from the arsenal. Meanwhile, the rioters kept strengthening the barricades between Thirty-seventh and Forty-third Streets, in Eighth Avenue, by lashing carts, wagons, and telegraph poles together with wire stripped from the latter. The cross streets were also barricaded. Time passed on, and yet the bayonets of the expected reinforcement from the arsenal did not appear. The two commanding officers now began to grow anxious; it would not do to defer the attack till after dark, for such work as was before them required daylight. At length, as the sun stooped to the western horizon, it was resolved to wait no longer, and the order to move forward was given. As they approached the first barricade, by Thirty-seventh Street, a volley was poured into them from behind it, followed by stones and brick-bats.

The police now fell back to the left, and the regulars advancing, returned the fire. The rioters, however, stood their ground, and for a time nothing was heard but the rapid roll of musketry. But the steady, well–directed fire of the troops, at length began to tell on the mob, and they at last broke, and fled to the next barricade. The police then advanced, and tore down the barricade, when the whole force moved on to the next. Here the fight was renewed, but the close and rapid volley of the troops soon scattered the wretches, when this also was removed. They kept on in this way, till the last barricade was abandoned, when the uncovered crowd broke and fled in wild disorder. The soldiers pressed after, breaking up into squads, and chasing and firing into the disjointed fragments as they drifted down the various streets.

There was more or less disturbance in this section, however, till midnight. At nine o'clock, an attack was made on a gun and hardware store, in Thirty-seventh Street, between Eighth and Ninth Avenues, but Sergeant Petty was sent thither with a small force, and scattered them at the first charge. At midnight, an attempt was made to destroy the colored church in Thirtieth Street, between Seventh and Eighth Avenues; but before the rioters had accomplished their work, Captain Walling, with his entire force and the regulars, came up, and though met with a volley, fell on them in such a headlong charge, that they scattered down the street.

All this time the arsenal presented the appearance of a regular camp; videttes were kept out, sentries established, howitzers commanded the streets, and everything wore the look of a besieged fortress.

Sandford, whom Wool wished to take command of all the troops, evidently thought that he had as much as he could do to hold that building, without doing anything to quell the riot in the city.

One of the first companies that came up from the forts the day before, and hence belonged to General Brown's force, got, no one could hardly tell how, into the arsenal, and were there cooped up as useless as though in garrison—for if seven hundred men with cannon sweeping every approach could not hold it, seven thousand could not. General Brown and Acton needed this company badly, but how to get it was the question. Governor Seymour held no direct communication with the Police Commissioners; for they were not on friendly terms, as they were holding their places in defiance of him, he having removed them some time before. Mr. Hawley, the chief clerk, who knew the Governor personally, acted, therefore, as the channel of communication between them. He now went to him, and asked him how things were at the arsenal. He replied, he did not know—no report had been sent him. Hawley then asked him to send an officer and ascertain, and get back the company belonging to General Brown's command. He replied he had no one to send. Hawley then offered to go himself, if he would give an order to this company of United States troops to report at once to General Brown at police head–quarters. He did so, and Hawley, reaching the arsenal in safety, gave the order to the adjutant–general, before calling on Sandford, so as to be sure it was obeyed.

On the northern limits of the city, serious disturbances had occurred during the day, especially in Yorkville, to which Acton was compelled to send a strong force. The mob also attempted to burn Harlem bridge, but the heavy rain of the night before had made it so wet that it would not ignite. Down town, likewise, mobs had assembled before the Western Hotel and other places, but were dispersed before they had inflicted any damage. Almost the last act in the evening was an attack on the house of Mr. Sinclair, one of the owners of the *Tribune*.

But rioters must eat and sleep like other people, and though knots of them could be seen in various parts of the city, the main portion seemed to have retired soon after midnight.

In the police head–quarters, men were lying around on the floor in the warm July night, snatching, as best they could, a little repose. General Brown and staff, in their chairs or stretched on a settee, nodded in this lull of the storm, though ready at a moment's notice to do their duty. But there was no rest for Acton.

He had not closed his eyes for nearly forty hours, and he was not to close them for more than forty to come.

With his nerves strung to their utmost tension, and resolved to put down that mob though the streets ran blood, he gave his whole soul to the work before him. He infused his determined, fearless spirit into every one who approached him. Anonymous letters, telling him he had not another day to live, he flung aside with a scornful smile, to attend to the telegraph dispatches from the different precincts.

Troops and men were stationed at various points, and gunboats were patrolling the rivers, and he must be on the alert every moment. The fate of a great city lay on his heart, and he could not sleep.

The Dead Sergeant in 22d Street.

• CHAPTER XVII •

Draft Riot—Third Day

SCENES IN THE CITY AND AT HEAD-QUARTERS.—FIGHT IN
EIGHTH AVENUE.—CANNON SWEEP THE STREETS.—NAR-
ROW ESCAPE OF CAPTAIN HOWELL AND COLONEL MOTT.—
BATTLE FOR JACKSON'S FOUNDRY.—HOWITZERS CLEAR THE
STREET.—STATE OF THINGS SHOWN BY TELEGRAPH
DESPATCHES.—GENERAL SANDFORD SENDS OUT A FORCE
AGAINST A MOB, AT CORNER OF TWENTY-NINTH STREET AND
SEVENTH AVENUE.—COLONEL GARDIN'S FIGHT WITH THE
MOB.—IS WOUNDED.—MOB VICTORIOUS. DEAD AND
WOUNDED SOLDIERS LEFT IN THE STREET.—CAPTAIN PUT-
NAM SENT TO BRING THEM AWAY.—DISPERSES THE MOB.—
TERRIFIC NIGHT.

TUESDAY HAD BEEN a day of constant success to the police and
military, and many thought that the rioters were thoroughly
disheartened, and but little more hard fighting would be done.
There had been two days of exhausting work, and both parties
were well tired out. The commissioners, certainly, could not
stand this terrible strain much longer. Forty–eight hours without
sleep or rest, and all the time under the intensest mental strain,
was telling on even the wiry Acton, though he would confess to
no fatigue.

To one who could take in all that was passing in New York on
this morning, the city would have presented a strange appearance.

The magnitude and demonstrations of the mob had aroused great fear for the Navy Yard and the naval property of the Government, and the marine company that had been on duty with the police was recalled by Admiral Paulding for their protection; and this morning six war–vessels, carrying in all over ninety guns, shotted and trained, could be seen drawn up, so as to command every avenue to the yard, while the ironclad battery *Passaic* and a gun–boat lay off the Battery to protect Fort Columbus during the absence of its garrison. Marines armed to the teeth, and howitzers, guarded all the entrances to the Navy Yard. Broadway was almost deserted—no stages were running, street–cars had disappeared—only here and there shutters were taken down from the stores, and it looked like Sabbath day in the city. But at police headquarters all was activity. The African church nearly opposite was filled with soldiers stretched on the seats and floor of the building. Another house, a few doors from the police building, was also crowded with soldiers. The owner of this empty house, having sent a flat refusal to Acton's request for the use of it, the latter quietly told the policemen to stave in the door. It took but a few minutes to send it from its hinges; and now the troops were quartered in it also; for all those in the service of the United States, under General Brown, had their head–quarters here.

In the basement of the police building was the telegraph, with the wires running like nerves to every part of the city, over which inquiries and answers were continually passing. Rooms all around were filled with rations obtained from a neighboring grocery and meat–market, taken with or without leave. On the main floor, on one side, in their office sat the weary commissioners; on the other, were Inspectors Carpenter, Dilks, and Leonard, fit, each one to be a general, while scattered around were police captains, detectives, and patrolmen. On the second story were the clerks, copyists, etc.; while the top floor was crowded with colored refugees, who had fled thither for protection. Some were standing and conversing, others sitting in groups on boxes, or walking from room to room; many of these sad and serious, as they thought of missing relatives and friends, while the colored man placed over them, with his shirt sleeves rolled up, was, with his assistants, dealing out provisions.

But soon it was announced that a vast crowd, numbering some five thousand, was assembled near Eighth Avenue and Thirty-second Street, sacking houses and hanging negroes. General Dodge and Colonel Mott, with Captain Howell, commanding Eighth Regiment Artillery, were at once despatched thither. As they marched up the avenue, they saw three negroes hanging dead, while the crowd around filled the air with fiendish shouts. As the firm, compact head of the column moved forward, the mob fell back, but did not scatter. Colonel Mott dashed forward on horseback and cut down one of the negroes with his sword. This seemed to be the signal for the mob to commence the attack, and the next moment they rushed forward on the soldiers with stones, brick–bats, and slung–shots. Colonel Mott then told Captain Howell to bring two pieces into battery on the corner of Thirty-second Street and Seventh Avenue, so as to sweep the streets; but he could not get through the dense crowd to do so. The infantry and cavalry were then ordered up and told to clear the way. The former, with level bayonets, and the latter with drawn sabres, charged on the mass, which parted and fell back some distance, and then halted. Captain Howell then advanced alone, and ordered the rioters to disperse, or he should fire on them. To this they replied in sullen silence. The apparent unwillingness of the captain to fire emboldened them to believe that he would not fire at all. Although they refused to disperse, the officers, as long as they made no assault, declined to give the word to fire. This delay encouraged the rioters still more; and either believing the guns, whose muzzles pointed so threateningly on them, were loaded with blank cartridges, or grown desperate and reckless with rage, they suddenly, as though moved by a common impulse, rushed forward and rained stones and missiles of every kind on the soldiers. Seeing that their object was to seize the guns and turn them on the troops, the word to fire was given. The next moment a puff of smoke rolled out, followed with a report that shook the buildings. As the murderous shot tore through the crowded mass, they stopped, and swayed heavily back for a moment, when the pieces were quickly reloaded, and again sent their deadly contents into their midst, strewing the pavements with the dead and dying. Those, however, in the rear, being protected by the mass in front, refused to give way, and it was not till five or six rounds had been fired that they finally broke and fled down the side streets. The military then broke into columns and marched up and down the streets, scattering everything before them, and arresting many of the rioters.

Having finished their work, they returned to headquarters. As they left the district, the mob, or a portion of it, gathered together again, and strung up afresh the lifeless bodies of the negroes.

A few hours later, Captain Brower, with a police force, was sent thither, to take down and remove the bodies of any negroes that might be still hanging. He did so without molestation.

Captain Howell's murderous fire on the mob came very near causing his death two days after. Having the curiosity to witness the scene of his struggle with the mob, he took his carriage, and drove over to it. A gang of seven or eight ruffians, seeing his uniform, cried out," There's the man who fired on us here—let us hang him." Their shouts called others to the spot, and almost before the captain was aware of his danger, some fifty men were assembled, and at once made a dash at the driver, and ordered him to stop. Captain Howell, quickly drawing his revolver, pointed it at the driver, and ordered him to turn down Thirty-first Street, and give his horses the whip, or he would shoot him on the spot. The man obeying, lashed his horses into a run. At this moment the crowd was all around the carriage, and one man was climbing up behind, when he fell and was run over. A shower of stones and brick–bats followed, breaking in the panels of the carriage, and narrowly missing the captain's head.

One stone struck an old wound in his side, and for a moment paralyzed his arm. The crowd with yells and shouts followed after, when he turned and emptied his revolver at them through the back window, which brought them to a halt. Colonel Mott had a similar escape the day before. Passing down one of the avenues in a carriage, he was recognized by some of the rioters, who immediately assailed him with stones, and fired at him. One of the bullets passed through the cushion on which he was sitting.

Soon after this affair in Seventh Avenue, word was telegraphed that Jackson's foundry, corner of Twenty-eighth Street, First and Second Avenues, was threatened. A military force was dispatched forthwith to it, piloted by four policemen. At Twenty-first Street and First Avenue, they were fired on by the mob. The attack was continued through the street to Second Avenue, and up this to Twenty-fifth Street, without any notice being taken of it by the troops. Made reckless by this forbearance, the rioters began to close up in more dangerous proximity, when the howitzer was unlimbered and pointed down the avenue. The mob not liking the looks of this, scattered, when the column resumed its march. The mob then rallied, and followed after, with shouts and distant shots, till the foundry on Twenty-eighth Street was reached. Here another mob came up from First Avenue, and the two made a simultaneous attack. The command was then given to fire, and a volley was poured into the crowd. Rapidly loading and firing, the troops soon stretched so many on the pavement, that the rest broke and fled. The military then entered the building and held it. The mob gathered around it, threatening to storm it, but could not pluck up courage to make the attempt. They seemed especially exasperated against the policemen, and had the effrontery to send a committee to the officer in command, demanding their surrender. If their request was refused, they declared they would storm the building at all hazards; but if complied with, they would disperse. The committee had to shout out their demands from the street. In reply, the officer told them if they did not take themselves off instantly, he would fire upon them; upon which they incontinently took to their heels.

As the day wore on, things began to wear a still more threatening aspect. Despatches came in from every quarter, announcing the activity of the mob. To a question sent to the Thirteenth Precinct, a little past twelve, inquiring how things were going on in Grand Street, was returned the following reply: "Lively; storekeepers have fired into the mob; force there yet."

"12.20. From Twenty-first. Building corner Thirty-third Street, Second Avenue, is set on fire by the mob."

"12.50. From Fifteenth. Send assistance to Twenty-first Precinct; they are about attacking it."

"12.55. From Twenty-sixth. It is reported that Government stores in Greenwich, near Liberty, are on fire; fired by mob."

"1.10. From Twenty-seventh. Send more men here forthwith."

"1.25. From Fourth. Fire corner of Catharine Street and East Broadway."

"1.45. A man just in from Eleventh Precinct, reports a number of bands of robbers, numbering from fifty to one hundred each, breaking into stores in Houston, near Attorney Street."

"1.47 p.m. From Twenty-ninth. The mob have cleared Twenty-first Precinct station-house."

"2 p.m. From Twenty-ninth. A large mob surrounded Captain Green's house, Twenty-eighth Street, Third Avenue. He escaped out of the back window; they threatened to hang him."

"3.10 p.m. To Eleventh. Send to foot of Fourteenth Street, East River, and if military is there, send word here forthwith."

"3.15. From Twenty-fourth. Mob are firing the building on Second Avenue, near Twenty-eighth Street. Immediate assistance is required. Houses occupied by negroes, who are fleeing for their lives."

"3.25. From Twentieth. The mob are sacking houses at Twenty-seventh Street and Seventh Avenue. We have no force to send."

"3.30. From Twenty-first. There is an attack on the colored people in Second Avenue, between Twenty-eighth and Twenty-ninth Streets."

"3.40. From Eleventh. Send to 242 Stanton Street, and take possession of cavalry swords forthwith."

There were five thousand cavalry swords there, and the mob were assembling to capture them; and the telegram announcing the fact, and the one ordering a force to seize them, were received and answered the same minute.

"3.55. To Twenty-first. How do things look?"

Ans. Very bad; large crowd in Thirty-fifth Street, near Third Avenue, and no assistance from adjoining precinct.

"4 o'clock. To Twenty-first. What is going on?"

Ans. The mob have captured some five or six negroes, and are preparing to hang them; be quick with reinforcements.

"4.43. From Twentieth. News have just come in that the mob are about to attack the Twenty-second Precinct station–house."

"5.15. From Sixteenth. Send us one hundred special shields and clubs; the citizens are arming up well."

"5.15. From Twenty-ninth. Who feeds the special men?"

Ans. You must, far as able.

Reply. No money.

Ans. It makes no difference; they must be fed; we are responsible.

"5.20. From Twenty-ninth. The rioters are now on Seventh Avenue and Twenty-eighth Street. They have just killed a negro; say they are going to cut off the Croton; they have pickaxes and crowbars; and also say they will cut off the gas; so reported by one of our men, who has been in the crowd; they were about to fire corner of Twenty-eighth Street and Seventh Avenue, when he came away."

To have cut off the water and extinguished the gas, would have been master–strokes; but the military arrived in time to prevent it.

"5.25. From First. Riot at Pier 4, North River; they have killed negroes there."

Thus, at the same moment, from the two extreme ends of the city, came the news of riots and calls for help. From points five miles apart, the wires would bring simultaneously tidings that showed the mob omnipresent.

In the midst of all these incessant exhausting labors, the following telegram came from the Twentieth Precinct:

"General Sandford says he has so many negroes at the arsenal, that he must get rid of them."

Acton's answer was characteristic. He had no time for formalities or courteous exchange of views. In an instant there flashed back over the wires the curt reply:

"Tell General Sandford he must do the best he can with them there."

General Sandford had at this time about the same number of men under his command at the arsenal that General Brown had at police head–quarters; yet the former, up to this morning, had not sent out a single company to assist the police to arrest the devastations of the mob. He apparently did not know what was going on, had hardly kept up any communication with the Police Commissioners or Governor Seymour, but now begs the former to relieve him of some colored refugees, as if the overworked commissioners had not enough on their hands already. This request is especially noteworthy, when taken in connection with his after report, in which he slates that on this morning the riot was substantially over; so much so, at least, that the police could do all that was necessary without the aid of the military. It would seem that if he really thought that the rest of the work should be left to them, he might have sent off some of his troops, and made room for the negroes in the arsenal.

At about two o'clock in the afternoon word was received that a large number of muskets were secreted in a store on Broadway, near Thirty-third Street; and Colonel Meyer was ordered to proceed thither, with thirty-three soldiers belonging to Hawkins' Zouaves, and take possession of them. Reaching the place, lie found a large mob gathered, which was momentarily increasing. He, however, succeeded in entering the building, and brought out the arms. An Irishman happening to pass by in his cart, the colonel seized it, and pitching in the guns, closed around it, and moved off.

Citizens offering their services were coming in all day, and a company was formed and placed under the command of Charles A. Lamont, and did good service. Others also were enrolled and placed on duty.

Colonel Sherwood's battery of rifled cannon arrived in the afternoon, and was put in position in front of the arsenal, where the firing of pickets all day would indicate that an attack was momentarily expected. This did not look as if General Sandford thought the riot substantially over.

At about five o'clock, it was ordered by Sandford, with an infantry force of one hundred and fifty, to corner of Twenty-seventh Street and Seventh Avenue, to quell a mob assembled in large numbers at that point, and which were gutting, and plundering, and firing houses. As they approached, they saw flames bursting from windows, while, to complete the terror of the scene, the body of a negro hung suspended from a lamp-post, his last struggle just ended. At the same time that the military arrived, firemen, who had come to put out the fire, reached the spot in another direction. One portion of the mob immediately took shelter behind the latter, so that the troops dared not fire and clear the streets, while another ran up to the house-tops, armed with guns and pistols, for the purpose of firing into the ranks below. The colonel told his men to keep a sharp lookout, and at the first shot fire. Scores of guns were immediately pointed towards the roofs of the houses. In the meantime, from some cause not fully explained, the imposing force, after this demonstration, marched away, leaving the mob in full possession of the field. It had hardly reached the protection of the arsenal again, when the plundering and violence recommenced; and in a short time two more negroes were amusing the spectators with their death throes, as they hung by the neck from lamp-posts. This was the second expedition sent out by Sandford, the commander-in-chief of the military, during the riot.

Towards evening word was brought to the Seventh Regiment armory that the mob had gathered in great force in First Avenue, between Eighteenth and Nineteenth Streets.

Colonel Winston, in command, immediately ordered out a force, composed in part of the military, and in part of enrolled citizens, and with a battery of two howitzers, under command of Colonel Jardine, of Hawkins' Zouaves, marched rapidly to the scene of disturbance. Passing down Nineteenth Street to the avenue, it halted, and unlimbering the pieces, trained them so as to command the avenue, while the infantry formed in line to support them. As soon as the rioters saw the guns bearing on them, they dodged into basements, and mounted to the windows and roofs of the tenement buildings that abounded in that vicinity. A number of them armed with muskets and pistols, and the rest with stones and brick-bats, began a fierce and determined attack on the troops. The howitzers, loaded with grape and canister, at once swept the street. After the first discharge, but few ventured to show themselves in the avenue, until after they heard the report, when they would dodge from behind corners and fire back. But from the tops of the houses an incessant fusillade was kept up. The soldiers endeavored to pick them off, but the rioters presented a small mark compared to that which the troops, massed in the open streets, furnished; and it was soon apparent that the fight was unequal. If they had only had a police force to enter the buildings, and hunt the men from the roofs, the fight would soon have been over. But the commander, thinking he could not spare a sufficient number to do this work, or that the soldiers, cumbered with their muskets, which, after the first discharge, would have to be clubbed, could make no headway in such a hand-to-hand fight, made no effort to dislodge the wretches, who loaded and fired with the most imperturbable coolness. One man was seen to step round the corner, after the discharge of the battery, and resting his gun on the shoulder of a fellow-rioter, take as deliberate aim at Colonel Jardine as he would at a squirrel on the limb of a tree, and fire. The ball struck the colonel in the thigh, and brought him to the pavement. Other officers shared his fate, while at every discharge, men would drop in the ranks. The howitzers rattled their shot on the deserted pavements and walls of the houses, but did no damage to the only portion of the enemy they had to fear, while the fight between the infantry and the rioters was like that between soldiers in the open field and Indians in ambush. Colonel Winston soon saw that it was madness to keep his men there, to be picked off in detail, and ordered a retreat. At the first sign of a retrograde movement, a cry rang along the avenue; and from the side streets, and basements, and houses, the mob swarmed forth so furiously, that it assumed huge proportions at once, and chased the retiring soldiers with yells and taunts, and pressed them so hotly that they could not bring off all their killed and wounded. Among those left behind was Colonel Jardine. lie took refuge in a basement, where the mob found him, and would have killed him on the spot, had not one of them recognized him as an old acquaintance, and for some reason or other protected him from further violence; and he was eventually carried to the house of a surgeon near by.

The mob were left masters of the field, and soon began their depredations. The state of things was at length reported to police head-quarters, and General Brown sent off Captain Putman, with Captain Shelby and a hundred and fifty regulars and two field-pieces, to disperse the mob and bring away the dead and wounded of Winston's force that might remain. They reached the spot between ten and eleven o'clock at night. The dimly lighted streets were black with men, while many, apprised of the approach of the military, mounted again to the roofs as before. Putnam immediately charged on the crowd in the street, scattering them like a whirlwind. He then turned his guns on the buildings, and opened such a deadly fire on them that they were soon cleared. Having restored order, he halted his command, and remained on the ground till half-past twelve.

At the same time a mob was pulling down the negro houses in York Street, which they soon left a heap of ruins. Houses plundered or set on fire in various parts of the city, combined with the ringing of fire-bells, thunder of cannon, and marching of troops, made this night like its predecessor—one of horror.

There was also a disturbance in Brooklyn. Shaw's and Fancher's elevators, and Wheeler's store on the docks, were set on fire, and a force ordered to put them out.

The illumination of the windows from the *Times* building this evening shed a brilliant glow over Printing-house Square, and flooded the Park to the City Hall with light, while an armed force within was ready to fire on any mob that should dare expose itself in the circle of its influence.

At 12.15 the following telegram was sent:

"To all stations. How are things in your precinct?"

Answer. "*All quiet.*"

Thus the third night of this terrible riot passed away still unsubdued, and still Acton sat at his post, awake, while others slept, and kept feeling through the telegraph wires the pulse of the huge, fevered city. The regiments coming back from Pennsylvania might arrive at any time, and he was anxious to know the moment they reached the New York docks. The Seventh Regiment, especially, he knew was expected to reach the city that night by special train. Policemen were therefore kept on the watch; but the regiment did not arrive till after daylight. About half-past four in the morning, the steady ranks were seen marching along Canal Street towards Broadway, and soon drew up in front of St. Nicholas Hotel.

• CHAPTER XVIII •

Draft Riot—Fourth Day

◈

PROCLAMATIONS BY THE GOVERNOR AND MAYOR.—CITY DISTRICTED.—APPEARANCE OF THE EAST SIDE OF THE CITY.—A SMALL SQUAD OF SOLDIERS CHASED INTO A FOUNDRY BY THE MOB.—FIERCE FIGHT BETWEEN THE MOB AND MILITARY IN TWENTY-NINTH STREET.—SOLDIERS DRIVEN FROM THE GROUND, LEAVING A DEAD SERGEANT BEHIND.—CAPTAIN PUTNAM SENT TO BRING THE BODY AWAY.—MOWS DOWN THE RIOTERS WITH CANISTER.—STORMS THE HOUSES.—UTTER ROUT OF THE MOB.—COLORED ORPHANS AND NEGROES TAKEN BY POLICE TO BLACKWELL'S ISLAND.—TOUCHING SCENE.—COMING ON OF NIGHT AND A THUNDER-STORM.—RETURNING REGIMENTS.—INCREASED FORCE IN THE CITY TO PUT DOWN VIOLENCE.—ARCHBISHOP HUGHES OFFERS TO ADDRESS THE IRISH.—CURIOUS ACCOUNT OF AN INTERVIEW OF A LADY WITH HIM AND GOVERNOR SEYMOUR.—STRANGE CONDUCT OF THE PRELATE.

ONLY THE PRINCIPAL disturbances of the third day were given, and of these the accounts were very succinct. The movements of the mobs and the conflicts with them were so similar in character, that a detailed description of them would be a mere repetition of what had gone before. After the police force, and the troops under General Brown had become organized so as to move and act together, each fight with the rioters was almost a repetition of its predecessor. Having adopted a plan of procedure, they seldom deviated from it, and the story of one fight became the story of all—a short struggle and a quick victory.

It was hoped this morning that the rioters would conclude that they could not carry out their mad designs; for the enrolment of large bodies of citizens, and the announcement of the speedy return of several regiments, showed that all the force necessary to subdue them was, or soon would be, on hand. The day before, the Governor had issued a proclamation, declaring the city to be in a state of insurrection; but this morning appeared a proclamation from Mayor Opdyke, announcing that the insurrection was practically ended. It is true he called on the citizens to form voluntary associations, with competent leaders, to patrol their separate districts, to protect themselves from roaming gangs of plunderers, and so spare the exhausted police and military. Yet he called on the citizens to resume their usual avocations, and directed the railroad and stage lines to resume their routes. This opinion of the Mayor was strengthened by the positive announcement that the draft had been suspended, and the passage of an ordinance by the City Council, appropriating $2,500,000 towards paying $300 exemption money to the poor who might be drafted. It was plain, if the draft was the cause of the continued riot, it would now cease. But in spite of all this, bad news came from Harlem, and Yorkville, and other sections. In fact, it was evident that the Police Commissioners did not share fully in the pleasant anticipations of the Mayor. Having ascertained that the leaders of the mob, learning from experience, had organized more intelligently, and designed to act in several distinct and separate bodies in different sections, they, with General Brown, divided the city into four districts, in each one of which were to be stationed strong bodies of the police and military, so that they could act with more expedition and efficiency than if they were sent out from the common head-quarters in Mulberry Street. It would, beside, save the fatigue of long marches. Those separate stations were in Harlem, Eighteenth, Twenty-ninth, and Twenty-sixth Precincts. A good deal was also expected by an invitation given by Archbishop Hughes, that appeared in the morning papers, to the Irish to meet him next day in front of his house, where, though crippled from rheumatism, he would address them from the balcony. The Eighth Avenue cars had been started, as well as those of the Third; and many stores were opened. Still, on the east side of the city, in the neighborhood of First Avenue, most of the shops were closed.

It should be here remarked to the credit of the German population, which were very numerous in certain localities on this side of the city, that they had no sympathy with the rioters; on the contrary, sent word to the Police Commissioners not to be concerned about their locality; they had organized, and would see that order was maintained there. No better title to American citizenship than this could be shown.

Though early in the morning, it was comparatively quiet on the east side of the city; yet near First Avenue knots of men could be seen here and there, engaged in loud and angry conversation. They looked exhausted and haggard, but talked defiant as ever, swearing terrible vengeance against the military; for, though hidden from sight, in the miserable tenement-houses near by, lay their dead, dying, and wounded friends by scores. Near Nineteenth Street, the scene of the conflict the evening previous, there were stones, brick-bats, shivered awning-posts, and other wrecks of the fight. The grog-shops were open, in which men with bloody noses, and bruised and battered faces, obtained the necessary stimulus to continue the desperate struggle. Dirty, slovenly-dressed women stood in the door-ways or on the steps, swearing and denouncing both police and military in the coarsest language. Though the immense gatherings of the preceding days were not witnessed, yet there was a ground-swell of passion that showed the lawless spirit was not subdued, though overawed. But the Police Commissioners were now prepared for whatever might occur. The Seventh Regiment had been stationed on the west side of the city, with a wide district to keep order, thus enabling them to concentrate larger forces in other directions. But, although everything wore this favorable aspect to the authorities, it was evident towards noon, from the steadily increasing size of the groups observed in the morning, that they had resolved to try again their strength with the military. The state of things was telegraphed to policy head-quarters, but the report making

The Rioters Dragging Col. O'Brien's Body Through The Street.

the mob not formidable, only a company of about twenty-five men were sent out. Finding the rioters numbered about two hundred or more, and not daring to fire their howitzer, lest, before it could be reloaded, the former would rush forward and seize it, they concluded to retire. The mob at once set furiously on them, and forced them to take refuge in Jackson's foundry. The following telegram to head-quarters announced the fact:

"1.25. From Twenty-first. The mob has charged our military, about twenty-five in number, and driven them into Jackson's foundry, First Avenue and Twenty-eighth Street. The mob are armed, and every time a regular shows himself they fire. A few good skirmishers would pick oil these riflemen and relieve the military."

This was soon succeeded by the following:

"1.54. From Twenty-first. Send military assistance immediately to First Avenue and Twenty-eighth Street. The mob increases, and will murder the military force."

Ans. "They are on their way up."

They soon arrived, and were at once furiously attacked by the mob. The soldiers fired into them, but they boldly held their ground, and were evidently bent on a desperate fight.

The former now took up their stations at the junction of the streets, and were about to sweep them with canister, when from some cause a delay was ordered. This increased the boldness of the mob, and they taunted and derided the soldiers. But in a few minutes a reinforcement of regulars arrived on the ground and charged bayonets. The rioters fell back, but rallying, forced the soldiers to retire in turn. The latter, however, returned to the charge, when the mob again gave way, but still stubbornly refused to disperse.

News of the magnitude of the struggle reached the Seventh .Regiment, and they rapidly marched to the spot. Their steady tramp along the pavement, and well-set ranks, discouraged the crowd, and they marched and counter-marched through the streets without molestation.

The mob, however, dispersed only to reassemble again in Twenty-ninth Street, and began to plunder the stores in the vicinity, and spread devastation on every side.

This being reported to head-quarters, a military force was despatched to disperse them. The rioters, however, instead of retreating, attacked them with the greatest fury. Almost every house was filled with them, and they lined the roofs with muskets and pistols, from which they poured down a deadly fire. For nearly a half an hour the fire was kept up without cessation, and many were killed. A sergeant was knocked down by a brick-bat, and then seized and beaten to death. The troops finding themselves unable to dislodge the assailants, retreated, leaving the body of the sergeant in the street, where it lay for three hours. General Brown not having a sufficient number of troops on hand, the mob all this time had it their own way. It was nine o'clock before he could despatch Captain Putnam with a strong force to put an end to the disgraceful scene. Arriving on the spot, the latter addressed the crowd, saying that he had come to carry away the dead body of the sergeant, and should do it at all hazards. But he had hardly placed it in a wagon, when the crowd began to assail his troops. He immediately unlimbered his pieces, when it scattered in every direction. But the rioters came together again at the corner of Thirty-first Street and Second Avenue, where they were met by reinforcements, and made a stand. They filled the houses, and mounted to the roofs, armed with muskets and revolvers, and as Putnam appeared, commenced a rapid fire. Placing his pieces in position, this gallant officer swept the street with canister, which soon cleared it. Eleven of the ring-leaders were shot down, and bodies lay thick on the pavement. But this did not intimidate those in the windows, or on the roofs, and they kept up a steady fire. Putnam, who showed by his cool courage that the fighting stock from which he came had not degenerated, now ordered his men to turn their fire on the buildings. At each discharge, the heavy volleys brought down many of the wretches, some pitching headlong from the roof, and dashing out their brains on the pavement and flagging below. But the fight was very unequal, for the assailants would expose their bodies as little as possible; Putnam saw that the houses must be stormed, and gave the order to do it. The fight was now transferred to the inside, and became close and murderous. In the narrow halls and on the stairways, numbers were of no avail, and the rioters fought with a desperation they had not before exhibited. There was no way of escape, and they seemed to prefer death to being taken prisoners, and for a half an hour maintained the conflict in the darkened rooms and passages with a ferocity that was appalling. At last, however, with their numbers sadly thinned, they were forced to yield, and took refuge in flight. Many, unable to got away, hid under beds and in closets, but the soldiers ferreted them out, and carried them to police head-quarters.

The arsenal had not been attacked, as Sandford seemed every day to think it would be. Many colored people, as before stated, took refuge in it; and about noon on this day, a body of police arrived before it, with the children of the Colored Orphan Asylum that had been burned on Monday, in charge. They had since that time been scattered round in station-houses, but were now to be escorted to Blackwell's Island, for better security. It was an impressive spectacle this army of children presented, as they drew up in line in front of the arsenal to wait for those within to join them. The block was filled with them. The frightened little fugitives, fleeing from they scarce knew what, looked bewildered at their novel position. It seemed impossible that they ever could have been the objects of any one's vengeance. With a strong body of police in front and rear, and a detachment of soldiers on either side, they toddled slowly down to the foot of Thirty-fifth Street, from whence they were taken by boats to the Island.

The Sixty-fifth New York Regiment arrived from Harrisburg in the afternoon, and just before midnight the One Hundred and Fifty-second also reached the city, and marched up Broadway to police headquarters, where they were stowed away to get some rest.

A heavy storm that set in during the evening, helped to scatter the crowd that would otherwise have gathered on this warm July night, but it at the same time gave a sombre aspect to the city. The crescent moon was veiled in black, and thunderous clouds that swept heavily over the city, deepened the gloom, and seemed portentous of greater evil. The closing of all the stores and shop-windows at nightfall, through fear, left the streets lighted only by the scattering lamps. This unusual stretch of blank dead walls, emitting no ray of light, rendered the darkness made by the overhanging storm still more impenetrable. Flashes of lightning would reveal small groups of men bent on plunder, in sections where the military and police were not stationed, but no open violence was attempted. In other directions, the bayonets of the soldiers would gleam out of the dense shadows, as they silently held the posts assigned them, ready to march at a moment's notice. This was the fourth night, and the cannon planted in the streets, and the increased military force, showed that peace was not yet fully restored. The Seventh Regiment was quartered in Thirty-fourth Street, part of the soldiers within a building, and crowding every window to catch the first sign of disturbance, and part stationed below, or marching back and forth in the street. Other troops and policemen were massed at head-quarters, ready to move, at the word of command, to any point threatened by the mob.

The fourth night was passing away, and still Acton clung to his post, and refused to take even a moment's rest. His whole nature had been keyed up to meet the grave responsibilities that lay upon him, and through the wires he still watched every threatened point in the city, with sleepless vigilance. In the meantime, over a thousand special policemen had been sworn in, and five hundred or more citizens had volunteered their services, while the steady arrival of returning regiments swelled the military force into formidable proportions.

During the day, Senators Connolly and O'Brien had waited on General Brown, and asked him to remove the military from their ward, as their presence excited the people. The General very bluntly refused, saying he should not permit his troops to retire from before an armed mob. He was asked also to order the troops to leave Jackson's foundry for the same reason, and gave an equally emphatic refusal. There was now to be no compromise with the rioters, no agreement entered into. They had got beyond the character of citizens with rights to be respected—they were assassins and murderers, to whom was submitted the simple question of subjection to law and authority, or death.

The fighting through the day had been severe, but the disturbance had not been so wide-spread and general. Outside of the city, there had been threatening rumors. It was reported that there was danger of an uprising in Westchester, where some leading Democrats had taken open opposition to the draft, and a gun-boat had gone up as far as Tarrytown; but nothing serious occurred.

The rioters being almost exclusively Irish, it was thought that an address from Archbishop Hughes would go far to quiet the ringleaders, and he had therefore issued the following call, already referred to:

To the men of New York, who are now called in many of the papers rioters.

MEN!

I am not able, owing to rheumatism in my limbs, to visit you, but that is not a reason why you should not pay me a visit in your whole strength. Come, then, tomorrow (Friday) at two o'clock, to my residence, northwest corner of Madison Avenue and Thirty-sixth street. There is abundant space for the meeting, around my house. I can address yon from the corner of the balcony. If I should not be able to stand during its delivery, you will permit me to address you sitting; my voice is much stronger than my limbs. I take upon myself the responsibility of assuring you, that in paying me this visit or in retiring from it, you shall not be disturbed by any exhibition of municipal or military presence. You who are Catholics, or as many of you as are, have a right to visit your bishop without molestation.

†John Hughes,

Archbishop of New York.

NEW YORK, *July* 16,1863.

A curious incident was related subsequently in one of the New York papers, respecting the manner in which an interview was brought about between him and Governor Seymour, and which resulted in the resolution of the Archbishop to address the rioters. The substance of the account was, that a young widow of high culture, formerly the wife of a well-known lawyer of this city—a woman living in an atmosphere of art, and refinement, and spending her time in study, became so excited over the violence and bloodshed that the authorities seemed unable to suppress, and finding that the Irish were at the bottom of the trouble, determined to appeal to Archbishop Hughes personally, to use his high authority and influence to bring these terrible scenes to a close.

Acting on this determination, she set out this morning for the Archbishop's residence, but on arriving was told that he was at the residence of Vicar-general Starrs, in Mulberry Street. Hastening thither, she asked for an interview. Her request was denied, when she repeated it; and though again refused, would not be repelled, and sent word that her business was urgent, and that she would not detain him ten minutes. The Archbishop finally consented to see her. As she entered the library, her manner and bearing—both said to be remarkably impressive—arrested the attention of the prelate. Without any explanation or apology, she told him at once her errand—that it was one of mercy and charity. She had been educated in a Roman Catholic convent herself, in which her father was a professor, and she urged him, in the name of God, to get on horseback, and go forth into the streets and quell the excitement of his flock. She told him he must, like Mark Antony, address the people; and in rescuing this great metropolis from vandalism, would become a second Constantine, an immortal hero. It was his duty, she boldly declared; and though she did not profess to be a Jeanne d'Arc or Madame Roland, but a plain woman of the present day, she would ride fearlessly by his side, and if he were threatened, would place her body between him and danger, and take the blow aimed at him. The cautious and crafty prelate was almost carried away by the impassioned and dramatic force of this woman, but he told her it would be presumption in him to do so; in fact, impossible, as he was so crippled with rheumatism and gout, that he could not walk. She then asked him to call the crowd, and address them from the balcony of his house. He replied that he was just then busy in writing an answer to an attack on him in the *Tribune*. She assured him that such a controversy was worse than useless—that another and higher duty rested on him. She pressed him with such importunity and enthusiasm, that he finally consented; but as a last effort to get rid of her, said he feared the military would interfere and attack the mob. She assured him they would not, and hurried off to the St. Nicholas to see Governor Seymour about it. She found the ante-room filled with officials and other personages on important business, waiting their turn to be admitted. But her determined, earnest manner so impressed every one with the importance of her mission, that precedence was granted her, and she found herself at once beside the astonished Governor. Without any preliminaries, she told him she had just come from the head of the church, and wanted his excellency to visit him immediately. No business was of such vital importance as this. The self-possessed Governor coolly replied that he should be glad to see the Archbishop, but business was too pressing to allow him to be absent even a half an hour from his duties. She hastened back to Archbishop Hughes, and prevailed on him to write a note to Governor Seymour, asking him to call and see him, as he was unable to get out. Fortified with this, she now took a priest with her, and providing herself with a carriage, returned to headquarters, and absolutely forced, by her energy and determination and persuasive manner, the Governor to leave his business, and go to the Archbishop's. The invitation to the Irish to meet him was the result of this interview.

Why Archbishop Hughes took no more active part than he did in quelling this insurrection, when there was scarcely a man in it except members of his own flock, seems strange. It is true he had published an address to them, urging them to keep the peace; but it was prefaced by a long, undignified, and angry attack on Mr. Greeley, of the *Tribune,* and showed that he was in sympathy with the rioters, at least in their condemnation of the draft. The pretence that it would be unsafe for him to pass through the streets, is absurd; for on three different occasions common priests had mingled with the mob, not only with impunity, but with good effect. He could not, therefore, have thought himself to be in any great danger. One thing, at any rate, is evident: had an Irish mob threatened to burn down a Roman Catholic church, or a Roman Catholic orphan asylum, or threatened any of the institutions or property of the Roman Church, he would have shown no such backwardness or fear. The mob would have been confronted with the most terrible anathemas

of the church, and those lawless bands quailed before the male-
dictions of the representative of "God's vicegerent on earth." It
is unjust to suppose that he wished this plunder and robbery to
continue, or desired to see Irishmen shot down in the streets; it
must, therefore, be left to conjecture, why he could not be moved
to any interference except by outside pressure, and then show so
much lukewarmness in his manner—in fact, condemning their
opponents almost as much as themselves.

The excitement consequent on the draft, exhibited in outbreaks in various parts of the country, and in the vicinity of New
York, was increased by the reports of violence and fighting in the
latter city. In Troy there was a riot, and the mob, imitating the
insane conduct of the rioters in New York, proceeded to attack
an African church. But a priest, more bold or more patriotic than
Archbishop Hughes, interfered and saved it. That the latter,
armed with nothing but the crucifix, could have effected as much
as the police and military together, there can be but little doubt.
This open and decided sympathy with law and order, and bitter
anathemas against the vandals who sought the destruction of the
city, were the more demanded, as such a large proportion of the
police force were Roman Catholics, and in their noble devotion
to duty, even to shooting down their own countrymen and men
of a similar faith, deserved this encouragement from the head of
the church.

Burning of the Second Avenue Armory.

· CHAPTER XIX ·

Closing Scenes.

TRANQUIL HOMING.—PROCLAMATION OF THE MAYOR.—
MOB COWED.—PLUNDERERS AFRAID OF DETECTION.—
DIRTY CELLARS CROWDED WITH RICH APPAREL, FURNITURE,
AND WORKS OF ART.—ARCHBISHOP HUGHES' ADDRESS.—
USELESS EFFORTS.—ACTON'S FORTY-EIGHT HOURS WITH-
OUT SLEEP OVER.—CHANGE IN MILITARY COMMANDERS IN
THE CITY.—GENERAL BROWN RELINQUISHES HIS COM-
MAND.—TRUE WORDS.—NOBLE CHARACTER AND BEHAV-
IOR OF THE TROOPS AND POLICE.—GENERAL BROWN'S
INVALUABLE SERVICES.

THIS WEEK OF horrors—a week unparalleled in the history of
New York—was drawing to a close. It had been one of terror
and dismay to the inhabitants, who thought only of the immediate effects on themselves of the triumph of the mob. A great
city laid in ashes, given up to robbers and cut-throats, is at any
time a terrible spectacle; but New York in ruins at this time was
a republic gone—a nation uncrowned and left desolate; but the
battle, both for the nation and city, had been nobly fought and won;
and Friday, the fifth day of this protracted struggle, dawned
bright and tranquil. The storm of the night before had passed
away, and the streets, thoroughly washed by the drenching rain,
stretched clean and quiet between the long rows of buildings,
emblematic of the tranquillity that had returned to the city.

The cars were seen once more speeding down to the business centres, loaded with passengers. Broadway shook to the rumbling of the heavy omnibuses; shutters were taken down, and the windows again shone with their rich adornments. The anxious look had departed from the pedestrians, for the heavy cloud, so full of present woe and future forebodings, had lifted and passed away.

The following proclamation of Mayor Opdyke will show the true state of things on this morning, and what the people had most to fear:

"The riotous assemblages have been dispersed. Business is running in its usual channels. The various lines of omnibuses, railway, and telegraph have resumed their ordinary operations. Few symptoms of disorder remain, except in a small district in the eastern part of the city, comprising a part of the Eighteenth and Twenty-first Wards. The police is everywhere alert. A sufficient military force is now here to suppress any illegal movement, however formidable.

"Let me exhort you, therefore, to pursue your ordinary business. Avoid especially all crowds. Remain quietly at your homes, except when engaged in business, or assisting the authorities in some organized force. When the military appear in the street, do not gather about it, being sure that it is doing its duty in obedience to orders from superior authority. Your homes and your places of business you have a right to defend, and it is your duty to defend them, at all hazards. Yield to no intimidation, and to no demand for money as the price of your safety. If any person warns you to desist from your accustomed business, give no heed to the warning, but arrest him and bring him to the nearest station-house as a conspirator.

"Be assured that the public authorities have the ability and the will to protect you from those who have conspired alike against your peace, against the government of your choice, and against the laws which your representatives have enacted.

"George Opdyke, Mayor."

Down-town there was scarcely anything to show that New York had for nearly a week been swept by one of the most frightful storms that ever desolated a city. Even in the disaffected districts, no crowds were assembled. In the corner groggeries, small groups of men might be seen, discussing the past, and uttering curses and threats; and ruined houses and battered walls and hanging blinds here and there arrested the eye, showing what wild work had been wrought; but it was evident that the struggle was over. The mob was thoroughly subdued, and the law-breakers now thought more of escaping future punishment than of further acts of violence. Bruised heads and battered forms were scattered through the low tenement-houses in every direction, which friends were anxious to keep concealed from the notice of the authorities. In dirty cellars and squalid apartments were piled away the richest stuffs—brocaded silks, cashmere shawls, elegant chairs, vases, bronzes, and articles of virtue, huddled promiscuously together, damning evidences of guilt, which were sure not to escape, in the end, the searching eye of the police, who had already begun to gather up the plunder. Thus the objects mostly coveted but a few hours ago now awakened the greatest solicitude and fear.

Even if the military under General Brown and the police had not shown the mob that they were its masters, the arrival of so many regiments, occupying all the infected districts, was overwhelming evidence that the day of lawless triumph was over, and that of retribution had come. Some acts of individual hostility were witnessed, but nothing more.

Archbishop Hughes had his meeting, and some five thousand assembled to hear him. They were on the whole a peaceable-looking crowd, and it was evidently composed chiefly, if not wholly, of those who had taken no part in the riot. None of the bloody heads and gashed faces, of which there were so many at that moment in the city, appeared. The address was well enough, but it came too late to be of any service. It might have saved many lives and much destruction, had it been delivered two days before, but now it was like the bombardment of a fortress after it had surrendered—a mere waste of ammunition. The fight was over, and to use his own not very refined illustration, he "spak' too late."

The reports that came in to Acton from all the precincts convinced him of this, and he began to think of rest.

The strain was off, and overtasked nature made her demand, and he was compelled to yield to it. The tremendous work that had been laid upon him had been right nobly accomplished. Had he been a weak and vacillating man, the rioters would have acquired a headway that could not have been stopped, without a more terrible sacrifice of life and property—perhaps even of half the city. Comprehending intuitively the gravity of the situation, and the danger of procrastination or temporizing, he sprang at once for the enemy's throat, and never ceased his hold until he had strangled him to death. If lie had waited to consult authorities about the legality of his action, or listened to the voice of pity, or yielded to the clamors of leading politicians or threats of enemies, both he and the city, in all human probability, would have been swept away in the hurricane of popular fury.

On this day a most remarkable announcement was published: that a sudden change had been made in the military command of the troops of the city and harbor. General Dix superseded General Wool, and Canby, General Brown. That Wool should have been removed at any time, might have been expected; not from incapacity, but on account of his age, and because any one could perform the mere nominal duties that devolved on him. But why General Brown should have been removed at this critical moment, when he and the Police Commissioners were performing their herculean task so faithfully and well, is not so plain; unless it was the result of one of those freaks of passion or despotic impulse, for which the Secretary of War was so ignobly distinguished. But unlike many other blunders which the War Department committed at this time, it did not result in any evil consequences, for the fight was over. But of this fact the Secretary of War was ignorant when he made out the order.

General Brown, in relinquishing his command, spoke warmly of the noble behavior of the troops during the riots, saying: "Engaged night and day in constant conflict with the mob, they have in some fifteen or twenty severe contests—in most of them outnumbered more than ten to one, many of the mob being armed—whipped and effectually dispersed them, and have been uniformly successful. In not a single instance has assistance been required by the police, when it has not been promptly rendered; and all property, public and private, which has been under their protection, has been perfectly and efficiently protected; and with pride he desires to record, that in this city, surrounded by grog-shops, but one single instance of drunkenness has fallen under his observation.

"To Lieutenant-colonel Frothingham, his able and efficient adjutant-general, he tenders his thanks for his untiring assistance.

"Having during the present insurrection been in immediate and constant co-operation with police department of this city, he desires the privilege of expressing his unbounded admiration of it. Never in civil or military life has he seen such untiring devotion and such efficient service.

"To President Acton and Commissioner Bergen he offers his thanks for their courtesy to him and their kindness to his command.

"Harvey Brown, *Brigadier-general.*"

The praise he bestows both on the police and soldiers was richly deserved; and he may well say that "with pride he desires to record that in this city, surrounded with grog shops, but one single instance of drunkenness has fallen under his observation." With all a soldier's tendency to indulge in spirituous liquor, to be thrown right amid drinking-places, which by harboring rioters had lost all claim to protection—part of the time suffering from want of food, and often drenched to the skin, and weary from hard fighting and want of sleep—not to step away occasionally in the confusion and darkness of night, and solace himself with stimulating drinks, was something marvellous. After hard fighting, and long marching, and short rations, a soldier feels he has a right to indulge in liquor, if he can get it; and their abstinence from it in such lawless times, not only speaks well for their discipline, but their character. A single instance shows under what perfect control the troops were. One day Colonel La-due, seeing that his men were exhausted and hungry, desired to let them have a little beer to refresh them, and the following telegram was sent from the precinct where they were on duty:

"5.45 p.m. From 9th. Colonel Ladue wishes his men allowed to have beer in station-house."

Answer. "Mr. Acton says he is opposed to beer, but the colonel can give his men as much as he pleases."

"Acton is opposed to beer," but the troops are not under his command, and he has no heart to deny the poor fellows the station-house in which to refresh themselves after their hard day's work. This incident also shows the strict discipline maintained in the police department.

General Brown had done a noble work. Taking his place beside the Police Commissioners, he bent all his energies to the single task of carrying out their plans, and save the city from the hands of the rioters. He never thought what deference might be due him on the score of etiquette, or on account of his military rank; he thought only of putting down the mob at all hazards. His refusal, at first, to serve under General Sandford was not merely that it was an improper thing to place a general of the regular army under the orders of a mere militia general,* having no rank whatever in the United States army, but ho knew it would paralyze his influence, and in all human probability result in the useless sacrifice of his troops. The absurdity of not moving until he received orders from his superior officer, cooped up in the arsenal, where he remained practically in a state of siege, was so apparent that he refused to countenance it. He was willing that President Acton should be his superior officer, and give his orders, and he would carry them out; for thus he could act efficiently and make his disciplined battalion tell in the struggle; but for the sake of his own reputation and that of his troops, he would not consent to hold a position that would only bring disgrace on both. His views are clearly expressed in his reply to a highly complimentary letter addressed to him by the mayor and

---

*Because he was especially assigned to the command of the city by the Secretary of War.

a large number of prominent citizens, for the signal services he had rendered. He says: "I never for a moment forgot that to the police was confided the conservation of the peace of the city; and that only in conjunction with the city authorities, and on their requisition, could the United States forces be lawfully and properly employed in suppressing the riot, and in restoring that peace and good order which had been so lawlessly broken. Acting in accordance with this principle, and as aids to the gallant city police, the officers and soldiers of my command performed the most unpleasant and arduous duty, with that prompt energy and fearless patriotism which may ever be expected from the soldiers of the Republic."

• CHAPTER XX •

Continued Tranquillity.—Strange Assortment of
Plunder Gathered in the Cellars and Shanties of
the Rioters.—Search for It Exasperates the Irish.—
Noble Conduct of the Sanitary Police.—Sergeant
Copeland.—Prisoners tried.—Damages Claimed
from the City.—Number of Police Killed.—Twelve
Hundred Rioters Killed.—The Riot Relief Fund.—
List of Colored People Killed.—Generals Wool
and Sandford's Reports.—Their Truthfulness
Denied.—General Brown vindicated.

On Saturday morning it was announced that the authorities at Washington had resolved to enforce the draft. It had
been repeatedly asserted during the riot that it was abandoned,
and the report received very general credence. Still, the official
denial of it produced no disturbance. The spirit of insurrection
was effectually laid.

It is a little singular, that, in all these tremendous gatherings
and movements, no prominent recognized leaders could be
found. A man by the name of Andrews had been arrested and
imprisoned as one, but the charge rested wholly on some exciting harangues he had made, not from any *active* leadership he
had assumed.

There were, perhaps, in the city this morning not far from ten thousand troops—quite enough to preserve the peace, if the riot should break out afresh; and orders therefore were given to arrest the march of regiments hastening from various sections to the city, under the requisition of the Governor. Still, the terror that had taken possession of men could not be allayed in an hour, and although the police had resumed their patrols, and dared to be seen alone in the streets, there was constant dread of personal violence among the citizens. Especially was this true of the negro population. Although many sought their ruined homes, yet aware of the intense hatred entertained toward them by the mob, they felt unsafe, and began to organize in self-defence. But the day wore away without disturbance, and the Sabbath dawned peaceably, and order reigned from the Battery to Harlem. The military did not show themselves in the street, and thousands thronged without fear the avenues in which the fighting had taken place, to look at the ruins it had left behind. On Monday there was more or less rebellious feeling exhibited by the rioters, on account of the general search of the police for stolen goods, and the arrest of suspected persons. It exhibited itself, however, only in threats and curses—not a policemen was assaulted. It was amusing, sometimes, to see what strange articles the poor wretches had stowed away in their dirty cellars. There was everything from barrels of sugar and starch to tobacco and bird-seed. Said a morning paper: "Mahogany and rosewood chairs with brocade upholstering, marble-top tables and stands, costly paintings, and hundreds of delicate and valuable mantel ornaments, are daily found in low hovels up-town. Every person in whose possession these articles are discovered disclaims all knowledge of the same, except that they found them in the street, and took them in to prevent them being burned. The entire city will be searched, and it is expected that the greatest portion of the property taken from the buildings sacked by the mob will be recovered." The rivers and outlets to the city were closely watched, to prevent its being carried off. In the meantime, arrests were constantly made.

It would be invidious to single out any portion of the police for special commendation, where all did their duty so nobly; but it is not improper to speak of the sanitary police, whose specific duties do not lead them to take part in quelling mobs.

They have to report all nuisances, examine tenement-houses and unsafe buildings, look after the public schools, but more especially examine steam-boilers, and license persons qualified to run steam-engines. Hence, it is composed of men of considerable scientific knowledge. But all such business being suspended during the riot, they at once, with their Captain, B. G. Lord, assumed the duties of the common policemen, and from Monday night till order was restored, were on constant duty, participating in .the fights, and enduring the fatigues with unflinching firmness, and did not return to their regular duties till Monday morning.

The drill-officer also, Sergeant T. S. Copeland, became, instead of a drill-officer, a gallant, active leader of his men in some of the most desperate fights that occurred. His military knowledge enabled him to form commands ordered hastily off, with great despatch. But not content with this, he led them, when formed, to the charge, and gave such lessons in drill, in the midst of the fight, as the police will never forget.

With the details of what followed we have nothing to do. The Grand Jury indicted many of the prisoners, and in the term of the court that met the 3d of August, twenty were tried and nineteen convicted, and sentenced to a longer or shorter terra of imprisonment Of course a large number on preliminary examinations got off, sometimes from want of sufficient evidence, and sometimes from the venality of the judges before whom they were brought. Claims for damages were brought in, the examination of which was long and tedious. The details are published in two large volumes, and the entire cost to the city was probably three millions of dollars. Some of the claims went before the courts, where they lingered along indefinitely. The number of rioters killed, or died from the effects of their wounds, was pat down by the Police Commissioners at about twelve hundred. Of course this estimate is not made up from any detailed reports. The dead and wounded were hurried away, even in the midst of the fight, and hidden in obscure streets, or taken out of the city for fear of future arrests or complications. Hence there was no direct way of getting at the exact number of those who fell victims to the riot. The loss of life, therefore, could only be approximated by taking the regular report of the number of deaths in the city for a few weeks before the riots, and that for the same length of time after. As there was no epidemic, or any report of increased sickness from any disease, the inference naturally was, that the excess for the period after the riots was owing to the victims of them. Many of these were reported as sunstrokes, owing to men exposing themselves to the sun with pounded and battered heads. The Police Commissioners took great care to keep all the wounded policemen indoors until perfectly cured. Only one ventured to neglect their orders, and he died of a sunstroke.

The difference of mortality in the city for the month previous to the riots, and the month during and subsequent, was about twelve hundred, which excess Mr. Acton thought should be put down to the deaths caused directly and indirectly by the riots. Although many policemen were wounded, only three were killed or died from the injuries they received.

Immediately after the riot, Mr. Leonard W. Jerome and others interested themselves in raising a fund for the relief of members of the Police, Militia, and Fire Departments who had sustained injuries in the discharge of their duty in suppressing the riots. Subscriptions to the amount of $54,980 were paid in, and $22,721.53 distributed by the Trustees of the Riot Relief Fund, in sums from $50 to $1,000, each, through Isaac Bell, Treasurer, to 101 policemen, 16 militiamen, and 7 firemen.

The balance was securely invested, to meet future emergencies, a portion of which was paid to sufferers by the Orange Riot of 1871.

The following is the list of colored people known to be killed by the mob, together with the circumstances attending their murder, as given by David Barnes, in his Metropolitan record, to which reference has heretofore been made.

COLORED VICTIMS OF THE RIOT.

WILLIAM HENRY NICHOLS (colored). Nichols resided at No. 147 East Twenty-eighth Street. Mrs. Staat, his mother, was visiting him. On Wednesday, July 15th, at 3 o'clock, the house was attacked by a mob with showers of bricks and stones. In one of the rooms was a woman with a child but three days old. The rioters broke open the door with axes and rushed in. Nichols and his mother fled to the basement; in a few moments the babe referred to was dashed by the rioters from the upper window to the yard, and instantly killed. The mob cut the water-pipes above, and the basement was being deluged; ten persons, mostly women and children, were there, and they fled to the yard; in attempting to climb the fence, Mrs. Staats fell back from exhaustion; the rioters were instantly upon her; her son sprang to her rescue, exclaiming, "Save my mother, if you kill me." Two ruffians instantly seized him, each taking hold of an arm, while a third, armed with a crowbar, calling upon them to hold his arms apart, deliberately struck him a savage blow on the head, felling him like a bullock. He died in the N. Y. Hospital two days after.

James Costello (colored).—James Costello, No. 97 West Thirty-third Street, killed on Tuesday morning, July 14th. Costello was a shoemaker, an active man in his business, industrious and sober. He went out early in the morning upon an errand, was accosted, and finally was pursued by a powerful man. He ran down the street; endeavored to make his escape; was nearly overtaken by his pursuer; in self-defence he turned and shot the rioter with a revolver. The shot proved to be mortal; he died two days after. Costello was immediately set upon by the mob. They first mangled his body, then hanged it. They then cut down his body and dragged it through the gutters, smashing it with stones, and finally burnt it. The mob then attempted to kill Mrs. Costello and her children, but she escaped by climbing fences and taking refuge in a police station-house.

Abraham Franklin (colored).—This young man, who was murdered by the mob on the corner of Twenty-seventh Street and Seventh Avenue, was a quiet, inoffensive man, of unexceptionable character. He was a cripple, but supported himself and his mother, being employed as a coachman. A short time previous to the assault, he called upon his mother to see if anything could be done by him for her safety. The old lady said she considered herself perfectly safe; but if her time to die had come, she was ready to die. Her son then knelt down by her side, and implored the protection of Heaven in behalf of his mother. The old lady said that it seemed to her that good angels were present in the room. Scarcely had the supplicant risen from his knees, when the mob broke down the door, seized him, beat him over the head and face with fists and clubs, and then hanged him in the presence of his parent. While they were thus engaged, the military came and drove them away, cutting down the body of Franklin, who raised his arm once slightly and gave a few signs of life. The military then moved on to quell other riots, when the mob returned and again suspended the now probably lifeless body of Franklin, cutting out pieces of flesh, and otherwise shockingly mutilating it.

Augustus Stuart (colored).—Died at Hospital, Blackwell's Island, July 22, from the effects of a blow received at the hands of the mob, on Wednesday evening of the Riot Week. He had been badly beaten previously by a band of rioters, and was frightened and insane from the effects of the blows which he had received. He was running toward the arsenal (State), Seventh Avenue and Thirty-seventh Street, for safety, when he was overtaken by the mob, from whom he received his death-blow.

Peter Houston.—Peter Houston, sixty-three years of age, a Mohawk Indian, dark complexion, but straight hair, and for several years a resident of New York, proved a victim to the riots. Houston served with the New York Volunteers in the Mexican war. He was brutally attacked and shockingly beaten, on the 13th of July, by a gang of ruffians, who thought him to be of the African race because of his dark complexion. He died within four days, at Bellevue Hospital, from his injuries.

Jeremiah Robinson (colored).—He was killed in Madison near Catharine Street. His widow stated that her husband, in order to escape, dressed himself in some of her clothes, and, in company with herself and one other woman, left their residence and went toward one of the Brooklyn ferries. Robinson wore a hood, which failed to hide his beard. Some boys, seeing his beard, lifted up the skirts of his dress, which exposed his heavy boots. Immediately the mob set upon him, and the atrocities they perpetrated are so revolting that they are unfit for publication. They finally killed him and threw his body into the river. His wife and her companion ran up Madison Street, and escaped across the Grand Street Ferry to Brooklyn.

William Jones (colored).—A crowd of rioters in Clarkson Street, in pursuit of a negro, who in self-defence had fired on some rowdies, met an inoffensive colored man returning from a bakery with a loaf of bread under his arm. They instantly set upon and beat him and, after nearly killing him, hung him to a lamppost. His body was left suspended for several hours.

A fire was made underneath him, and he was literally roasted as he hung, the mob revelling in their demoniac act. Recognition of the remains, on their being recovered, was impossible; and two women mourned for upwards of two weeks, in the case of this man, for the loss of their husbands. At the end of that time, the husband of one of the mourners, to her great joy, returned like one recovered from the grave. The principal evidence which the widow, Mary Jones, had to identify the murdered man as her husband, was the fact of his having a loaf of bread under his arm, ho having left the house to get a loaf of bread a few minutes before the attack.

Joseph Reed (colored).—This was a lad of seven years of age, residing at No. 147 East Twenty-eighth Street, with an aged grandmother and widowed mother. On Wednesday morning of the fearful week, a crowd of ruffians gathered in the neighborhood, determined on a week of plunder and death. They attacked the house, stole everything they could carry with them, and, after threatening the inmates, set fire to it. The colored people who had the sole occupancy of the building, fled in confusion into the midst of the gathering crowd. And then the child was separated from his guardians. His youth and evident illness, even from the devils around him, it would be thought, should have insured his safety. But no sooner did they see his unprotected, defenceless condition, than a gang of fiendish men seized him, beat him with sticks, and bruised him with heavy cobblestones. But one, tenfold more the servant of Satan than the rest, rushed at the child, and with the stock of a pistol struck him on the temple and felled him to the ground. A noble young fireman, by the name of John F. Govern, of No. 39 Hose Company, instantly came to the rescue, and, single-handed, held the crowd at bay. Taking the wounded and unconscious boy in his arms, he carried him to a place of safety. The terrible beating and the great fright the poor lad had undergone was too much for his feeble frame; he died on the following Tuesday.

Joseph Jackson (colored), aged nineteen years, living in West Fifty-third Street, near Sixth Avenue, was in the industrious pursuit of his humble occupation of gathering provender for a herd of cattle, and when near the foot of Thirty-fourth Street, East River, July 15, was set upon by the mob, killed, and his body thrown into the river.

Samuel Johnson (colored).—On Tuesday night Johnson was attacked near Fulton Ferry by a gang who mercilessly beat and left him for dead. A proposition was made to throw him into the river, but for some reason the murderers took fright and fled. He was taken by some citizens to his home, and died the next day.

————Williams (colored).—He was attacked on the corner of Le Roy and Washington Streets, on Tuesday morning, July 14th, knocked down, a number of men jumped upon, kicked, and stamped upon him until insensible. One of the murderers knelt on the body and drove a knife into it; the blade being too small, he threw it away and resorted to his fists. Another seized a huge stone, weighing near twenty pounds, and deliberately crushed it again and again on to the victim. A force of police, under Captain Dickson, arrived and rescued the man, who was conveyed to the New York Hospital. He was only able to articulate "Williams" in response to a question as to his name, and remained insensible thereafter, dying in a few days

Ann Derrickson.—This was a white woman, the wife of a colored man, and lived at No. 11 York Street. On Wednesday, July 15th, the rioters seized a son of deceased, a lad of about twelve years, saturated his clothes and hair with camphene, and then procuring a rope, fastened one end to a lamp-post, the other around his neck, and were about to set him on fire, and hang him; they were interfered with by some citizens and by the police of the First Ward, and their diabolical attempt at murder frustrated. While Mrs. Derrickson was attempting to save the life of her son she was horribly bruised and beaten with a cart-rung. The victim, after lingering three or four weeks, died from the effects of her injuries.

Reports from the captains of the several precincts, with all the details of their operations, were made out—also from the subordinate military officers to their immediate superiors. The final reports of General Wool, commanding the Eastern Department, and Major-general Sandford, commanding the city troops, caused much remark in the city papers, and called forth a reply from General Brown, who considered himself unjustly assailed in them. Explanation of the disagreement between him and General Wool having been fully given, it is not necessary to repeat it here. The same may be said of the statement of General Wool, regarding his orders on Monday the 13th, respecting the troops in the harbor. But in this report of General Wool to Governor Seymour, there are other statements which General Brown felt it his duty to correct. General Wool says, that finding there was a want of harmony between Generals Sandford and Brown in the disposition of troops, he issued the following order:

Major-general Sandford, Brevet Brigadier-General Brown.

Gentlemen:—It is indispensable to collect your troops not stationed, and have them divided into suitable parties, with a due proportion of police to each, and to patrol in such parts of the city as may be in the greatest danger from the rioters. This ought to be done as soon as practicable.

John E. Wool, *Major-general.*

After this had been issued, General Sandford reporting to me that his orders were not obeyed by General Brown, I issued the following order:

"All the troops called out for the protection of the city are placed under the command of General Sandford."

General Brown in his reply says, that he "*never saw or heard of this first order.*" The only explanation of this, consistent with the character of both, is that General Wool sent this order to General Sandford alone—either forgetting to transmit it to General Brown, or expecting General Sandford to do it.

At all events, sent or not, it was a foolish order. One would infer from it that the whole task of putting down the riots belonged to the military, the commanders of which were to order out what co-operating force of police they deemed necessary and march up and down the disaffected districts, trampling out the lawlessness according to rule. This might be all well enough, but the question was, how were these troops, strangers to the city, to find out where "*such parts of the city*" were in which was "*the greatest danger from the rioters?*" It showed a lamentable ignorance of mobs; they don't stay in one spot and fight it out, nor keep in one mass, nor give notice beforehand where they will strike next. Such knowledge could only be obtained from police head-quarters, the focus of the telegraph system, and *there* the troops should have been ordered to concentrate at once, and put themselves Tinder the direction of the Police Commissioners. Again, General Wool says he issued the following order to General Brown, on Tuesday:

"Sir:—It is reported that the rioters have already recommenced their work of destruction. To-day there must be no child's play. Some of the troops under your command should be sent immediately to attack and stop those who have commenced their infernal rascality in Yorkville and Harlem."

This order, too, General Brown says he never received. Thinking it strange, he addressed a note to General Wool's assistant adjutant-general, respecting both these orders, which had thus strangely wandered out of the way. The latter, Major Christensen, replied as follows:

"The orders of General Wool published in his report to Governor Seymour, viz.: 'That patrols of military and police should be sent through the disaffected districts;' and the one July 14th, 'To-day there must be no child's play,' etc., were not issued by me, and I cannot therefore say whether copies were sent to you or not. They were certainly *not* sent by me.

C. F. Christensen,
"Major, Assistant Adjutant-general."

We have explained how the error may have occurred with regard to the first order. But there is no explanation of this, except on the ground that General Wool perhaps sketched out this order, without sending it, and afterwards seeing it amid his papers, thought it was a copy of one he had sent. He was well advanced in years, and might easily fall into some such error.

It is not necessary to go into detailed account of all the statements contained in General Wool's letter which General Brown emphatically denies; but the following is worthy of notice. lie says that General Brown issued orders that General Sandford countermanded, and that General Brown acted through the riots under his (Wool's) orders; whereas the latter says, he never received but three orders from Wool during the whole time, and only *one* of those referred to any action towards the rioters, and that was to bring off some killed and wounded men left by a military force sent out either by Sandford or Wool, and which had been chased from the field by the mob.

But the statements of General Wool are entirely thrown into the shade by the following assertion of General Sandford, in his report. He says: "With the remnant of the [his] division (left in the city), and the first reinforcements from General Wool, detachments were sent to all parts of the city, and the rioters everywhere beaten and dispersed on Monday afternoon, Monday night, and Tuesday morning. In a few hours, but for the interference of Brigadier-general Brown, who, in disobedience of orders," etc.

The perfect gravity with which this assertion is made is something marvellous. One would infer that the police was of no account, except to maintain order after it was fully restored by the military on Tuesday morning. General Sandford might well be ignorant of the state of things in the city, for he was cooped up in the arsenal, intent only on holding his fortress. So far as he was concerned, the whole city might have been burned up before Tuesday noon, and he would scarcely have known it, except as he saw the smoke and flames from the roof of the arsenal. He never sent out a detachment until after the Tuesday afternoon, when, as he says, but for General Brown's action, the riot would have been virtually over. The simple truth is, these reports of Generals Wool and Sandford are both mere afterthoughts, growing out of the annoyance they felt on knowing that their *martinetism* was a total failure, and the whole work had been done by General Brown and the Police Commissioners from their head-quarters in Mulberry Street. Acton and Brown had no time to grumble or dispute about etiquette. They had something more serious on hand, and they bent their entire energies to their accomplishment. General Sandford held the arsenal, an important point, indeed a vital one, and let him claim and receive all the credit due that achievement; but to assume any special merit in quelling the riots in the streets is simply ridiculous. That was the work of the police and the military under the commissioners and General Brown.

The statement of the Police Commissioners, Acton and Bergen, on this point is conclusive. They say that General Sandford's error consisted in "not choosing to be in close communication with this department, when alone through the police telegraph, and other certain means, trustworthy information of the movements of the mob could be promptly had."

That single statement is enough to overthrow all of General Sandford's assertions about the riot. It was hardly necessary for them to declare further in their letter to General Brown:

"So far from your action having had the effect supposed by General Sandford, we are of the opinion, already expressed in our address to the police force, that through your prompt, vigorous, and intelligent action, the intrepidity and steady valor of the small military force under you, acting with the police force, the riotous proceedings were arrested on Thursday night, and that without such aid mob violence would have continued much longer."

WELL-EARNED PRAISE.

ON THE WEEK after the riot the Board of Police Commissioners issued the following address to the force, in which a well-earned tribute is paid to the military:

To the Metropolitan Police Force.

On the morning of Monday, the 13th inst., the peace and

good order of the city were broken by a mob collected in several quarters of the city, for the avowed purpose of resisting the process of drafting names to recruit the armies of the Union.

Vast crowds of men collected and fired the offices where drafting was in progress, beating and driving the officers from duty.

From the beginning, these violent proceedings were accompanied by arson, robbery, and murder.

Private property, unofficial persons of all ages, sexes, and conditions, were indiscriminately assailed—none were spared, except those who were supposed by the mob to sympathize with their proceedings.

Early in the day the Superintendent was assaulted, cruelly beaten, robbed, and disabled by the mob which was engaged in burning the provost marshal's office in Third Avenue, thus in a manner disarranging the organization at the Central Department, throwing new, unwonted, and responsible duties upon the Board.

At this juncture the telegraph wires of the department were cut, and the movement of the railroads and stages violently interrupted, interfering seriously with our accustomed means of transmitting orders and concentrating forces.

The militia of the city were absent at the seat of war, fighting the battles of the nation against treason and secession, and there was no adequate force in the city for the first twelve hours to resist at all points the vast and infuriated mob. The police force was not strong enough in any precinct to make head, unaided, against the overwhelming force. No course was left but to concentrate the whole force at the Central Department, and thence send detachments able to encounter and conquer the rioters. This course was promptly adopted on Monday morning. Tine military were called upon to act in aid of the civil force to subdue the treasonable mob, protect life and property, and restore public order.

Under such adverse circumstances you were called upon to encounter a mob of such strength as have never before been seen in this country. The force of militia under General Sandford, who were called into service by the authority of this Board, were concentrated by him at and held the arsenal in Seventh Avenue, throughout the contest. The military forces in command of

Brevet Brigadier-general Harvey Brown reported at the Central Department, and there General Brown established his headquarters, and from there expeditions, combined of police and military force, were sent out that in all cases conquered, defeated, or dispersed the mob force, and subjected them to severe chastisement. In no instance did these detachments from the Central Department, whether of police alone or police and military combined, meet with defeat or serious check.

In all cases they achieved prompt and decisive victories. The contest continued through Monday, Tuesday, Wednesday, Thursday, and till 11 o'clock on Thursday night, like a continuous battle, when it ended by a total and sanguinary rout of the insurgents.

During the whole of those anxious days and nights, Brigadier-general Brown remained at the Central Department, ordering the movements of the military in carefully considered combinations with the police force, and throughout the struggle, and until its close, commanded the admiration and gratitude of the Police Department and all who witnessed his firm intelligence and soldierly conduct.

It is understood that he had at no time under his immediate command more than three hundred troops, but they were of the highest order, and were commanded by officers of courage and ability. They cordially acted with, supported, and were supported by, the police, and victory in every contest against fearful odds, was the result of brave fighting and intelligent command.

In the judgment of this Board, the escape of the city from the power of an infuriated mob is due to the aid furnished the police by Brigadier-general Brown and the small military force under his command. No one can doubt, who saw him, as we did, that during those anxious and eventful days and nights Brigadier-general Harvey Brown was equal to the situation, and was the right man in the right place.

We avail ourselves of this occasion to tender to him, in the most earnest and public manner, the thanks of the department and our own.

To the soldiers under his command we are grateful as to brave men who perilled all to save the city from a reign of terror. To

Captains Putnam, Franklin, and Shelley, Lieutenant Ryer, and Lieutenant-colonel Berens, officers of corps under the command of Brigadier-general Brown, we are especially indebted, and we only discharge a duty when we commend them to their superiors in rank and to the War Department for their courageous and effective service.

Of the Inspectors, Captains, and Sergeants of police who led parties in the fearful contest, we are proud to say that none faltered or failed. Each was equal to the hour and the emergency. Not one failed to overcome the danger, however imminent, or to defeat the enemy, however numerous. Especial commendation is due to Drill-sergeant Copeland for his most valuable aid in commanding the movements of larger detachments of the police.

The patrolmen who were on duty fought through the numerous and fierce conflicts with the steady courage of veteran soldiers, and have won, as they deserve, the highest commendations from the public and from this Board. In their ranks there was neither faltering nor straggling. Devotion to duty and courage in the performance of it were universal.

The public and the department owe a debt of gratitude to the citizens who voluntarily became special patrolmen, some three thousand of whom, for several days and nights, did regular patrolmen's duty with great effect.

In the name of the public, and of the department in which they were volunteers, we thank them.

Mr. Crowley, the superintendent of the police telegraph, and the attaches of his department, by untiring and sleepless vigilance in transmitting information by telegraph unceasingly through more than ten days and nights, have more than sustained the high reputation they have always possessed.

Through all these bloody contests, through all the wearing fatigue and wasting labor, you have demeaned yourselves like worthy members of the Metropolitan Police.

The public judgment will commend and reward you. A kind Providence has permitted you to escape with less casualties than could have been expected. You have lost one comrade, whom you have buried with honor. Your wounded will, it is hoped, all recover, to join you and share honor. It is hoped that the severe but just chastisement which has been inflicted upon those guilty of riot, pillage, arson, and murder, will deter further attempts of that character. But if, arising out of political or other causes, there should be another attempt to interrupt public order, we shall call on you again to crush its authors, confident that yon will respond like brave men, as you ever have, to the calls of duty; and in future, whenever the attempt may be made, you will have to aid you large forces of military, ably commanded, and thus be enabled to crush in the bud any attempted riot or revolution.

To General Canby, who, on the morning of Friday, the 17th inst., took command of the military, relieving Brigadier-general Brown, and to Gen. Dix, who succeeded General Wool, the public are indebted for prompt, vigorous, and willing aid to the police force in all the expeditions which have been called for since they assumed their commands. Charged particularly with the protection of the immense amount of Federal property and interests in the Metropolitan district, and the police force charged with the maintenance of public order, the duties of the two forces are always coincident.

Whatever menaces or disturbs one equally menaces and disturbs the other.

We are happy to know that at all times the several authorities have co-operated with that concert and harmony which is necessary to secure vigor and efficiency in action.

Sergeant Young, of the detective force, aided by Mr. Newcomb and other special patrolmen, rendered most effective service in arranging the commissary supplies for the large number of police, military, special patrolmen, and destitute colored refugees, whose subsistence was thrown unexpectedly on the department. The duty was arduous and responsible, and was performed with vigor and fidelity. All the clerks of the department, each in his sphere, performed a manly share of the heavy duties growing out of these extraordinary circumstances. The Central Department became a home of refuge for large numbers of poor, persecuted colored men, women, and children, many of whom were wounded and sick, and all of whom were helpless, exposed, and poor. Mr. John H. Keyser, with his accustomed philanthropy, volunteered, and was appointed to superintend these wretched victims of violence and prejudice, and has devoted unwearied days to the duty. The pitiable condition of these poor people appeals in the strongest terms to the Christian charity of the benevolent and humane. The members of the force will do an acceptable service by calling the attention to their condition of those who are able and willing to contribute in charity to their relief.

• CHAPTER XXI •

Orange Riots of 1870 and 1871.

RELIGIOUS TOLERATION.—IRISH FEUDS—BATTLE OF
BOYNE WATER.—ORANGEMEN.—ORIGIN AND OBJECT OF
THE SOCIETY.—A PICNIC AT ELM PARK.—ATTACKED BY
THE RIBBONMEN.—THE FIGHT.—AFTER SCENES.—RIOT
OF 1871.—CONSPIRACY OF THE IRISH CATHOLICS TO PRE-
VENT A PARADE OF ORANGEMEN.—FORBIDDEN BY THE CITY
AUTHORITIES.—INDIGNATION OF THE PEOPLE.—MEETING
IN THE PRODUCE EXCHANGE.—GOVERNOR HOFFMAN'S
PROCLAMATION.—MORNING OF THE 12TH.—THE
ORANGEMEN AT LAMARTINE HALL.—ATTACK ON THE
ARMORIES.—THE HARPERS THREATENED.—EXCITING
SCENES AROUND LAMARTINE HALL AND AT POLICE HEAD-
QUARTERS.—HIBERNIA HALL CLEARED.—ATTACK ON AN
ARMORY.—FORMATION OF THE PROCESSION.—ITS
MARCH.—ATTACKED.—FIRING OF THE MILITARY WITHOUT
ORDERS.—TERRIFIC SCENE.—THE HOSPITALS AND
MORGUE.—NIGHT SCENES.—NUMBER OF KILLED AND
WOUNDED.—THE LESSON.

IN A FREE country like ours, where toleration of all religions alike
is one of the fundamental principles of the Government, one
would naturally think that open persecution of any sect or body
of religionists was impossible. But the Irish, unfortunately, have

brought with them to this country not merely many of their old customs and national fêtes, but their old religious feuds.

Nearly two hundred years ago, William of Nassau, Prince of Orange, or William the Third, a Protestant, met the Catholic King, James the Second, of England, in deadly battle, in the vales of Meath, through which the Boyne River flows, and utterly routed him, and compelled him to flee to the Continent for safety. According to old style, this was on the first day of July, as the old ballad says:

> "'Twas bright July's first morning clear,
>   Of unforgotten glory,
> That made this stream, through ages dear,
>   Renowned in song and story."

According to new style, however, this has become the twelfth of the month. The Ulster Protestant Society, known as Orangemen, was founded in 1795. It was a secret political organization, founded, it is said, to counteract the Ribbonmen, or Protectors, as they were called. Its object in this country, it is asserted, is entirely different, and more in harmony with other societies that have their annual celebration in New York City and other places.

It is not necessary to go over the bitter feuds between these and the Catholic Irish in the old country. The hates they engendered were brought here, but kept from any great outward manifestation, because the Orangemen indulged in no public displays. We believe that there had been only one procession previous to this. In this year, however, an imposing display was resolved upon, but no trouble was anticipated, and no precautions taken by the police. It was not proposed to parade the streets, but to form, and march in procession up Eighth Avenue, to Elm Park, corner of Ninetieth Street and Eighth Avenue, and have a picnic, and wind up with a dance. As the procession passed Fourth Street, in full Orange regalia, and about twenty-five hundred strong (men, women, and children), playing "Boyne Water," "Derry," and other tunes obnoxious to the Catholics, some two hundred Irishmen followed it with curses and threats.

Violence was, however, not feared, and the procession continued on, and at length reached the new Boulevard road, where a large body of Irishmen were at work. Beyond, however, the interchange of some words, nothing transpired, and it entered the park, and began the festivities of the day.

In the meanwhile, however, the rabble that had followed them came upon the Ribbonmen at work on the Boulevard road, and persuaded them to throw up work and join them, and the whole crowd, numbering probably about five hundred, started for the park. The foreman of the gang of three hundred workmen saw at once the danger, and hurried to the Thirty-first Precinct station, corner of One Hundredth Street and Ninth Avenue, and told Captain Helme of the state of things.

The latter immediately thought of the picnic, and, anticipating trouble, telegraphed to Jourdan for reinforcements. In the meanwhile, the mob, loaded with stones, advanced tumultuously towards the park, within which the unsuspecting Orangemen were giving themselves up to enjoyment. Suddenly a shower of stones fell among them, knocking over women and children, and sending consternation through the crowd. Shouts and curses followed, and the Orangemen, rallying, rushed out and fell furiously on their assailants. Shovels, clubs, and stones were freely used, and a scene of terrific confusion followed. The fight was close and bloody, and continued for nearly half an hour, when Sergeant John Kelly, with a force of sixteen men, arrived, and rushing in between the combatants, separated them, and drove the Orangemen back into the park. The mob then divided into two portions, of between two and three hundred each. One party went by way of Ninth Avenue, and, breaking down the fence on that side, entered the park, and fell with brutal fury on men, women, and children alike. A terrible fight followed, and amid the shouts and oaths of the men and screams of the women and children, occasional pistol-shots were heard, showing that murder was being done. The enraged, unarmed Orangemen, wrenched hand rails from the fence, tore up small trees, and seized anything and everything that would serve for a weapon, and maintained the fight for a half an hour, before the police arrived. The second portion went by Eighth Avenue, and intercepted a large body of Orangemen that had retreated from the woods, and a desperate battle followed. There were only two policemen here, and of course could do nothing but stand and look on the murderous conflict. In the meantime, the force telegraphed for by Captain Helme arrived. It consisted of twenty men, to which Captain Helme added the reserve force, with a sergeant from the Eighth, Ninth, Fifteenth, Sixteenth, and Nineteenth Precincts, making in all some fifty men. These he divided into two portions, one of which he sent over to Eighth Avenue to protect the cars, into which the fugitives were crowding, while the other dashed furiously into the park, and fell on the combatants with their clubs. They soon cleared a lane between them, when turning on the Ribbonmen, they drove them out of the park. They then formed the Orangemen into a procession, and escorted them down the city. A portion, however, had fled for the Eighth Avenue cars; but a party of Ribbonmen were lying in wait here, and another fight followed. Huge stones were thrown through the windows of the cars, the sides broken in, over the wreck of which the mob rushed, knocking down men, women, and children alike, whose shouts, and oaths, and screams could be heard blocks off. The scene was terrific, until the arrival of the police put an end to it, and bore the dead and wounded away.

About seven o'clock, Superintendent Jourdan arrived in the precinct, accompanied by Inspectors Dilks and Walling, and Detectives Farley and Avery. In the basement of the Thirty-first Precinct station, on a low trestle bed, three bloody corpses were stretched, while the neighboring precincts were filled with the wounded. Two more died before morning. The street near each station was crowded with Orangemen inquiring after friends.

Although no more, outbreaks occurred, the most intense excitement prevailed among the Irish population of the city, and it was evident that it needed only a suitable occasion to bring on another conflict.

THE RIOT OF 1871

WHEN THE NEXT anniversary of the Orangemen came round, it was discovered that a conspiracy had been formed by a large body of the Catholic population to prevent its public celebration. The air was full of rumors, while the city authorities were in possession of the fullest evidence that if the Orangemen paraded, they would be attacked, and probably many lives be lost. They were in great dilemma as to what course to pursue. If they allowed the procession to take place, they would be compelled to protect it, and shoot down the men whose votes helped largely to place them in power. If they forbade it, they feared the public indignation that would be aroused against such a truckling, unjust course. As the day drew near, however, and the extensive preparations of the Irish Catholics became more apparent, they finally determined to risk the latter course, and it was decided that Superintendent Kelso should issue an order forbidding the Orangemen, to parade. This ludicrous attempt on the part of the Mayor to shift the responsibility from his own shoulders, awakened only scorn, and the appearance of the order was followed by a storm of indignation that was appalling. The leading papers, without regard to politics, opened on him and his advisers, with such a torrent of denunciations that they quailed before it. Processions of all kinds and nationalities were allowed on the streets, and to forbid only one, and that because it was *Protestant,* was an insult to every American citizen. Even Wall Street forgot its usual excitement, and leading men were heard violently denouncing this cowardly surrender of Mayor Hall to the threats of a mob. An impromptu meeting was called in the Produce Exchange, and a petition drawn up, asking the president to call a formal meeting, and excited men stood inline two hours, waiting their turn to sign it. The building was thronged, and the vice-president called the meeting to order, and informed it that the rules required twenty-four hours' notice for such a meeting. The members, however, would listen to no delay, and with an unanimous and thundering vote, declared the rules suspended. The action of the city authorities was denounced in withering terms, and a committee of leading men appointed to wait on them, and remonstrate with the Mayor. One could scarcely have dreamed that this order would stir New York so profoundly. But the people, peculiarly sensitive to any attack on religious freedom, were the more fiercely aroused, that in this case it was a Catholic mob using the city authority to strike down Protestantism. The Mayor and his subordinates were appalled at the tempest they had raised, and calling a council, resolved to revoke the order. In the meantime, Governor Hoffman was telegraphed to from Albany. Hastening to the city, he, after a consultation with Mayor Hall, decided to issue the following proclamation:

Having been only this day apprised, while at the capital, of the actual condition of things here, with reference to proposed processions to-morrow, and having, in the belief that my presence was needed, repaired hither immediately, I do make this proclamation:

The order heretofore issued by the police authorities, in reference to said processions, being duly revoked, I hereby give notice that any and all bodies of men desiring to assemble in peaceable procession tomorrow, the 12th inst., will be permitted to do so. They will be protected to the fullest extent possible by the military and police authorities. A police and military escort will be furnished to any body of men desiring it, on application to me at my head-quarters (which will be at police head-quarters in this city) at any time during the day. I warn all persons to abstain from interference with any such assembly or procession, except by authority from me; and I give notice that all the powers of my command, civil and military, will be used to preserve the public peace, and put down at all hazards, every attempt at disturbances; and I call upon all citizens, of every race and religion, to unite with me and the local authorities in this determination to preserve the peace and honor of the city and State. Dated at New York, this eleventh day of July, A. D. 1871.

John T. Hoffman.

It was thought by many that this would counteract the effects of the cowardly order of the police superintendent. But whatever its effect might have been, had it been issued earlier, it now came too late to do any good. The preparations of the Roman Catholics were all made. A secret circular had fallen into the hands of the police, showing that the organization of the rioters was complete—the watchwords and signals all arranged, and even the points designated where the attacks on the procession were to be made. Arms had been collected and transported to certain localities, and everything betokened a stormy morrow. Consequently, General Shaler issued orders to the commanders of the several regiments of militia, directing them to have their men in readiness at their respective armories at 7 o'clock next morning, prepared to march at a moment's warning. His head-quarters, like those of General Brown in the draft riots, were at the police head-quarters, so as to have the use of the police telegraph, in conveying orders to different sections of the city. Meanwhile, detachments were placed on guard at the different armories, to frustrate any attempt on the part of the mob to seize arms.

The night, however, wore quietly away, and in the morning the Governor's proclamation appeared in the morning papers, showing the rioters the nature of the work before them, if they undertook to carry out their infamous plans. It seemed to have no effect, however. Early in the morning sullen groups of Irishmen gathered on the corners of the streets, where the Irish resided in greatest numbers, among which were women, gesticulating and talking violently, apparently wholly unaware that the authorities had any power, or, at least, thought they dared not use it. Other groups traversed the streets, while at the several rendezvous of the Hibernians, many carried muskets or rifles without any attempt at concealment. In the upper part of the city, a body of rioters began to move southward, compelling all the workmen on their way to leave work and join them. One or two armories were attacked, but the rioters were easily repulsed. The demonstrations at length became so threatening, that by ten o'clock the police seized Hibernia Hall.

About the same time, the Orangemen—who on the issue of Kelso's order had determined not to parade but on the appearance of the Governor's proclamation changed their mind—began to assemble at Lamartine Hall, on the corner of Eighth Avenue and Twenty-ninth Street. Their room was in the fourth story, and the delegates from the various lodges brought with them their badges and banners, which they displayed from the windows. This brought a crowd in front of the building, curious to know what was going on in the lodge room. Soon five hundred policemen, ten or fifteen of them on horseback, appeared under the command of Inspectors Walling and Jamieson, and occupied both sides of Twenty-ninth Street, between Eighth and Ninth Avenues. Several policemen also stood on Eighth Avenue, while the door of the hall was guarded by others. Inside the hall there were probably sonic seventy-five or a hundred Orangemen, discussing the parade. Some stated that a great many, concluding there would be none, had gone to their usual work, while others, alarmed at the threats of the Hibernians, would not join it. But after some discussion, it was resolved, that although the number would be small, they would parade at all hazards; and at eleven o'clock the door was thrown open, and the Orangemen, wearing orange colors, were admitted, amid the wildest cheering. An invitation was sent to the lodges of Jersey City to join them, but they declined, preferring to celebrate the day at home.

Two o'clock was the hour fixed upon for the parade to begin, and the authorities at police head-quarters were so advised. In the meantime a banner had been prepared on which was inscribed in large letters,

"AMERICANS! FREEMEN!! FALL IN!!!"

in order to get accessions from outsiders, but without success.

The line of march finally resolved upon was down Eighth Avenue to Twenty-third Street, and up it to Fifth Avenue, down Fifth Avenue to Fourteenth Street, along it to Union Square, saluting the Lincoln and Washington statues as they passed, and then down Fourth Avenue to Cooper Institute, where the procession would break up.

About one o'clock, a party of men came rushing down Eighth Avenue, opposite Lamartine Hall, cheering and shouting, led by a man waving a sword cane. As he swung it above his head it parted, disclosing a long dirk. The police immediately advanced and swept the street. Eighth Avenue was cleared from Thirtieth Street to Twenty-eighth Street, and the police formed several deep, leaving only room enough for the cars to pass.

In the meantime, around police head-quarters, in Mott Street, things wore a serious aspect. From six o'clock in the morning, the various detachments of police kept arriving until Bleecker, Houston, Mulberry, and Mott Streets were dark with the massed battalions, ready to move at a moment's notice. Rations were served out to them standing. Early in the day, Governor Hoffman and staff arrived, and were quartered in the Superintendent's room, while General Shaler and staff were quartered in the fire marshal's office. Commissioners Manierre, Smith, and Barr were in their own rooms, receiving reports from the various precincts over the wires. A little after nine a dispatch came, stating that the quarrymen near Central Park had quitted work, and were gathering in excited groups, swearing that the Orangemen should not parade. Immediately Inspector Jamieson, with two hundred and fifty policemen, was despatched in stages to Forty-seventh Street and Eighth Avenue, to watch the course of events. Another dispatch stated that an attack was threatened on Harper's building, in Franklin Square, and Captain Allaire, of the Seventh Precinct, was hurried off with fifty men to protect it. A little later came the news that the Orangemen had determined to parade at two o'clock, and a police force of five hundred, as we have already stated, were massed in Eighth Avenue, opposite Lamartine Hall. About noon, a body of rioters made an attack on the armory, No. 19 Avenue A, in which were a hundred and thirty-eight stands of arms. Fortunately, the janitor of the building saw them in time to fasten the doors before they reached it, and then ran to the nearest police-station for help, from which a dispatch was sent to headquarters. Captain Mount, with a hundred policemen, was hurried off to the threatened point. He arrived before the doors were broken in, and falling on the rioters with clubs, drove them in all directions. During the forenoon, Drill-captain Copeland was given five companies, and told to seize Hibernia Hall, where arms were being distributed. As he approached, he ordered the mob to disperse, but was answered with taunts and curses, while the women hurled stones at his face. He then gave the order to charge, when the men fell on the crowd with such fury, that they broke and fled in wild confusion. Meanwhile, the detectives had been busy, and secured eighteen of the ringleaders, whom they marched to police head-quarters.

As the hour for the procession to form drew near, the most intense excitement prevailed at police head-quarters, and the telegraph was watched with anxious solicitude. The terrible punishment inflicted on the rioters in 1863 seemed to have been forgotten by the mob, and it had evidently resolved to try once more its strength with the city authorities. Around the Orange head-quarters a still deeper excitement prevailed. The hum of the vast multitude seemed like the first murmurings of the coming storm, and many a face turned pale as the Orangemen, with their banners and badges, only ninety in all, passed out of the door into the street. John Johnston, their marshal, mounted on a spirited horse, placed himself at their head. In a few minutes, the bayonets of the military force designed to act as an escort could be been flashing in the sun, as the troops with measured tread moved steadily forward. Crowds followed them on the sidewalks, or hung from windows and house-tops, while low curses could be heard on every side, especially when the Twenty-second Regiment deliberately loaded their pieces with ball and cartridge. The little band of Orangemen looked serious but firm, while the military officers showed by their preparations and order that they expected bloody work. The Orangemen formed line in Twenty-ninth Street, close to the Eighth Avenue, and flung their banners to the breeze. A half an hour later, they were ready to march, and at the order wheeled into Eighth Avenue. At that instant a single shot rang out but a few rods distant. Heads were turned anxiously to see who was hit; More was expected as the procession moved on. A strong body of police marched in advance. Next came the Ninth Regiment, followed at a short interval by the Sixth. Then came more police, followed by the little band of Orangemen, flanked on either side, so as fully to protect them, by the Twenty-second and Eighty-fourth Regiments. To these succeeded more police. The imposing column was closed up by the Seventh Regiment, arresting all eyes by its even tread and martial bearing. The sidewalks, doorsteps, windows, and roofs were black with people. The band struck up a martial air, and the procession moved on towards Twenty-eighth Street. Just before they reached it, another shot rang clear and sharp above the music. No one was seen to fall, and the march continued. At

the corner of Twenty-seventh Street, a group of desperate-look-
ing fellows were assembled on a wooden shed that projected
over the sidewalk. Warned to get down and go away, they hesitated, when a company of soldiers levelled their pieces at them.
Uttering defiant threats, they hurried down and disappeared. As
the next corner was reached, another shot was fired, followed by
a shower of stones. A scene of confusion now ensued. The police
fell on the bystanders occupying the sidewalks, and clubbed
them right and left without distinction, and the order rolled
down the line to the inmates of the houses to shut their windows.
Terror now took the place of curiosity; heads disappeared, and
the quick, fierce slamming of blinds was heard above the uproar
blocks away. The procession kept on till it reached Twenty-fourth
Street, when a halt was ordered. The next moment a shot was
fired from the second-story windows of a house on the northeast
corner. It struck the Eighty-fourth Regiment, and in an instant a
line of muskets was pointed at the spot, as though the order to
fire was expected. One gun went off, when, without orders, a sudden, unexpected volley rolled down the line of the Sixth, Ninth,
and Eighty-fourth Regiments. The officers were wholly taken by
surprise at this unprecedented conduct; but, recovering themselves, rushed among the ranks and shouted out their orders to
cease firing. But the work was done; and as the smoke slowly lifted
in the hot atmosphere, a scene of indescribable confusion presented itself. Men, women, and children, screaming in wild terror, were fleeing in every direction; the strong trampling down
the weak, while eleven corpses lay stretched on the sidewalk,
some piled across each other. A pause of a few minutes now followed, while the troops reloaded their guns. A new attack was
momentarily expected, and no one moved from the ranks to suc-
cor the wounded or lift up the dead. Here a dead woman lay
across a dead man; there a man streaming with blood was creep-
ing painfully up a doorstep, while crouching, bleeding forms
appeared in every direction. Women from the windows looked
down on the ghastly spectacle, gesticulating wildly. The police
now cleared the avenue and side streets, when the dead and
wounded were attended to, and the order to move on was given.
General Varian, indignant at the conduct of the Eighty-fourth in

firing first without orders, sent it to the rear, and replaced it on the flank of the Orangemen with a portion of the Ninth. The procession, as it now resumed its march and moved through Twenty-fourth Street, was a sad and mournful one. The windows were filled with spectators, and crowds lined the sidewalks, but all were silent and serious. Not till it reached Fifth Avenue Hotel were there any greetings of welcome. Here some three thousand people were assembled, who rent the air with cheers. No more attacks were made, and it reached Cooper Institute and disbanded without any further incident.

In the meantime, the scene at the Bellevue Hospital was a sad and painful one. The ambulances kept discharging their bloody loads at the door, and groans of distress and shrieks of pain filled the air. Long rows of cots, filled with mangled forms, were stretched on every side, while the tables were covered with bodies, held down, as the surgeons dressed their wounds. The dead were carried to the Morgue, around which, as night came on, a clamorous crowd was gathered, seeking admission, to look after their dead friends. A similar crowd gathered at the door of the Mount Sinai Hospital, filling the air with cries and lamentations. As darkness settled over the city, wild, rough-looking men from the lowest ranks of society gathered in the street where the slaughter took place, among whom were seen bare-headed women roaming about, making night hideous with their curses.

A pile of dead men's hats stood on the corner of Eighth Avenue and Twenty-fifth Street untouched, and pale faces stooped over pools of blood on the pavement. The stores were all shut, and everything wore a gloomy aspect. The police stood near, revealed in the lamplight, but made no effort to clear the street. It seemed at one time that a serious outbreak would take place, but the night passed off quietly, and the riot was ended, and the mob once more taught the terrible lesson it is so apt to forget.

Two of the police and military were killed, and twenty-four wounded; while of the rioters thirty-one were killed, and sixty-seven wounded—making in all one hundred and twenty-eight victims.

There was much indignation expressed at the troops for firing without orders, and firing so wildly as to shoot some of their own men. It was, of course, deserving the deepest condemnation, yet it may have saved greater bloodshed. The fight evidently did not occur at the expected point, and doubtless the result here, prevented one where the mob was better organized, and would have made a more stubborn resistance. That innocent persons were killed is true; but if they will mingle in with a mob, they must expect to share its fate, and alone must bear the blame. Troops are called out to fire on the people if they persist in violation of the peace and rights of the community. Of this all are fully aware, and hence take the risk of being shot. Soldiers cannot be expected to discriminate in a mob. If the military are not to fire on a crowd of rioters until no women and children can be seen in it, they had better stay at home.

To a casual observer, this calling out of seven hundred policemen and several regiments of soldiers, in order to let ninety men take a foolish promenade through a few streets, would seem a very absurd and useless display of the power of the city; and the killing of sixty or seventy men a heavy price to pay for such an amusement. But it was not ninety Orangemen only that those policemen and soldiers enclosed and shielded. They had in their keeping the laws and authority of the city, set at defiance by a mob, and also the principle of religious toleration and of equal rights, which were of more consequence than the lives of ten thousand men. The day when New York City allows itself to be dictated to by a mob, and Protestants not be permitted to march as such quietly through the streets, her prosperity and greatness will come to an end. The taking of life is a serious thing, but it is not to weigh a moment against the preservation of authority and the supremacy of the law.

One thing should not be overlooked—the almost universal faithfulness of the Roman Catholic Irish police to their duty. In this, as well as in the draft riots, they have left a record of which any city might be proud. To defend Protestant Irishmen against Roman Catholic friends and perhaps relatives, is a severe test of fidelity; but the Irish police have stood it nobly, and won the regard of all good citizens.[*]

Receiving and Removing Dead Bodies at the Morgue.

· AFTERWORD ·

PUBLISHER'S NOTE: *On page 250 in the footnote, the authors of the afterword refer to Mary Burton—the teenaged primary informant during the Negro Riots of 1712-1741—as a slave. Headleyhimself refers to Burton in his text as a colored servant girl (page 12). There is ample scholarly literature available today to prove that Mary Burton was not a slave and not colored. She was a white (possibly even Irish) indentured servant.*

I

"That's the reason I dislike the Irish so much," resumed the New-Yorker. "They are scarcely a year in the country before they pretend to be equal to our born citizens. I should have no objection to their coming here, provided they would be contented to remain servants—the only condition, by the by, they are fit for; but when they come without a cent in their pockets, pretending to enjoy the same privileges as our oldest and most respectable citizens, my blood boils with rage; and I would rather live among the Hottentots at the Cape of Good Hope, than in the United States, where every cart-man is as good as myself."[1]

Francis Grund's observations on the reluctance of upper class New Yorkers to accept the democratic standards for which America claimed to stand is merely one of the many reactions of Europeans to the realities of American life as recorded between 1830 and 1850. Dickens noticed in particular the seamier aspects of New York, which struck him as shocking even though he was already familiar with the London slums:

What place is this, to which the squalid street conducts us? A kind of square of leprous houses, some of which are attainable only by crazy

---

[1] Francis J. Grund, *Aristocracy in America: From the Sketchbook of a German Nobleman* (New York: Harper Torchbooks, 1959), 51.

wooden stairs without. What lies beyond this tottering flight of steps, that creak beneath our tread?—A miserable room, lighted by one dim candle, and destitute of all comfort, save that which may be hidden in a wretched bed. . . . Here, too, are lanes and alleys, paved with mud knee-deep; . . . hideous tenements which take their name from robbery and murder; all that is loathsome, drooping, and decayed is here.[2]

The clear contrast of these two extremes—the pretension of the rich and the desperation of the poor—frequently appears in the pages of European observers and just as frequently is absent in American observations of the nineteenth century. We owe the astuteness of de Tocqueville and Lord Bryce to the fact that they were aristocrats and therefore not subject to the leveling pressures of American democracy, the dangers of which they saw in the tendency to homogenize experience and deplore intellectual variety and dissent. Thus, each man was more sensitive to the realities of class and social distance than most Americans precisely because neither needed to prove how well democracy worked. In contrast, Americans generally have ignored these realities of conflict, especially when they manifested themselves openly and violently. As a result, the subject of violence has always aroused great fear and antagonism in America, apparently from the wish that if we refuse to take it seriously, violence will somehow disappear.

The roots of our present attitudes towards violence derive partially from a long-standing tradition that the American colonial experience was essentially simple and peaceful. As Howard Mumford Jones points out:

The Courtship of Miles Standish pictures, not without humor, an orderly little society. Evangeline gives us a village of pastoral simplicity ruined by the unseemly British, and though the village is French, we have adopted the Acadian legend. . . . True, there are Indian massacres and wars against the French, but our side always wins. By and by, a shortsighted Parliament and stubborn King, beginning in 1765, enact a series of measures that violate the principle of no taxation with-

---

[2] Charles Dickens, *American Notes* (London: Chapman and Hall, 1855), 61–62.

out representation, and after ten years of patient remonstrance we begin a war for independence in 1775. Virginia is settled by gallant gentlemen; Pilgrim and Puritan come to Massachusetts to escape religious tyranny; Lord Baltimore provides a refuge for persecuted Catholics in Maryland; the jolly Dutch, knowing that Irving is going to write about them, found New Amsterdam; William Penn launches a "holy experiment" in Pennsylvania in which any Christian can participate, and the noble Oglethorpe creates Georgia in 1733 as a refuge for oppressed debtors who are not to own slaves.

But the men who were brought to the New World in the era of English exploration and discovery were . . . an unruly lot, obeying orders when they felt like it, disobeying them when they did not, conspiring against their leaders and presenting problems of discipline to their superiors that are, so to speak, handed on to the days of the vigilantes and the lynchers.[3]

As a substitute for the image of the American Adam, which has become an accepted feature of American cultural analysis, Jones suggests the more fundamental reality of duplicity, violence, and conflict, which characterized the grasping for power in the New World.[4] But while some historians, like Beard and Parrington, acknowledged the importance of conflict in the formation of American society, most American historians, particularly those who emerged prominently since the Second World War, have stressed consensus and continuity rather than convulsions and cleavages in our national past. As one recent dissenting historian has suggested, "With the exception of the Civil War and often the New Deal, there were, according to this school of thought, no significant discontinuities in American history."[5]

---

[3] O Strange New World, American Culture: The Formative Years (New York: Viking Press, 1968), 276–77.

[4] See Jones's chapter, "Renaissance Man in America," which argues that the true model for political morality in the New World was that of Machiavelli's Prince, who combined the talents of the lion and the fox in his search for power.

[5] Barton J. Bernstein, ed., Towards a New Past: Dissenting Essays in American History (New York: Pantheon, 1968), vii-viii.

It seems useful, given the drift of contemporary events, to examine whether this consensual notion of the nature of our experience, which our written history conveys, seems realistic. Any historian who seeks to recapitulate the American past must, at least, justify this view of America by scrutinizing the nature of conflict and violence. It is not merely that America is violent, for violence is found in every society and in every culture; but the failure to recognize the often central role that it plays in American history may mitigate the social realities from which historical changes arise. As Richard Hofstadter suggests in *The Progressive Historians,* we have lost sight of "the ethnic, racial, religious, moral conflict with which American life is permeated."[6] Hofstadter, who has generally dismissed the importance of conflict and violence, urges that historians study why violence has flourished in our culture, but serious systematic study of violence in America simply does not exist and has only recently become the subject of scholarly concern.[7] A book like Headley's *The Great Riots of New York: 1712–1873* provides one of the few glimpses, sys-

---

[6] The Progressive Historians: Turner, Beard, Parrington (New York: Alfred A. Knopf, 1968), p. 462. However, Hofstadter's assertion that "the extraordinary American penchant for violence has been so sporadic, channeled, and controlled that it has usually bled itself out in the isolated, the local, and the partial, instead of coalescing into major social movements" begs the question of violence. It does not necessarily follow that the failure to coalesce into major social movements automatically makes the violence which occurred sporadic, channeled, and controlled. In effect, Hofstadter generalizes about the effects of this violence without examining the causes, which is a strange procedure for historical analysis.

[7] Some recent examples of scholarly concern with violence are *Violence in America,* Thomas Rose, ed. (New York: Random House and Vintage, 1969); Bernard Bailyn, *Ideological Origins of the American Revolution* (Cambridge: Harvard University Press, 1968); Patrick Renshaw, *The Wobblies: The Story of Syndicalism in the United States* (Garden City: Anchor Books, 1968); Arthur Waskow, *From Race Riot to Sit-in, 1919 and the 1960's* (Garden City: Anchor Books, 1967): Richard Drinnon, *Rebel in Paradise: A Biography of Emma Goldman* (Chicago: University of Chicago Press, 1961); Hugh Davis Graham and Ted Robert Gurr, *Violence in America: Historical and Comparative Perspectives* (A Report to the National Commission on the Causes and Prevention of Violence), 2 vols. (Washington: United States Government Printing Office, 1969); Jerome Skolnick, *The Politics of Protest: Violent Aspects of Protest and Confrontation* (A Report to the National Commission on the Causes and Prevention of Violence) (Washington: United States Government Printing Office, 1969).

tematic or otherwise, of violence as a significant historical factor in shaping American society; moreover, it offers a striking formulation of attitudes that typified the reaction of the social and political elite of the nineteenth century—attitudes still prevalent today—to the violent displays of the lower classes.

II

EDGAR ALLAN POE described Joel Tyler Headley as the "Autocrat of all the Quacks."[8] Headley was, in fact, one of the most popular writers of the nineteenth century and must be seriously considered as an important influence on the popular taste of the period. But in spite of his enormous popularity, the details of his career remain obscure. Headley was born in Walton, New York in 1813 to Isaac and Irene Headley; his father's family had emigrated from England to New Jersey in 1665, and his mother was from the prominent Benedict family of New York. By his own account, Headley passed an unspectacular youth. In a letter written in 1846 to R. W. Griswold, an influential critic to whom Headley was applying for help in launching his literary career, he described himself as "fond of sports, especially of the field, and hence my great love at the present day of hunting and fishing. It is a wild and romantic spot on the banks of the Delaware where I first saw the light and I attribute to the glorious and grand scenery of my birthplace much of my love of mountain-climbing and indeed my descriptive power."[9]

Headley graduated from Union College in 1839, studied at Auburn Theological Seminary and apparently was offered a large congregation in New York City; but his health was poor and he

---

[8] Edgar Allan Poe, Collected Works, VI (New York: Chesterfield Society, 1909), 47.

[9] Rufus W. Griswold, *Passages from the Correspondence & Other Papers of Ritfus W. Griswold* (Cambridge, Mass.: W. M. Griswold, 1898), 211. For a brief glimpse of Headley's place among the New York literati, see Perry Miller, *The Raven and the Whale: The War of Words and Wits in the Era of Poe and Melville* (New York: Harcourt, Brace and World, 1959).

was urged not to take up the responsibilities of so large a parish. Instead, Headley went to Stockbridge, Massachusetts, where he took charge of a small congregation. His health continued to suffer, however, and in 1842 he went to Italy as the first stop of an intended three- or four-year European stay. From Italy he sent back a series of letters published as *Italy and the Italians* (1844), which was popular enough to induce him to come out with a second volume, *Letters from Italy* (1845).[10] At this point, having returned to America after less than two years in Europe, Headley decided to pursue a literary career. He became associate editor of the New York *Tribune* in 1846, though only for about a year, and from 1846 on Headley produced a tremendous volume of work, most of which was popular history.

In 1854 Headley was elected to the New York Assembly and the next year was chosen to serve as Secretary of State of New York on the Know-Nothing ticket. He remained as secretary until 1858, having done little more, apparently, than supervise the census. He returned to writing, spending most of the next forty years of his life in Newburgh, New York. Headley's output and popularity barely diminished, and it was during this period— between the outbreak of the Civil War and the end of Reconstruction—that Headley produced his best and historically most interesting work.

His particular interest for us lies in his great fascination with war and conflict, the acceptance of which was fed generally by the nationalistic and militaristic tone of the Jacksonian period and to which his development as a writer remains attached. For in spite of his Whig politics, Headley clearly shared with the Jacksonians a fervent belief in America's "manifest destiny." His first major book other than travel sketches was *Napoleon and His Marshals* (1846), which by 1861 went into its fiftieth edition. He followed this with *Washington and His Generals* (1847), which was

---

[10] Headley's first book was actually a translation of Charles Sealsfield's *Scenes and Adventures in Mexico,* which he was too afraid to acknowledge publicly because of the bad language used by the author. On Sealsfield's view of America, see *America, Glorious and Chaotic Land,* E. L. Jordan, trans, and ed. (Englewood Cliffs, N.J.: Prentice-Hall, 1969).

modeled directly on the study of Napoleon and which was possibly his most popular book.[11] Except for some sentimental writing that reflected much of the strongly feminist taste of the period, Headley's books up to the Civil War continue to focus on military or heroic exploits: *The Life of Oliver Cromwell* (1848), *Luther and Cromwell* (1850), *The Imperial Guard of Napoleon* (1851), *The Lives of Winfield Scott and Andrew Jackson* (1852), *The Second War with England* (1853), *The Life of General H. Havelock, K.C.B.* (1859), *The Illustrated Life of Washington* (1859).

The rate at which Headley turned out material frequently weakened his style, and some of his critics blasted him for lapses of literary taste. One reviewer noted of *Napoleon and His Marshals* and *Washington and His Generals*: "Mr. Headley has exhibited his shrewdness in the choice of subjects and the mode of treating them; and has betrayed the low grade of his genius by its wonderful fecundity."[12] He added that the increased interest in war was nourished by writers like Headley, in whom he saw a frank catering to low tastes and the commercial value of a book. Another reviewer, writing in the *United States Magazine and Democratic Review* of 1848, flatly condemned Headley's *Oliver Cromwell*— "It shows neither learning, taste, nor judgment"—and also objected to Headley's overwhelming interest in war.[13]

But for the most part, Headley received substantial support from magazine reviewers, who recognized in his style the elements of mass appeal:

Mr. Headley is in very many respects—we think he might become in nearly all—fitted to be the writer of that history [of Napoleon]. He has a rapid, clear and vigorous style, much skill in delineating and dissecting character, a quick philosophy to discern the causes that produced great results, and a power of description on occasions of "pith and

---

[11] Frank Luther Mott, *Golden Multitudes: The Story of Best Sellers in the United States* (New York: R. R. Bowker, 1947).

[12] "Headley's Histories," *Methodist Review*, 8 (3rd series, 1848), 84.

[13] *United States Magazine and Democratic Review*, 23 (July–December, 1848), 333–40.

moment," in scenes of swift and thrilling action, that we do not remember to have seen surpassed by any writer.[14]

In effect, Headley thrilled his audience with pictures of valor and the glories of war at a time of growing nationalism, when the Mexican War was just bursting upon the public consciousness.[15]

The most notable difference in Headley's work during and after the Civil War derives from his greater concern for the actualities of violence and conflict rather than for their more glorified aspects on which he had built his reputation. This more realistic view of war developed, undoubtedly, as a result of the profound impact of the Civil War, which seared in the memory of the generation that fought it an intense awareness of the passion of violence. The reaction of Oliver Wendell Holmes, Jr. seems to embody the widespread feeling that his generation had been "set apart by its experience. Through our great good fortune, in our youth our hearts were touched with fire. It was given to us to learn at the outset that life is a profound and passionate thing."[16]

It is clear that Headley views the war with the same passionate commitment that swept all the participants headlong into the violent conflict, and that his history of the conflict, *The Great Rebellion,* the very title of which underscores his attitude towards the southern cause, concerns itself primarily with explaining to the civilian population the details of the battles in all their heroic splendor. Headley mirrors the widely accepted feeling shared and promulgated by other popular historians, such as John S. Cabot Abbott, Robert Tomes, and Charles E. Lester, that the nation was dragged into war by the ambitions of power-mad southern politi-

---

[14] "Napoleon and His Marshalls," *American (Whig) Review* 3 (May 1846), 539–540.

[15] Those reviewers hostile to Headley's treatment of war pointed especially to the popular agitation towards Mexico, and attributed the general eagerness for the war to popular historians like Headley. See notes 11 and 12 above for articles that argue this position.

[16] Thomas F. Pressley, *Americans Interpret their Civil War* (New York: Collier Books, 1962), 18. Holmes made the remark in 1884. For a full discussion of Holmes's attitudes towards his civil war experience, see Edmund Wilson, *Patriotic Gore: Studies in the Literature of the American Civil War* (New York: Oxford University Press, 1962), 743–796.

cians—opinions echoed by Lincoln, Douglas[17] and Edward Everett. But we see that, in spite of the tendency towards prolixity, much of the sentimentality which colored his treatment of Washington disappears in the face of the singular horrors of the war. Look, for instance, at this description of the battle of Shiloh, which Headley refers to as the battle of Pittsburg Landing:

> . . . the dead of both the contending hosts lay in heaps on every side. Scattered through the woods, gathered in groups on open spots where there had been hard struggles for the possession of important batteries, stretched along the road, they lay in every conceivable shape, and disfigured by every form of wound. Here the rifle and musket had done its deadly work—leaving the slain like so many sleepers, with nought but the purple spot, or the pool of blood to show how they met their fate—there, headless bodies, disemboweled corpses, and shattered limbs, told where the heavy shot and shell had ploughed through the ranks. Among this mighty multitude of dead, hundreds of artillery horses lay scattered, with their harness upon them. It was a ghastly spectacle, such as was never before seen on this continent, . . .[18]

In this passage we glimpse the beginning of those changes in American prose style that would emerge during and after the war and that would mark the irrevocable split between pre- and post-war America.

For as Edmund Wilson points out, the creation of such a style—the chastening and purging of the sloppiness and pomposity of American prose and the substitution instead of the language of responsibility and decisiveness dictated by the demands

---

[17] Pressley, *op. cit,* The first chapter, "The War of the Rebellion," thoroughly reviews union attitudes towards the war. For Headley's view of the causes of the war, see his preface to *The Great Rebellion,* vol. I, in which he says, "The *great, moving cause was the desire of power—slavery the platform* on which they worked their diabolical machinery." 11 [emphasis Headley's].

[18] *The Great Rebellion,* vol. I (Hartford: Hurlbut, Williams & Company, 1863) 360–61.

of war—was not merely a probability but almost a necessity.[19] It would have been inconceivable for Headley to have written this kind of passage prior to his experience of the war; and the war gave to Headley a quality often missing in his work: a practical sense of brutality and violence. The man who extolled the virtues of combat and the splendor of men at war in the service of a good cause now recoils from the bloodshed. And with this new edge to his sensibilities, Headley turns after the war to examine violence itself, for which he has greater respect and fear than before.

III

THE GREAT RIOTS of New York: 1712–1873 differs from every other book that Headley wrote in its concern with forms of violence that were bred in cities, that reflected the animus of the lower classes and that, unlike war, which is institutionalized and legal violence, seemed to attack the foundations of the society without justification.[20] Although Headley was undoubtedly stimulated to write the book because of its inherent commercial appeal—the Civil War still lingered vividly in the minds of many people—and although he was also probably capitalizing on the recent outbreaks of violence during the Orange Riots of 1870–1871, *Great Riots* springs most immediately from the fears aroused by the unpredictable behavior of the poor, whose numbers were increasing in the cities. Headley never really liked the city: his books reveal a passion for the countryside, and his choosing to live in Newburgh for the last forty years of his life, on a country estate that smacked of English gentry living, attests his basic hostility

---

[19] *Patriotic Gore,* 649 ff.

   [20] *The Great Riots of New York: 1712–1873* (New York: E. B. Treat, 1873), hereafter cited as Great Riots. A later version of Great Riots, published as Pen and Pencil Sketches of the Great Riots (New York: E. B. Treat, 1877), also includes a long section on the railroad strikes of 1877 and underlines Headley's hostility towards the worker whose violence he considered entirely unjustified. Both books had local and limited sales.

towards the city. But the current of uneasiness that runs through *Great Riots* stems not only from a long-standing and personal malaise; it epitomizes the general, social dislocation felt by others who saw in the city the destruction of basic American values.[21] By the 1870s, the pressures that emerged after the Civil War to accelerate the growth of cities and the decline of the town signified a major shift in the development of the United States from an agrarian to an industrial state.

In addition, the immediate reason for writing this book—to provide a historical account of the Draft Riots of 1863 in terms of the personal experiences of the major participants—becomes in effect a glorification of the role of the police, who clearly stood for the forces of order and decency in the minds of the wealthier and more educated people.[22] Equally important is the fact that Headley regarded the Draft Riots as an instrumental battle of the Civil War, practically an extension of the battles he described in *The Great Rebellion* (1866), which was his defense of the Union policies. Specifically, he wished to give the riots "the prominence they deserved . . . of having a vital bearing on the fate of the war and the nation."[23]

Seen from this perspective, Headley's concern with riots as a general phenomenon of cities coincides with his attitude towards the men who led the rebellion of the South. To Headley, the greatness of the United States rested on its utter devotion to the republican principles established by the Revolution and consolidated by the Constitution. All of his historical writing reflects this position, informing his view of Washington and providing the basis for his sympathy for Napoleon, whom he saw as a republican gone astray. Headley's chauvinism fundamentally inhibits his ability to examine any historical situation except in somewhat grandiose terms, so that his understanding of the nature of conflict and the violence that grows out of it is predicated on a patrician and conservative

---

[21] For an account of anti-urbanism see Morton and Lucia White, The Intellectual vs. the City (New York: Mentor, 1964).

[22] Great Riots, 17–18.

[23] Great Riots, 17.

point of view.[24] Headley's book was not meant merely as a historical study, but as a warning to an audience which was likely to feel threatened by the apparent ease with which violence occurred and the relative difficulty with which it was put down. *Great Riots* can thus be seen as skillful propaganda, a prelude to the fear of and violent resistance to the labor movement that emerged over the next two decades of the nineteenth century.[25]

We can connect Headley's strong bias against the poor and the efforts of workingmen to organize with his earlier political career of the 1850s, when he ran successfully for the state legislature and for the position of New York's Secretary of State on the Know-Nothing ticket. The Know-Nothing party developed, like many other third party movements in America, because the major parties failed to offer sufficient ideological as well as practical commitment to certain popular values. In this case, strong anti-Catholic and anti-immigrant prejudices coalesced with the often vague but nevertheless profound sentiment that traditional standards were being assaulted by alien forces. Headley probably entered the Know-Nothing movement for the same reasons as those of other politicians who did not necessarily share nativist prejudices. The surge of popularity for the Know-Nothings was especially strong in New York, which, like many other states in the North, was witnessing the collapse of traditional party lines. The Know-Nothing tickets during the years of its greatest strength, 1854–1856, constantly pulled in former Whigs and Democrats who were seeking new political bases from which to operate.[26]

---

[24] In The Reconstruction of American History (New York: Harper Torchbooks, 1962), John Higham notes that "From the early 18th to the late 19th century, the best history came from the pens of independent gentlemen, who did not write in the service of church or from any institutional incentive. They had a high respect for the dignity of history, in the writing of which they exhibited a generalized sense of responsibility to society. Theirs was the period of patrician history." 10. Headley was by no means so detached, although certainly patrician in his habits and ideas.

[25] Headley's venomous hatred of the strikers is expressed many times in *Pen and Pencil Sketches of the Great Riots* (see note 20).

[26] For a detailed account of the Know-Nothing movement in New York, see Lewis Dow Scisco, *Political Nativism in New York State* (New York: Columbia University Press, 1901).

The new party particularly attracted Whigs, many of whom identified the Jacksonian Democrats as responsible for the breakdown of law and order and the political difficulties of the country. Indeed, most Whigs saw the turmoil of the second quarter of the nineteenth century, which J. B. McMaster described as one of the most disorderly periods in American history, as a premonition of the collapse of republican principles and the subsequent demise of American society. Moreover, most Whigs resented the Democratic party, which had gained substantial success in New York City by manipulating the vote of the foreign population, particularly the Irish, and had helped to destroy the efforts of the Whigs to challenge this Democratic hegemony.[27] The Know-Nothings cut into the Tammany hold on the working-class population, and appealed naturally to those who opposed the policies and wished to reform the corrupt electoral practices of the Tammany machine.

The interest of the Know-Nothings in a man like Headley parallels Headley's interest in them. In order to build broad political support, the movement could not rely merely on the appealing novelty of a secret organization; it required the presence of names that the public could recognize, and Headley possessed in addition to his political visibility the added virtue of being untarnished by previous political associations. Headley had worked assiduously to thwart Seward's reelection as senator in 1854, and his talents as a popular writer combined with these other factors to make him a strong candidate at the top of the ticket in 1855.

Headley, who was clearly a Whig, also took an expedient position. His strong Whig sympathies compelled him to regard the men who supported the Democrats as political mongrels, whose presence threatened the noble experiment to establish a republic of free men, the failure of which "will be owing to the exten-

---

[27] See Walter Hugins, *Jacksonian Democracy and the Working Class: A Study of the New York Workingmen's Movement, 1828–1837* (Stanford: Stanford University Press, 1960), for an account of the period's politics. See also Lee Benson, *The Concept of Jacksonian Democracy: New York as a Test Case* (New York: Atheneum, 1965).

sion of the political franchise to whites and blacks who were unfit to use it, and cared for it not because of its honor, or the good use to which it might be put, but as a piece of merchandise to be sold to the highest bidder or used as a weapon of assault against good order and righteous laws."[28] Expediency, however, can not account for all of Headley's feelings, since he was, like other nativists, strongly anti-Catholic in his political attitudes and implicitly distrusted the large numbers of lower class Irish who were flooding into the country.[29] Thus, from the few details we know about Headley's politics, we can infer that he agreed with many of the principles enunciated by the Know-Nothings in their Cincinnati Council of 1854, and that he almost certainly supported the oath of the third degree, which attempted to consolidate pro-Union sentiment and isolate anti-slavery elements in the movement.[30]

Headley's implicit prejudices therefore appear in *Great Riots* because of long-standing rather than haphazard attitudes; and it is these attitudes, as well as his more general view of history as a series of struggles, that form the basis of his ideas about the role of violence in the evolution of a society. To Headley, the riots that occurred in New York City since 1712 represented a fundamental factor in the growth and moral climate of the city:

> The history of the riots that have taken place in a great city from its foundation, is a curious and unique one, and illus-

---

[28] *Great Riots*, 68.

[29] Ray Allen Billington calls two of Headley's books, *Letter from Italy* (1845) and *History of the Persecutions and Battles of the Waldenses* (1852), anti-Catholic in sentiment. *The Protestant Crusade, 1800–1860: A Study of the Origins of American Nativism* (Chicago: Quadrangle Books, 1964). Although this charge is somewhat circumstantial and ignores the strong anti-clerical strain in republican ideas, which goes back to radicals like Thomas Paine, Headley does fail to criticize the pro-clerical spirit of Know-Nothing rhetoric and behavior. Headley's interest in and usefulness to the Know-Nothing Party, as well as the Know-Nothing ideology itself, is strongly paralleled by George Wallace's appeal and his choice of General LeMay as an easily recognized public figure. Note that both parties called themselves the American Party and shared similar platforms.

[30] Scisco, *Political Nativism*, chap. VI.

trates the peculiar changes in tone and temper that have come over it in the course of its development and growth. They exhibit also one phase of its moral character—furnish a sort of moral history of that vast, ignorant, turbulent class which is one of the distinguishing features of a great city, and at the same time the chief cause of its solicitude and anxiety, and often dread.[31]

Even though this observation could be the basis for an interesting theoretical discussion about the roots of violent behavior, it rapidly becomes obvious that Headley is expressing a generalized fear, touched off essentially by the war and post-war riots, that New York and, by implication, the rest of the country, would become a victim of "mob violence." In effect, he raises the issue of "law and order" that draws on many of the same hatreds which permeated the Know-Nothing movement: the growth of a disreputable class in the cities, the threat of violence and subsequent destruction of property, the loss of political power to those who favor the despised minority, and the more or less undefined threat to an American way of life.[32]

As we examine Headley's attitudes towards violence in the light of this stereotyped vision of American society, we can predict when he approves of and when he rejects its use. For instance, in his account of the Negro Riots of 1712 and 1741,[33] Headley describes the black population in the following terms:

The population numbered only about ten thousand, one-fifth of which was negroes, who were slaves. Their education being wholly neglected, they were ignorant and debased,

---

[31] *Great Riots*, 17.

[32] John Higham's *Strangers in the Land: Patterns of American Nativism, 1860–1925* (New York: Atheneum, 1963), surveys these trends and their impact on the immigrant population.

[33] For other sources on these riots see Herbert Aptheker's *A Documentary History of the Negro People in the United States*, vol. I (New York: Citadel Press, 1962), 4; and *Negro Slave Revolts in the United States, 1526–1860* (New York: International Publishers, 1939), 18–23. See also Richard B. Morris, *Government and Labor in Early America* (New York: Harper Torchbooks, 1965).

and addicted to almost every vice. They were, besides, restive under their bondage and the severe punishments often inflicted on them, which caused their masters a great deal of anxiety.[34]

Headley's superficial sympathy hardly obscures his sense of superiority, which does not question why the Negroes are "debased," nor what justifies their punishment, but seems rather more concerned for the masters' peace of mind. And his account of the riot, which in fact only consisted of a series of mysterious fires that the slaves were accused of starting, and for which 18 persons (including a Catholic Priest) were hanged, 13 were burned at the stake and 71 transported, fails significantly, in spite of a tone of shock at the brutality of the proceedings, to distinguish between violence against property and violence against persons.

Throughout this discussion Headley assumes that the poor, the Negroes, the Irish, and the lower classes in general cause riots, without seeing that people riot in response to particular conditions that are the true causes of violence. Headley's inability to see that the only true violence that occurred was the official violence of the court, the conduct of which was bestial and hysterical to a degree reminiscent of the Salem Witch Trials, demonstrates his willingness to rationalize certain forms of violence as an expression of "the weakness of human nature under certain circumstances [which] have been witnessed since the world was made, and probably will continue to the end of time, or until the race enters on a new phase of existence."[35]

This was turning the tables on them in a manner the upper class did not expect, and they began to reflect what the end might be . . .

---

[34] Great Riots, 26.

[35] *Great Riots,* 44.

In what is perhaps the most astute insight of the book, Headley pinpoints the essential mechanism of class and race prejudice in operation, showing how the court used the testimony of a slave, Mary Burton, to condemn the other slaves, but then rejected her accusations against prominent white citizens:

Robespierre and his friends cut off the upper-crust of society without hesitation or remorse; but unfortunately the crust next below this became in turn the upper-crust, which also had to be removed, until at last they themselves were reached, when they paused. They had advanced up to their necks in the tide of revolution, and finding that to proceed farther would take them overhead, they attempted to wade back to shore. So here, so long as the accusations were confined to the lowest class, it was well enough, but when *they* were being reached, it was high time to stop. The proceedings were brought to a close, further examinations were deemed unnecessary, and confessions became flat and unprofitable; and this strange episode in American history ended.[36]

But Headley fails to investigate the reasons for this "strange episode"; he seems unwilling or unable to recognize the profound gulf between the rich and the poor and the ease with which the former control the opportunities of the latter. He lacks the empathy of a writer like Jacob Riis in whose hands the lower classes emerge as distinctly human subjects. Instead, he assumes automatically that violence derives typically from an instinctive hatred of those who are better off, and that rarely can violence be justified unless the responsible elements of society approve. Indeed, his overriding concern with essentially conservative forms of social control manifests itself all the more clearly as he moves closer to the central episode of the book: the Draft Riots.

As a result of this class-ridden conception of the purposes of and justification for violence, Headley tends to identify social and political tyranny only in terms of accepted norms. Thus, he can view the Stamp Act Riots of 1765 as fundamentally justified, because the issuing of stamps violated the right to representation in all tax matters. Furthermore, he suggests that, since the colonies assembled in Congress condemned the act, "the open,

---

[36] *Great Riots,* 42–43.

violent opposition to it by the people rises above the level of a common riot, and partakes more of the nature of a righteous revolution."[37] But in spite of his admiration for the colonials and his belief that these riots initiated the first steps towards the American Revolution, Headley nevertheless labels these Stamp Act protests riots. Given this hesitancy on his part to accept any form of extra-legal action, including the early stages of the American Revolution, it is not surprising that Headley never specifically defines "riot." We can guess that, generally, he means lawless, destructive behavior on the part of large numbers of persons. Sometimes a riot is organized but usually it bursts forth spontaneously, dying out only when the threat or application of force is used. This constant association between violence and disorder, on the one hand, and organized force and order, on the other, warps all of Headley's discussions of riots by instantly undercutting the possible legitimacy of violent demonstrations.

Except for his less biased account of the Stamp Act Riot, his treatment of the Spring Election Riots of 1834, the Flour Riot of 1837, and the Bread Riot of 1857 illustrates clearly his prejudices towards the poor, immigrant classes, whose social behavior he describes in the narrowest possible terms. Not only does he criticize the poor for rioting in 1837 because of a shortage of bread, he categorizes their response—the destruction of barrels of flour—as a perfect illustration of the "insensate character of a mob,"[38] a heedless, destructive mass. In doing so, Headley ignores two crucial factors that might have made the actions of the crowd intelligible. First, he scorns the fact that the poor rioted because

---

[37] *Great Riots,* 47. For other sources on the Stamp Act Riots, see Arthur M. Schlesinger, "Political Mobs and the American Revolution, 1765–1776," *American Philosophical Society Proceedings,* 99 (August 1955), 244–250. Irving Mark, *Agrarian Conflicts in Colonial New York, 1711–1775* (New York: Columbia University Press, 1940). Alfred F. Young has an excellent bibliographical essay on the second half of the 18th century in his *The Democratic Republicans of New York* (Chapel Hill: University of North Carolina Press, 1967).

[38] *Great Riots,* 110. On the Spring Election Riots, see Leo H. Hirsch, "Negroes and New York, 1783–1865," *Journal of Negro History,* 16 (1931), 382–473, and Billington, *The Protestant Crusade, op. cit.* On the Flour Riot see vol. 6 of J. B. McMaster's *History* (New York: Appleton, 1913), 392–94.

they believed that the shortage of bread was caused by hoarding on the part of merchants, who were trying artificially to keep the prices up. While this explanation no doubt seemed novel to the economic views of some nineteenth century historians, the technique of monopolizing a vital commodity in order to create higher profits was familiar both to the merchants and to the poor. By sneering at the analysis promulgated by the poor that the flour was unfairly priced, and by blaming the unrest and subsequent violence on the agitations of political demagogues, Headley adopts a classic apology for the rich and an equally traditional explanation for the behavior of the poor, which deprives them of all political initiative. Second, Headley does not recognize the symbolic importance of the act. Howard Zinn points out that man "will do violence against a symbol which stands for, or which he believes stands for, that which prevents him from satisfying his needs."[39] When the poor attacked the merchants and destroyed the barrels of flour, they were not, as Headley suggests, foolishly wasting good flour, but actually striking out against the symbol of the forces that controlled and oppressed them.

Headley's reluctance to see political consciousness behind these riots, which pervades most analyses of crowd behavior, is echoed in his description of the Bread Riot of 1857. Then, as in 1837, conditions among the poor were particularly miserable, and they suffered greatly from the depression of that year. The exasperation of the "mob" with the shortage of bread led to threats of violence, which was prevented by the formation of a number of public works projects and the granting of relief through a num ber of private agencies. In addition to omitting mention that this was not a riot, Headley also leaves out the significant fact that the poor themselves organized a series of demonstrations, which attracted the attention of city authorities and prompted the formation of these relief measures; and this was the first time "the unemployed had an important political impact as the [common]

---

[39] "The Force of Nonviolence," *The Nation* (March 17, 1962), 228. This article also appears in *Violence in America,* Thomas Rose, ed. (New York: Random House and Vintage, 1969).

council [of New York] appropriated money for public works projects and passed numerous resolutions expressing concern over the plight of the unemployed."[40]

Even his treatment of those riots which were not ostensibly motivated by political or economic considerations—such as the Doctors' Riot of 1788 or the Astor Place Riot of 1849, both of which in fact had their roots in many of the same grievances that the poor and uneducated share towards the rich—suggests that Headley wishes to describe violent behavior. This is not principally because he wants to observe it and understand it, but because he wants to reinforce his argument for devising effective methods to contain violence, no matter what its origins.[41]

IV

HEADLEY'S INTEREST FOR us lies, primarily, in his treatment of the Draft Riots, for in this long section he reveals his most deeply rooted beliefs about the relation between an individual, or groups of individuals, and the state. Headley's analysis of the riots underscores an ambivalence that appeared in rudimentary form in some of his early work but here emerges clearly for the first time. Previously, he had fought as an opponent, however misguided his political choices seem to us, what he considered to be the forces of demagogy and tyranny: this explains his otherwise contradictory position both as a Know-Nothing and an ardent republican

---

[40] Frank R. Breul, "Early History of Aid to the Unemployed in the United States," in *In Aid of the Unemployed*, Joseph M. Becker, S.J., ed. (Baltimore: Johns Hopkins University Press, 1965), 10.

[41] For an account of the Astor Place Riot, see Richard Moody, *The Astor Place Riot* (Bloomington: University of Indiana Press, 1958). More interesting is a contemporary pamphlet which makes this remarkable statement about the riot: "This terrible tragedy is a lesson to us all. None can escape its warning. We are all responsible, all guilty; for we make a part of a society that has permitted thousands of its members to grow up in poverty and ignorance, and exposed to the temptations of vice and crime. This mob is but a symptom of our social condition, and it points out a disease to which we should lose no time in applying a proper remedy." *Account of the Terrific and Fatal Riot at the New York Astor Place Opera House* (New York: H. M. Ranney, 1849), 32.

who supported the French Revolution as a historical necessity. But during the Civil War, under the threatened collapse of the Union to which he was so devoted, his concern for the expressed needs for manpower that the newly designed Conscription Act of 1863 was intended to meet runs violently counter to the concern he might have had for individual freedom. The Draft Riots were apparently the catalyst that forced him to reject the liberties of the individual for the prerogatives of the state: "The government, whether wrong or right, must be supported, or abandoned and given over to revolution."[42] The collapse of his republican principles in the face of the exigencies of the war reinforces Headley's already familiar social and political prejudices. Although he makes the riots more comprehensible and readable than other commentators,[43] the nature of his interpretation of the events and the method by which he selected his factual material raise a number of serious questions about Headley's methodological and theoretical limitations.

Like most of the writers who have examined the behavior of crowds, Headley tends to assume that men in crowds lose their reason and become willing slaves to political demagogues. This view was reinforced by Headley's class bias, which naturally inhibited his sympathy for disorderly behavior. In addition, few analyses of crowd behavior existed before the twentieth century, and these tended to reflect a generalized fear of "the mob" and mob rule. Certainly this feeling has persisted since Gustave Le Bon's influential study of the crowd, which was published in 1895 and which reflected the feeling that crowds were essentially mobs whose political influence would undermine the advances of civilization.[44] Just as Le Bon derived many of his ideas about crowd

---

[42] *Great Riots*, 141.

[43] Some other sources are: Herbert Asbury, *The Gangs of New York: An Informal History of the Underworld* (Garden City: Doubleday, 1928); James McCague, *The Second Rebellion: The Story of the New York City Draft Riots of 1863* (New York: Dial Press, 1968); Irving Werstein, *July 1863* (New York: Julian Messner, 1957); two 19th century accounts are David M. Barnes, *The Draft Riots in New York, 1863* (New York: Baker and Godwin, 1863) and *Appleton's Annual Cyclopedia, 1863,* an excellent summary.

[44] *The Crowd: A Study of the Popular Mind* (New York: Viking Press, 1967).

behavior from his personal knowledge of the Paris Commune of 1871, so Headley mirrors his age's fears and obsessions and views the behavior of the draft rioters as the true image of lower-class crowds. But more recent studies of crowd behavior suggest that personal prejudices have exaggerated the irrationality of crowds although that aspect cannot be denied, and that many crowds which have been described as destructive mobs sought to attain concrete political goals through violence.[45] We can assess Headley's true strengths and weaknesses by using some of the criteria by which George Rudé measures crowd behavior: what actually happened; in what context did the incident occur; what was the size of the crowd, the nature of its actions, the goals of its promoters, and the role of its leaders and members; what were the social origins, ages, and occupations of its members; at whom were the activities of the crowd aimed; how effectively did the authorities repress the activities of the crowd; and what were the consequences of the event and its historical significance."[46]

Characteristically, Headley offers little insight into the conditions that promoted the riots. He assumes, generally, that "Most of the riots of New York have grown out of causes more or less local, and wholly transient in their nature."[47] Thus, when he speaks about the causes of the riots, he treats the 300 dollar exemption clause, which was cited by many as the symbol that incited the poor to riot against the inequities of the draft, merely as an unfortunate example of the gap between the rich and the

---

[45] For a sampling of views that regard crowds as purposeful and political, see the following: George Rudé, *The Crowd in History* (New York: John Wiley & Sons, 1964); Elias Canetti, *Crowds and Power* (New York: Viking Press, 1966); E. J. Hobsbawm, *Primitive Rebels: Studies in Archaic Forms of Social Movement in the 19th and 20th Centuries* (New York: W. W. Norton, 1959); E. P. Thompson, *The Making of the English Working Class* (New York: Vintage, 1963); Jesse Lemisch, "The Radicalism of the Inarticulate: Merchant Seamen in the Politics of Revolutionary America" in Alfred F. Young, ed., *Dissent* (DeKalb: University of Northern Illinois Press, 1968); Hadley Cantril, *The Psychology of Social Movements* (New York: John Wiley & Sons, 1941); Neil Smelser, *Theory of Collective Behavior* (Englewood Cliffs, N.J.: Prentice-Hall, 1963).

[46] Rudé, 10–11.

[47] *Great Riots,* 79.

poor that will be corrected "When society gets in that happy state, that the rich man has no advantages over the poor, [and when] there will be no need either of drafting or volunteering."[48] Not only does Headley ignore the objective conditions of poverty that prevailed in New York City and that frequently served as a source of conflict and violence;[49] he also fails to admit the right of the poor to challenge these inequalities. Moreover, because Headley does not conceive of the lower classes as capable of viable political behavior, he cannot see the violence of the poor as a form of political action. Thus he explains the hostility to the draft as the response of those who opposed Lincoln and who were unwilling to fight against their old political friends.

His reluctance to see specific political goals behind the violence of the crowd compels Headley to describe the activities of the crowd in most arbitrary terms. Not only are the rioters uninformed, irrational, destructive and purposeless; they belong to a "mob"—a "wild, savage, and heterogenous looking mass—"[50] that, having accomplished its original objective to disrupt the calling of names by the federal marshals, then proceeds on an indiscriminate path of destruction. Aside from the attacks on the Draft offices and the attempts made against the *Tribune* and Horace Greeley, Headley construes the riots as fundamentally non-political and even anti-political; and he sees the essence of the crowd's irrationality in the burning of a Postmaster's house, a man whose wife "was noted for her kindness to the poor and wretched, who now repaid her by sacking and burning her house."[51]

If Headley sees the rioters as lacking concrete political goals, he nevertheless details the racial excesses of the crowd. Traditionally, most observers have treated the Draft Riots as fundamentally anti-Negro in tone, and have pointed to the violence directed against the Negro population of the city by the Irish as an instance of northern bigotry. Headley concurs with this analy-

---

[48] *Great Riots,* 139–40.

[49] For a view of poverty in New York, see Seymour Mandelbaum, *Boss Tweed's New York* (Englewood Cliffs, N.J.: Prentice-Hall, 1965).

[50] *Great Riots,* 153.

[51] *Great Riots,* 181.

sis up to a point, lashing the rioters for destroying the Colored Orphan Asylum and ridiculing the perverse logic that rationalized the violence against Negroes as just punishment for those who were supposedly the cause of the war.[52] But on the whole he does not see the riots in racial terms, although he accepts the belief that Negroes were widely resented by the Irish because they were somehow responsible for the war.

In fact, the violent attacks by the Irish against the Negro population were motivated by specific, deep-rooted, economic grievances, much as the attacks against the houses of wealthy people and against Brooks Brothers symbolized the passionate sense of frustration and deprivation aroused by poverty:

> The competition offered by negroes was small, but in many places it called forth opposition which frequently passed beyond mere protest into bloodshed and murder. Longshoremen especially took offense at this invasion. These laborers were Irish, who at that time in the industrial world seldom got beyond the pick and shovel, and therefore felt the threatened competition keenly; furthermore, the two opposing classes felt a violent racial antipathy toward each other. Along the docks of Chicago, Detroit, Cleveland, Buffalo, Albany, New York, Brooklyn, Boston, and other places, the introduction of negro strike breakers was often the signal for fierce riots, in which striking Irishmen sought by stones and brickbats to prevent the new hands from taking their places. In the spring of 1863, in the months immediately preceding the draft riots in New York, the two races on a number of occasions clashed in this way on the waterfront of the city, and murders were frequent. In June, the month before the riots, 3,000 longshoremen began a strike for higher wages, which for most of them ended in failure, and in this, their supreme effort, the sons of Erin saw their black rivals, under police protection, taking their places. It was the heaping of insult upon injury, the culmination of months

---

[52] *Great Riots*, 169.

of bad blood and ugly feeling. In another month's time came the drafts, which in the minds of a large part of the industrial classes, already deeply stirred, was another name for forced military service in behalf of the hated negro rivals, and at the head of the rioting mobs were the angry and defeated longshoremen. Industrial discontent was a fundamental cause of the riots.[53]

In order to put the violence of the rioters into such a context, Headley would have needed a sympathetic sense of the suffering engendered by poverty and reinforced by class barriers. But as we have seen, Headley speaks almost exclusively from an elite point of view, denying that the riots stemmed from fundamental grievances of the poor, insisting that, in fact, political demagogues had stirred up the lower classes. Thus, ultimately, Headley proposes to treat the rioters sternly:

> When men begin to burn and plunder dwellings, attack station-houses, hang negroes, and shoot down policemen, it is too late to attempt to restore peace by talking about the constitutionality of laws. The upholding of laws about the constitutionality of which there is no doubt, is the only thing deserving of consideration.[54]

The police played an instrumental role in suppressing the Draft Riots, and it is not surprising that Headley dedicated his book to them. Speaking in a tone that parallels many contemporary views of violence and the police, Headley calls for a return to law and order and the establishment of a tactical patrol force trained to put down riots as efficiently as possible. Throughout

---

[53] Emerson David Fite, *Social and Industrial Conditions in the North during the Civil War* (New York: Frederick Ungar, 1962), 189–90. Also note Fite's comments on the way industrialization put men out of work, 197. For a similar account see John Hope Franklin, *From Slavery to Freedom* (New York: Knopf, 1967), 3rd edition.

[54] *Great Riots*, 222. Compare this with Henry Raymond's editorial in the New York *Times,* July 15, 1863, in which he urges the police and military to "give them grape and plenty of it."

his discussions of the methods that the police used to break up the crowds, Headley never questions the relationship between the level of violence that preceded the police action and that which followed.[55] Even as the police are literally driving some of the more desperate rioters off of the roofs of buildings, we get no sense of outrage from Headley, who seems to enjoy the bloody progress of the police. Only when troops fight pitched battles with rioters does Headley express concern over excessive force, and that seemingly is due to his conviction that the militia are hopelessly disorganized and usually encourage the rioters by their repeated inability to disperse them.

It is because of Headley's general hostility towards the rioters and his sympathy with the police action that he is eager to claim that by Friday, the 17th of June, the "spirit of insurrection was effectually laid."[56] But correspondence between Lincoln and Governor Seymour indicates that the unrest which provoked the riots continued well into August.[57] In addition, since Headley failed to see the root causes of the riot in terms of the actual conditions that thrust a large portion of the lower class population into open rebellion against the city, state, and federal government, it is unlikely that he understood what effect the military repression of the riots had on the feelings of those involved; for the brutal extinguishing of the violence probably served to deepen the already profound animosities of the poor.

---

[55] For an account of a riot that was actually a police riot, see Herbert Gutman, "The Tompkins Square 'Riot' in New York City on January 13, 1874: A Reexamination of its Causes and its Aftermath," *Labor History*, 6, No. 1 (Winter 1965), 44–70.

[56] *Great Riots.* 267.

[57] "Secret societies organized for the encouragement of desertion and for resistance to the draft. Obstruction was manifest in widely separated parts of the country, and disaffection spread wide and deep. Enrolling officers were rudely handled and some were shot in performance of duty. The property of others was destroyed. The drawing of names from the wheel, a public proceeding, often resulted in violence, while the making of an arrest was likely to create a riot." J. G. Randall and David Donald, *The Divided Union* (Boston: Little, Brown, 1961), 315. Randall and Donald note that 46,000 conscripts and 118,000 substitutes were actually drafted. See Edward Needles Wright, *Conscientious Objectors in the Civil War* (New York: A. S. Barnes, 1961), for the impact that the draft had on the numbers of conscientious objectors.

In contrast with the government's failure to locate and isolate the spirit of the insurrection, the rioters achieved their most immediate goal—the interruption of the draft—through violence. And although the draft was eventually continued, the widespread opposition that flamed up all over the North, much of which involved attacks against the marshals supervising the calling of names, was officially supported by a number of state governments, which manipulated the quotas and interfered so successfully with the whole process that only about 6 percent of the Union forces were actually obtained through conscription.[58] Perhaps most significant was the fact that, in revising the original draft law of 1863, Lincoln withdrew the objectionable $300 exemption clause, which was subsequently applied only to conscientious objectors, and replaced it with a series of incentive bounties that were designed to attract more long-term enlistments.

These important effects escaped Headley's notice, since he apparently was more concerned about the extent of damage done to the city by the rioters. He does mention that a great number of people were killed, at least one thousand, and that uncounted others were injured. Most other writers on the riots have accepted these figures, but one scholar has disputed both the numbers killed and the extent of the riots, charging that the threat to the city was really created by the partisan political reporting of the newspapers.[59] But although Headley may have

---

[58] Randall and Donald, op. cit. 314.

[59] Robert Stewart Mitchell, *Horatio Seymour of New York* (Cambridge: Harvard University Press. 1938), is the only scholar to dismiss the seriousness of the draft riots. He bases his opinion on the small number of deaths, 74, which were officially attributed to the riots. His source is David Valentine, *New York City Manual,* 1864. But aside from the fact that statistical records were, according to the United States Bureau of the Census, full of inaccuracies and omissions, Mitchell's whole argument is tendentiously weighted as a defense of Seymour's role during the riots, for which he was accused of treason by some. It is possible that some papers exaggerated the violence and killing, but political partisanship does not compensate for the enormous difference between Mitchell's claims, which no contemporary observer supports, and those of Headley and David Barnes, who drew on police reports.

In the final analysis, Headley stresses the issue of law and order and misses the essential significance of all the riots. The draft, after all, did not really cause

exaggerated his figures somewhat, the riots clearly threatened the ability of the federal government to implement the draft. On the other hand, Headley's notion that the riots were a prelude to mob rule and endangered the financial center of the North, the loss of which would have fatally undermined the Union cause, appears distorted; for there is nothing to indicate that rioters either intended or attempted to destroy Wall Street, disrupt the Union and assure victory for the Confederacy. And while there is some correlation between men who were active Copperheads like Samuel F. B. Morse, their previous activities in the Know-Nothing party and their opposition to Lincoln's policies, other ex-Know-Nothings like Henry Raymond of the *Times* continued to express strong dislike of the Irish while supporting the Union cause. Headley probably falls into this latter group, since he was both an ardent Unionist and opponent of the rioters. And his

---

the ensuing violence any more than the hoarding of flour caused the riots of 1837. These events merely catalyzed the social, political and economic fears of the poor, the unemployed, and the rejected elements of the society. The throngs of Irish who pillaged and burned buildings and who also stood up to well-armed troops during the last days of the riots, when it was clear that only desperation remained, were expressing the accumulated frustration of living under oppressive conditions. And the political exploitation of the Irish by Tammany Hall, while feared by the upper classes, never gave the masses of poor Irish the political power to deal with the causes of their frustration.

Although historical analogies are susceptible of great distortion. Headley's willingness to treat violence as social threat, rather than as a legitimate and functional political signal that is a vital part of the political process, seems symptomatic of most historical writing.[60] Most historians of the Draft Riots of 1863 tend to emulate Headley's assumptions and judgments, while the attitudes of most contemporary writers towards violence in our society suggest a ready desire to condemn it, a continued failure to perceive the roots of violence, and a refusal to see its necessary role in creating social change when non-violent methods fail. So long as writers insist on viewing violence from the top rather than from the bottom—instead of writing history from the bottom up, in Jesse Lemish's perceptive phrase—the actualities of violence will persist all the while that its critics ignore and deprecate its existence.

[60] Both Howard Zinn, "History as Private Enterprise," in *The Crucial Spirit: Essays in Honor of Herbert Marcuse,* Kurt H. Wolff and Barrington Moore, Jr., eds. (Boston: Beacon Press, 1967), and Irving Louis Horowitz, *Three Worlds of Development: The Theory and Practice of International Stratification* (New York: Oxford University Press, 1966), chap. 12, point out why historians and social scientists fail to recognize violence and to see its legitimacy and function.

anti-Abolitionist feelings may also account for his tolerance towards Governor Seymour, who was roundly accused of coddling the mob by the Republican press, for whom Headley had little sympathy because of its abolitionist views. Nevertheless, he does dismiss the idea that the riots resulted from a plot between southern agents and northern sympathizers, although many wild charges filled the press at the time of the riots.

In spite of his limitations, Headley's value as a social commentator is obviously significant because he did not reject or obscure the importance of violence as a political and social phenomenon. In a sense, his readiness to speak in terms of his class makes his work even more useful, since it measures at least partially some of the irreducible distance between the rich and the poor. It is not, of course, certain that Headley's view of violence adequately represents the attitudes of the upper classes. Other gentlemen historians like George Bancroft were much more sympathetic to the poor than was Headley. Yet Headley remains one of the few decent sources of information about violence, and until modern historians begin to treat it systematically, Headley's pejorative view must stand as a singular example of American writing on the subject of violence.

Thomas Rose
James Rodgers

Washington, D.C.
1969

Bibliographical Note

THIS NOTE INCLUDES a listing of riots that Headley does not discuss, and a bibliography of Headley's books on the date first issued, although many went into a number of editions.

ADDITIONAL RIOTS, 1745–1858

THERE WERE MANY riots before 1712, and during the period Headley writes about, riots occurred that are not mentioned in his book. The incidents listed below were termed riots by the press and those few who wrote about them. It is possible that Headley didn't include them because he didn't consider them riots, didn't know about them, or wanted to minimize certain forms of violence, especially riots against Irish and Catholics. We include this long list because more research is needed about early riots and violence, and because, even today, most writers do not define what they mean by riot in precise terms.

1745—"Unruley or drunken mariners, privateersmen," including many transient soldiers and sailors, formed mobs and rioted. (Carl Bridenbaugh, *Cities in Revolt*, New York: Capicorn, 1964, p. 117.)

August 18, 1760—Impressment riots. (This and all other references to David Maydole Matteson are to his carefully documented, unpublished manuscripts on riots, Manuscript Division, Number 9356, Library of Congress, Washington, D.C.)

April 24 and July 11, 1764—Impressment riots: Matteson; Jesse Lemisch. ("The Radicalism of the Inarticulate: Merchant Seamen in the Politics of Revolutionary America" in Dissent, *edited by Alfred Young, DeKalb: University of Northern Illinois Press, 1968, pp. 51–52) Lemisch writes that the impressment riots were purposeful, disciplined, and radical. "The pattern of rioting as political expression, established as a response to impressment, was adapted and broadened as a response to the Stamp Act." Richard Morris calls the impressment riots in both 1764 and 1765 an insurrection which was "supported by great numbers of Sailors headed by Captains of Privateers, and other Ships." They were organized. (Richard B. Morris,* Government and Labor in Early America, New York: Harper Torch Books, 1965, p, 189.)

February 5, 1770—The Battle of Golden Hill: This two day battle resulted from antagonism between troops and the population. British soldiers took off-duty civilian employment and undercut wages given to American workingmen. (See Bridenbaugh, *Cities in Revolt*, p. 312; and Jesse Lemisch, "The American Revolution Seen From the Bottom Up," in Barton J. Bernstein, ed., *Towards a New Past: Dissenting Essays In American History*, New York: Pantheon, 1963, p. 22.)

1766—Various manors ejected tenants who would not accept "onerous leases." Two thousand armed tenants refused to pay rent, some were jailed, and in protest they marched on New York City and were finally dispersed by redcoats with cannons. (Staughton Lynd, *Class Conflict, Slavery, and the U.S. Constitution*, Indianapolis: Bobbs-Merrill, 1967, pp. 31, 66.) See also Irving Mark, Agrarian Conflicts in Colonial New York, 1711–1775, *Columbia University Press, 1940, pp. 131–163.*

1790–1803—Liberty-Pole riots in many cities including New York City (Matteson; John Bach McMaster, A History of the People of the United States from the Revolution to the Civil War, New York: Appleton, 1913, Vol. 2, pp. 401–402).

July 4, 1788—Federalist—Anti-Federalist riots: There were pitched battles fought with swords, bayonets, clubs, stones, brick–bats, and paving stones, which spread from New York City to the countryside, including a huge parade on July 23 in New York City where mobs broke down doors and marched on houses of anti-Federalists. (Alfred F. Young, *The Democratic Republicans of New York,* Chapel Hill: University of North Carolina Press, 1967, pp. 119–120.)

October 1793—Field riots occurred when authorities could not stop a mob of "boy apprentices, and Negroes, as well as Sailors who demolished two bawdy houses." Young, p. 471, describes the wretched jobs and horrible housing which contributed to this riot, also described in detail by Matteson.

December 24, 1806—Riot, including attacks on Catholic churches, and general rioting between Catholics and Protestants. (Matteson) Stokes describes the Augustus Street Riot which was of a similar nature, and which took place the next day. (I. N. Phelps Stokes, comp., *The Iconography of Manhattan Island,* 1498–1909, New York: McGraw-Hill, 1967.)

April 1810—Election riots in New York including rioting between Irish Catholics and Protestants. (Matteson)

June 29, 1812—St. James Street Riot, also involving Catholics and Protestants. (Stokes)

July 1830—Hog Cart Riots, where carts were overturned and covered with mud in protest against their being in the streets. (Stokes)

October 13–15, 1831—Park Theater Riots, sometimes called the Anderson Riots. Anderson was a singer and actor, a recently arrived immigrant, but when he went on stage at the Park Theater, a riot broke out. Matteson argues that the public would only accept native actors.

March 13, 1835—Broadway Hall riots involving immigrant Catholics and native Americans, caused in part by the publication of twelve letters signed by "Brutus" (identified as Samuel F. B. Morse), explaining that Catholicism was a foreign conspiracy that had to be dealt with by patriotic nativist action. (These were eventually published as a book called *Foreign Conspiracy Against The Liberties of The United States.* New York: Leavitt, Lord and Co., 1835. See also Matteson; Ray Allen

Billington, *The Protestant Crusade, 1800–1860,* Chicago: Quadrangle, 1964; and Louis Dow Scisco, *Political Nativism in New
York State.* New York: Columbia University Press, 1901.)

1836—Includes many riots: McMaster, p. 369, writes about tailors
who struck, marched in the streets, "raised a riot," and committed enough violence so that the militia had to be called out.
Louis Adamic (*Dynamite: The Story of Class Violence in America.*
New York: Harper, 1931, p. 6) wrote that Irish harbor workers
rioted for higher wages, and in order to quell the disturbances
the militia were called out. Matteson writes about riots in July
against abolitionists and at the Chatham Street Chapel involving Irish and Protestants.

March 28, 1840—Loco Foco Riot; March 29, rioters attacked a
beer garden. This became a German-Irish riot, but was dispersed by the mayor without the militia. In April 1840 there
were riots and strikes for higher wages. Troops were called in
to protect workers and laborers willing to work. (Matteson)

April 1842—Scisco writes, "After the polls were closed on election night the city streets were filled with a mob which drove
before it the hated Irish, and stoned the windows of the
Catholic bishop. Mayor Morris placed militiamen on duty to
guard the Catholic churches from violence." p. 37.

August 29, 1851—Rowdies attacked a house on Greenwich Street
where Hungarian offices were located. The police attacked the
mob and the Hungarians, who were a symbol of Catholics
and Irish. On September 11 there was a German celebration
that turned into a Catholic-Protestant riot. (Matteson)

July 4, 1852—Catholic-Protestant riots, involving knives, shovels, and pickaxes, which the police were able to quell. (Matteson)

July 4, 1853—Hibernian riot involving Catholics and Protestants.
(Matteson)

1854—During 1854 there were many riots: February 26 in a
dance hall; May 28 between Irish and Protestants; June 4, Irish
and native Americans where the military was called out; September 3, an Irish riot against the street preaching which happened almost every Sunday. Protestant preachers, often
flanked by bodyguards and mobs, went into Irish neighbor-

hoods and harangued people about the horrors of Romanism. Gustavus Myers writes that on May 28, the riotous crowd reached 20,000, police and guardsmen were called, and sixty were arrested. (Myers, *History of Bigotry in the United States,* New York: Capricorn, 1960, pp. 140–160.)

November 4, 1856—Election riots where ballot boxes and ticket stands were destroyed in many wards, and the police were called.

1857—Many people were hurt, and the police were called, during riots in 1857. On January 16 there was a riot involving Irish and native Americans; on June 28 there were riots in two different parts of the city between the same groups; the same thing happened on July 4 and September 3, 1857. (Matteson)

1858—There were riots between native Americans and Catholics on March 18, April 1, and October 3. The last was an Irish-Italian riot. The April riot involved a workers' strike for higher wages at the water works, and the refusal to let others work. The sheriff, who attempted to make arrests, was assaulted. (Matteson)

BIBLIOGRAPHY OF BOOKS BY JOEL TYLER HEADLEY

The Adirondack; or Life in the Woods. New York: Baker and Scribner, 1849.

The Alps and the Rhine. New York: Baker and Scribner, 1848.

The Beauties of Joel Tyler Headley. New York: J.S.Taylor, 1851.

History of the Persecutions and Battles of the Waldenses. New York, 1852. (Publisher unknown)

The Chaplains and Clergy of the Revolution. New York: Scribner, 1864.

Farragut, and our Naval Commanders. New York: E. B. Treat, 1867.

Grant and Sherman; Their Campaigns and Generals. New York: E. B. Treat, 1866.

The Great Celebration Ordered by Washington at Newburgh in 1783. New York: Newburgh, 1881.

The Great Rebellion; a History of the Civil War in the United States. New York: E. B. Treat, 1863.

The Great Riots of New York, 1712–1873. New York: E. B. Treat, 1873.

H. M. Stanley's Wonderful Adventures in Africa (with Willis Fletcher Johnson). Milwaukee: Excelsior Publishing Company, 1890.

The Home Annual. New York, 1855.

The Illustrated Life of Washington. New York: G. andF. Bill, 1859.

The Imperial Guard of Napoleon. New York: C. Scribner, 1851.

Italy and the Italians, in a Series of Letters. New York: I. S. Platt, 1844.

Letters from Italy. New York: Wiley and Putnam, 1845.

Letters from the Backwoods and the Adirondack. New York: J. S. Taylor, 1850.

The Life and Travels of General Grant. Boston: W. H. Thompson, 1879.

The Life of General H. Havelock. New York: C. Scribner, 1859.

The Life of Oliver Cromwell. New York: Baker and Scribner, 1848.

The Life of Ulysses S. Grant. New York: E. B. Treat, 1885.

The Life of Winfield Scott. New York: C. Scribner, 1861.

The Lives of Winfield Scott and Andrew Jackson. New York: C. Scribner, 1852.

Luther and Cromwell. New York: J. S. Taylor, 1850.

Miscellaneous Works. New York, 1849.

Mountain Adventures in Various Parts of the World. New York: C. Scribner, 1872.

Napoleon and his Marshals. New York: Hurst and Company, 1846.

The One Progressive Principle. New York: J. S. Taylor, 1846.

Our Army in the Great Rebellion. New York: E. B. Treat, 1891.

Our Navy in the Great Rebellion. New York: E. B. Treat, 1891.

Pen and Pencil Sketches of the Great Riots. New York: E. B. Treat, 1877.

The Power of Beauty. New York: S. J. Taylor, 1850.

Reasons for the Centennial at Washington's Headquarters, Newburgh. New York: Journal Book and Job Printing Establishment, 1881.

Rumbles and Sketches. New York: J. S. Taylor, 1850.

Sacred Heroes and Martyrs. New York: E. B. Treat, 1870.

The Sacred Mountains. New York: Baker and Scribner, 1847.

Sacred Mountains, Characters and Scenes in the Holy Land. New York: Scribner, Armstrong and Company, 1875.

The Second War with England. New York: C. Scribner, 1853.

Stanley's Adventures in the Wilds of Africa. Philadelphia: Edgewood Publishing, 1882.

Washington and His Generals. New York: Baker and Scribner, 1847